My Turn To Spin

Know The Score Books Publications

CULT HEROES	Author	ISBN
CHELSEA	Leo Moynihan	1905449003
MANCHESTER CITY	David Clayton	9781905449057
NEWCASTLE	Dylan Younger	1905449038
SOUTHAMPTON	Jeremy Wilson	1905449011
WEST BROM	Simon Wright	190544902X

MATCH OF MY LIFE	Editor	ISBN
ENGLAND WORLD CUP	Massarella & Moynihan	1905449526
EUROPEAN CUP FINALS	Ben Lyttleton	1905449577
FA CUP FINALS 1953-69	David Saffer	9781905449538
FULHAM	Michael Heatley	1905449518
LEEDS	David Saffer	1905449542
LIVERPOOL	Leo Moynihan	190544950X
SHEFFIELD UNITED	Nick Johnson	1905449623
STOKE CITY	Simon Lowe	9781905449552
SUNDERLAND	Rob Mason	1905449607
SPURS	Allen & Massarella	9781905449583
WOLVES	Simon Lowe	1905449569

GENERAL FOOTBALL	Author	ISBN
BURKSEY	Peter Morfoot	1905449496
The Autobiography of a Football God		
HOLD THE BACK PAGE	Harry Harris	1905449917
2006 WORLD CUP DIARY	Harry Harris	1905449909

AUTOBIOGRAPHY	Author	ISBN
TACKLES LIKE A FERRET	Paul Parker	190544947X
(England Cover)		
TACKLES LIKE A FERRET	Paul Parker	1905449461
(Manchester United Cover)		

CRICKET	Author	ISBN
GROVEL!	David Tossell	9781905449439
The Story & Legacy of the Summer of 1976		
MOML: THE ASHES	Pilger & Wightman	1905449631
WASTED?	Paul Smith	9781905449453

Forthcoming Publications in 2007

CULT HEROES	Author	ISBN
CARLISLE UNITED	Mark Harrison	9781905449095
CELTIC	David Potter	9781905449088
NOTTINGHAM FOREST	David McVay	9781905449064
RANGERS	Paul Smith	9781905449071

MATCH OF MY LIFE	Editor	ISBN
ASTON VILLA	Neil Moxley	9781905449651
BOLTON WANDERERS	David Saffer	9781905449644
DERBY COUNTY	Johnson & Matthews	9781905449682
MANCHESTER UNITED	Brian Hughes	9781905449590

GENERAL FOOTBALL   Author   ISBN

2007/08 VODAFONE CHAMPIONS LEAGUE YEARBOOK
Harry Harris   9781905449934

OUTCASTS   Steve Menary   9781905449316
The Lands That FIFA Forgot

PARISH TO PLANET   Dr Eric Midwinter   9781905449309
How Football Came To Rule The World

MY PREMIERSHIP DIARY   Marcus Hahnemann   9781905449330
Reading's Season in the Premiership

CRICKET	Author	ISBN
LEAGUE CRICKET YEARBOOK		
Midlands edition	Andy Searle	9781905449729
North East edition	Danny Pugsley	9781905449712
North West edition	Andy Searle	9781905449705

3

Know The Score Books Limited
118 Alcester Road
Studley, Warwickshire, B80 7NT
Tel: 01527 454482 Fax: 01527 452183
info@knowthescorebooks.com
www.knowthescorebooks.com

A CIP catalogue record is available for this book from the British Library

ISBN: 978-1-905449-42-2

Jacket Design by Lisa David
Book Designed and Edited by Andy Searle

Printed and bound in Great Britain
by Cromwell Press, Trowbridge, Wiltshire

Mixed Sources
Product group from well-managed
forests and other controlled sources
www.fsc.org Cert no. TT-TOC-2082
© 1996 Forest Stewardship Council
FSC

My Turn To Spin

The Shaun "Shaggy" Udal Story

As told to Pat Symes

To my Grandfather, Geoffrey, for getting me started on this wonderful journey. To Mum and Dad for doing everything in their power to help me succeed, I hope I've made you proud along the way.

To Hampshire CCC for giving me the chance to play the great game and play it for the best club in the world!

And lastly, leaving the best to last, to my family, Emma, Katherine, Rebecca and Jack, you are my world and I cannot put into words how much you mean to me, I would be lost without you and can't imagine life without all of you. We have been through a lot recently and it's been hard at times but I think it has made us closer. Emma, I don't know how you have stuck with me, but am glad you have, you are an amazingly strong person who I love to bits. All three of my children are the most precious things in the world to me, I would and will do anything for you. All my love goes to you.

Contents

Acknowledgements

HAMPSHIRE County Cricket Club has been my life for the best part of two decades. Inevitably there have been ups and downs but, in the main, more high points than low. Many people at Hampshire and in the England set-up have made my cricket life memorable and I thank them for providing me with plenty of material to help fill this book.

My gratitude goes also to Simon Lowe and Andy Searle at Knowthescorebooks for giving me the chance to write about my career and putting it in some kind of cohesive order, to Pat Symes and his faltering shorthand for recording it all, and to Jim Baldwin for his detailed statistics and for correcting all the factual mistakes made by myself and my floundering ghost.

There are numerous other people who have played a part in my life, my brother Gary, Robin Smith , Rod Bransgrove, Mark Nicholas, Warney, all the people from my club Camberley who have always supported me, a massive thanks for being great mates. I could name so many more, but these few have played significant roles in my cricketing life.

What a journey it's been, there may be a few more years yet, who knows, but if there's not then I've lived my dream for 21 seasons, who'd have thought that? Certainly not me!

Foreword

By Shane Warne

I FIRST CAME across Shaggy when he came to Australia on the 1994-95 Ashes tour, but got to know him far better, of course, when I joined Hampshire a few years later at the start of my stint in county cricket. I like to think I have helped him fulfil his talent, which was evident on that Ashes tour but which has lain dormant for far too long. There is no doubt Shaggy always had the potential and the ability and if I was able to improve him in any way then I am pleased. We all benefited, not least his county.

My greatest contribution, maybe, was in convincing him how good he could be. He had either lost confidence or incentive and was in danger of allowing his career to drift. There were one or two technical areas I felt he could improve but what made the difference was that even in his 30s he was prepared to listen and learn, and not all players would do that.

I like bowling with another spinner at the other end. In Australia I had Tim May and Stuart MacGill often working in tandem with me, and it was good to have Shaggy sharing the spinning load when I came to Hampshire because we helped each other.

One of his great assets is his captaincy. As Hampshire captain I have never been slow to seek his advice if I felt I needed it and I know that when I was not leading the side, Shaggy would do an excellent job as my replacement. The players respected him for his leadership qualities, tactical appreciation and determination to win and because they knew he would always lead from the front. Captaining the county to the C & G Trophy triumph at Lord's was his proper reward and I think the responsibility brought the best out of him as a player. I played in the first two rounds and he was kind enough to make sure I later got a medal.

Shaggy and Emma, his wife, made me and my family very welcome when I first came to England and for that I shall always be thankful. It is not easy uprooting to the other end of the world and coming to terms with a whole new cricketing culture and way of life.

My Turn To Spin

I know Shaggy had his ups and downs in 2006. There was the great success he enjoyed in India, winning the Mumbai Test on the last afternoon, but there was also the shock of discovering that his beloved son Jack was suffering from autism. What he and his family went through can only be guessed at.

Shaggy has always given me 100 per cent backing as a friend and as a player and his commitment to Hampshire has never been in doubt. These days players shift from county to county without thinking twice but Shaggy has always been a Hampshire man and has proved it time and again over his 20 years and more with the club. I applaud loyalty and in Shaun Udal, Hampshire have a player who has shown it in abundance.

We keep in contact throughout the close season and I am sure we will always be friends. No one was happier than I was when he got his England caps at 36 years of age, too late to get the full international career I felt he deserved.

I know he loved his time in the limelight and if in any small way I contributed to that, then I am truly delighted. Shaggy has a good few years left in him because the fires still burn bright. Perhaps there are some twists and turns still to come. Don't rule it out.

Chapter 1

Selected

BOB WILLIS will go down in cricket history as one of England's greatest fast bowlers. His 325 Test wickets put him ahead of legends like Fred Trueman and the Bodyline destroyer Harold Larwood and many others. As a 12-year old I vividly recall watching his eight for 43 slice through the Australians at Headingley in 1981 to earn England one of the most spectacular Test triumphs of all time. But it was Bob Willis, the television commentator and pundit, who so damaged my family with his ill-considered remarks and his scathing analysis of my part in England's tour of Pakistan in the autumn of 2005.

As a professional cricketer of some 20 years standing I have never minded criticism, providing it was constructive and well-intended. But Willis went too far, causing my 14 year old daughter to be ridiculed and humiliated at school and my wife, Emma to have to report to the year head the play-ground incidents which had reduced Katherine to tears. It needed the kindly intervention of a big man in all senses to bring to an end an unhappy incident, which all but had me on the plane home. Thank goodness for Freddie Flintoff.

I should explain the background. At 36 I became the fourth oldest player to represent England in Tests, some ten years after my last flirtation with international cricket and long after even I, a great optimist, had thought my chances of playing for England had gone. I was not a popular choice, statistically the best of a small crop of county off spinners available to the selectors and hoisted out of county obscurity to take on those masters of spin, the Pakistanis on their own dry, dusty and dead wickets.

I was on a hiding to nothing in retrospect, but I love a challenge and this was the biggest of my life. I was by some distance the oldest member of the touring party and what I had willingly taken on was hard, very hard, for a whole variety of reasons. Leaving Emma and my three children was difficult enough, adjusting to life in the international arena was never going to be easy and trying to get out the Pakistani batsmen day after day in the sweltering heat and choking atmosphere was a colossal task for all of us, let alone someone new to cricket at this level, like me. I played in all three Tests and while I know I did not bowl badly, I ended with three wickets at 92.33, figures, which I admit, on the face of it hardly justified my controversial selection. Importantly, the England coach Duncan Fletcher and all the players knew I had done as well as could be expected in the extraordinary circumstances, but that was not how some influential commentators saw it, not least Willis.

I have always got on well with Willis socially, so it was not as though there was any lingering animosity, and myself and my family would have accepted any technical criticism without the slightest hesitation. It's part of the job. All sports-lovers have their opinions on players and now that I was playing for England, I had to accept that my inclusion and my performances were being scrutinised by a critical sporting nation. In my view Willis went too far. "Shaun Udal should not be wearing the three Lions," was one such utterance, implying that I was hopelessly out of my depth, a county trundler playing beyond his true station in life. At home in Basingstoke, north Hampshire, Katherine became the laughing stock of her contemporaries as they repeated his mocking comments, surrounded and cornered by so-called school friends and taunted to tears. Katherine's way out of this problem was to text her mother and it was a deeply worried Emma who drove to the school to make sure our daughter's tormentors dispersed.

The school's year head was alerted and there was no repeat, but Katherine was clearly shaken and crying when she called me in Lahore to tell me of the whole sorry incident. It was then that Freddie came to the rescue. Grabbing the phone from my hand, Freddie told her: "Don't let them get to you. You stand up to them. Your dad has been great." Needless to say, she was cheered immediately and her kudos rose to dizzy heights among those very same children who had sometimes made her school life a misery. But that's Freddie for you. He's by nature a generous, lovely bloke who got involved even more directly, I understand, when the son of his manager, Neil Fairbrother, was the victim of some bullying at school. So Freddie met the boy at the school gates, to the shock of his tormentors, and his street cred soared, like Katherine's, through the roof. Problem solved.

None of which gets away from the fact commentators like Willis have huge power to hurt. He may have felt genuinely that I was not an England-class player but there are ways and methods of saying such things without causing such damage beyond the cricket field. Perhaps he felt he had to be controversial, I can respect that, and I know also that some of the English newspapers were less than complimentary at times, but the broadsheets got my task in perspective, pointing out the lifeless state of the wickets and how the conditions hardly favoured the finger spinners. It was not as though I alone struggled to cope in Pakistan. Soon after our tour, India played on the same wickets and the experienced off spinner Harbhajan Singh did not get even one and at large personal cost.

But then everything at Test level is magnified and I was merely grateful late in my career to build on an international career which started with an Ashes tour in 1994-95, continued with an England A tour of Pakistan the following year and was interspersed with ten limited overs internationals. I came close around that time to playing a Test match or two but there is no getting away from the fact that my prospects faded over the years and had all but been extinguished by the time the Pakistan tour came to be considered.

The summer of 2005 had been outstanding for me in domestic cricket, but even more outstanding for England. In the absence of Shane Warne, I was Hampshire's captain when we won the C & G Trophy at Lord's. To hold the trophy aloft as the winning captain at cricket's headquarters was the high point of my career and I would have been happy to take the memories of that magnificent occasion with me into retirement a few years down the line as the best day of my cricket life. Many outstanding players have never so much as appeared in a Lord's final. I had played in three, winning them all. Most players, denied the opportunity to play for their country, would have settled for that sort of record.

At the same time England were engaged in the most enthralling Ashes series of all time in terms of closeness of results and for sheer excitement. Even non-cricket fans were gripped by the enormity of the matches and the entire nation seemed to come to a stand still as the final drama was played out at the Oval. Among the England supporters, no less fervent than those who followed the series ball by ball, was me. I am an England fan in all sports and it was no different because I had played with and against the players who were to become overnight heroes. I shared from afar the highs and lows of that series, and wondered what it must have been like to wave from an open-topped bus at the jubilant hordes in central London and to visit Buckingham Palace to meet the Queen.

Not for one moment did I think I should have been up there on the bus with Freddie, Kevin Pietersen and the others. They had deserved their glory and, as a supporter, I was very, very happy. Two months later I was walking out for my Test debut at Multan in the company of those same Ashes heroes, hardly daring to believe what was going on. It was as if I had been a lucky punter in a competition to spend a day with the England team, a feeling as surreal as it gets in cricket.

Even now I wonder how the whole episode unfurled, how on earth it was that I was plucked from the autumn of a contented county career to spearhead the England spin attack surrounded by Freddie Flintoff and the other household names. In fact it all began the day after England had won the Ashes at the Oval. As the Ashes' winners paraded through Trafalgar Square, Hampshire were engaged in a run-of-the-mill totesport National League match at Cardiff. Shane Warne joined us in Cardiff but he was in no mood to play after giving body and soul in defeat the previous day and watched as we were absolutely hammered by 151 runs. That can have done nothing for his humour, but, for some reason, the match was being televised.

The television was on in our dressing room at Sophia Gardens but the sound was mute so that it was only later that my father Robin, who had been watching the match at home with sound properly turned up, told me that my name had cropped up as a possible candidate for the Pakistan tour. My captaincy performance at Lord's and a productive summer in the championship had not gone unnoticed. There were doubts about Ashley Giles and his hip injury, Robert Croft, who had stood in my path before, had retired from international cricket, and I was seen as the best of the rest. My figures were far better than younger rivals like Graeme Swann and Gareth Batty, I could bat and my fielding was still a strong point. I actually finished the season with 44 championship wickets at 18.90, in the top four ahead of some prominent bowling names.

Selected

The one-day match at Cardiff was followed by a four-day championship match and it was then that the plot began to thicken. Eddie Bevan, a prominent Welsh journalist, told me that he had spoken to David Graveney, the chairman of selectors, and he was privately pushing for me to be included. Warne had recovered his composure and renewed his strength enough to play in this match and Graveney sought him out to ask his opinion of me at the end of the third day. Warne did not tell me details of their conversation, but he said to me, "If I had to put money on it, I would say you are on the plane to Pakistan." What was I to believe? After a decade of dashed hopes and getting so close to selection, I refused to raise my expectations without greater evidence.

The Glamorgan match was by no means one of my better ones that summer, one wicket and a handful of runs in an easy win, and over the weekend that followed the phone did not ring. I took this as a bad sign until I was alerted to an article in the Sunday Telegraph written by Steve James, a former Glamorgan opening batsman who had become a successful journalist. My father-in-law, Graham Joblin, spotted references to me while he was enjoying a morning coffee and rang me instantly. More to the point, James enjoyed a close relationship with Duncan Fletcher and, in surmising who might be among the Pakistan tour party, my name was prominently mentioned. Had any other journalist written about me in such a way, I would have taken it as educated guess work but James, who was with Fletcher at Glamorgan, appeared to have the England coach's ear.

The next day, a Monday, is one I will never forget. The conjecture was over and it was time for the selectors to announce their squad for Pakistan. The Ashes team picked itself and so, too, did most of the fringe players. The big problem was that injury to Giles, which was showing no signs of improvement. To go to Pakistan without a recognised spin bowler of any variety would have been unthinkable and suddenly, from nowhere, I was the favourite. Even so, after so many setbacks, I was mentally prepared to be overlooked again. The squad was being announced at 10am so I took my daughters, Katherine and Becky, to school, pausing occasionally to stare at my mobile, willing it to ring and yet not expecting it to. Then just before the appointed hour, the phone burst into song, and the caller was using a mobile number I didn't recognise. My hands were trembling as the mystery caller made himself known, "Shaggy, it's David Graveney. This is one of the nicer phone calls I have to make. It's to tell you that you have been picked to play in Pakistan in a month's time. We'll see you at Loughborough for the medical tests and from now on your phone is going to be busy."

Busy, that was an understatement to end all understatements. I was still replying to messages and texts days later but before all hell broke loose, I had just enough time to make some calls of my own prior to the official announcement. All I could respond to the chairman of selectors was an inadequate ' thanks', but in the proper meaning of the words I was absolutely gob-smacked. "I'm in," I said to Emma as we embraced and, I'm not ashamed to admit, I burst into uncontrollable tears. Ever since I was a small boy, running around my cricket- mad grandad's garden, I had dreamed of this moment, those dreams being raised and dashed constantly over the years since I made my professional debut in 1989. Now it was a reality and how I wished he was here now so I could tell him my news.

The first action of which I have any meaningful memory was to ring my father, my mentor and greatest supporter. "I'm in," I said, my hands and voice still wobbling. "In what?" he asked, a not unreasonable question, and when I told him, his response was "fucking hell". Dad had never pushed me beyond what we both realised was my true capabilities, never lived his life through me, but I knew how much he cared and it must have been as big a moment for him as it was for me. For years I had watched him out of the corner of my eye from the middle as he paced the boundary of countless sometimes empty county grounds, willing me to succeed, alternatively critical and praising whether batting, bowling or fielding. I always looked for him, always knew where he was. Here, also, was his reward.

The next call was to my mother, Mary who was working in the British Aerospace catering department a few miles away at Farnborough. She was convinced there was something wrong when I showed up and again I was choking back the tears when I told her the news. We drank company champagne as word got around and it was then that the mobile exploded into action, a constant stream of media exploring the line about England's fourth oldest player, a statistic which will be forever etched on my brain. I did a live spot for Sky TV and Warne, a staunch advocate of mine, was the first to congratulate me. Still absolutely elated, we headed for Katherine's school - where we were later to have that momentary spot of trouble - and where the headmistress, Mrs Lawson, kindly pulled her out of lessons. We did the same at Becky's school, Castle Hill Junior School, and then it was on to the Rose Bowl for a press conference delayed by my determination to tell my girls the glad tidings. Draped in an England flag, I was the hero of the day as the cameras clicked, and an inspiration to all county players who had laboured for years, nurturing the diminishing hope that they might one day also get the chance to play for England.

The formal letter of my selection duly arrived, informing me of two training camps at Loughborough, which I was to attend, and a day of medical tests. My county colleague Chris Tremlett went with me as he sought to convince in vain the England selectors and training staff that he could overcome the latest of many injuries to have beset such a promising career. I was undeniably worried about the physical work, not least the bleep tests. Perhaps I had begun to believe all that publicity about my age. There were, after all, players ten or more years younger than me and competing with them in the sprints was not going to be easy. I was concerned that my 36 years might show before we had even boarded the plane. We were given vitamin C supplements, jabbed for typhus and typhoid and warned not to touch the fruit and salads once we had got to Pakistan. Fletcher was in Cape Town on a deserved holiday but Phil Neale, the team operations manager, analyst Tim Boon, physiotherapists Dean Conway and Kirk Russell, massage therapist Mark Saxby and bowling coach Troy Cooley all kept a watchful eye on our fitness efforts and no allowances were made for my extra years on the clock. I think I acquitted myself reasonably well but what worried me almost as much was how I would be received and treated by the other players. My previous experience of England touring sides was in Australia almost eleven years previously when I was conversely one of the younger players and where I discovered how the squad quickly broke down into cliques. Being uncapped, I felt excluded at times by the battle-hardened older players like Mike Gatting and Graham Gooch, although I should say that they were never unfriendly, just remote and living in their own worlds. I feared this might happen again, bearing in mind I was still uncapped but now a great deal older than most of those around me.

When we arrived at Loughborough I was not looking forward to our first meeting. Most of the lads had the Ashes in common and there was still a sense of achievement among them. Of course I had come to know the England players over the years but I wondered if they would see me, understandably, as a sort of ageing interloper. I need not have worried. Michael Vaughan thrust out a hand of welcome straight away, "Well done, mate. Congratulations on your selection." Strauss, Collingwood, Jones and Giles all did the same and, from that moment, I was one of the lads. It was noticeable how they all got on, all enjoyed each other's company and I was accepted among them as if I had been an international for years. Vaughan was a revelation, putting me at ease by telling me "they are all human", to wear what I wanted, to have a drink if that was what I also wanted and said he treated us all as adults. This had not always been the case in my previous experience. I was issued with all the kit, a sponsors' mobile phone and other perks but there was one very strong message: "When it comes to cricket, you must give everything." That was fine by me because that was my philosophy anyway.

I gave everything in a compulsory swimming test in the Olympic-sized pool at Loughborough, but it was still probably not quite good enough. I was really frightened of this because I knew I would be badly exposed. Chris Tremlett, for one, swam like the proverbial fish while I and, thankfully, Ashley Giles were quickly revealed to be the poorest, plodding on as best we could while others seemingly frolicked around us. It was all about endurance and after only a short time my shoulder began to cause me problems, but I resolved not to give up under any circumstances. For 35 or 40 minutes I battled on, up and down that pool which seemed to get longer and deeper with every painful lap. Never have I been more glad to hear a whistle calling a halt and our efforts had not gone unnoticed. "Congratulations to Shaggy and Ashley for doing so well," said one of the training staff and there was a minor ripple of applause. Well deserved, if I say so myself. At the end of the sessions, I felt very much at home, part of the squad and well accepted. Freddie called me grandad occasionally, in jest, and once in a while there would be a minor, good-natured jibe about my age but overall I was more conscious of it than anyone else and it all passed more smoothly than I had imagined.

A year or two before I had had a little confrontation with Collingwood when our counties clashed in a Sunday league match. Colly said something to me and I responded with: "You think you are a big man now you play for England." Robin Smith had to intervene but the incident never developed because Colly apologised and the game continued. But it had occurred to me that Colly might still bear a grudge and I was relieved that he obviously did not.

The England A side used Loughborough at the same time and it was here that I came face-to-face with Gareth Batty, a big rival of mine for the spinning spot and who had played for England in the same year, 2005. He must have been very disappointed but he was gracious enough not to show it in congratulating me and shaking me warmly by the hand. To be honest, I thought Swann was the more unlucky but I reminded Gareth that at 28 he had a decade of cricket in him and plenty more chances to keep alive the art of off spin bowling at Test level. At the end of the sessions I rang Emma to tell her how much kit England expected me to carry with me to Pakistan. I drove home in my England tracksuit, stopping to buy petrol I didn't need just to show it off.

Had England not called me, I would have spent the winter in the printing trade, which was my alternative profession, plodding up the overcrowded M3 to my company's base at Fleet, Hampshire, avoiding the rain and listening to events in Pakistan on the radio as I drove. It was how I had spent the majority of winters since I became a professional cricketer, as seasonal an occupation as Father Christmas's, and that's how I expected life to continue. After a summer on the road, I was always glad to see more of my family, while at the same time envying those players who were wintering in warmer climes. Knowing deep down I was as good as them did not make it any harder to bear.

The terms of employment by the ECB for the Pakistan tour came as a pleasant shock. Since touring Australia in 1994-95, the fees paid to the players had doubled in a decade and, without divulging figures, was a magnificent sum and a most welcome out-of-season bonus. I reckon that four or five years playing for England should set players up for life and for anything more than five years, should mean never having to work again. For me it was a reminder of what I had missed financially and what might have been if my career had taken off after 1995 instead of temporarily going backwards at an alarming rate. Having said all that, my salary for playing in Pakistan and, later, in India would have amounted to two weeks' wages for a good-average Premiership footballer.

My Turn To Spin

I am an emotional man and my family are my world. I found it hard saying goodbye to Emma and the girls in 1994 when I went to Australia. Now it was eleven years on and there was one- year-old Jack to consider, a late and much loved arrival. I knew saying goodbye would be the hardest part of going to Pakistan and as the big day approached the mood at home became more and more subdued. I made the choice to leave the family at home when I met the other players at the Heathrow Marriott on the eve of our departure because I knew I would not be able to face the final cheerio so publicly.

On the morning of my last day, I discovered three hours before I was due to go that my 'England' trousers were too long, even for someone of 6ft 2 inches. I raced down to a shop in Basingstoke in a desperate late attempt to get them altered and while that was being done for me I bought four cards and wrote a little message each for Emma, Katherine, Becky and Jack, saying how much I would miss them and how much I loved them. I sat in my vehicle in a car park opposite the town's post office and as I wrote, the tears poured down my cheeks, threatening to smudge my shakily-written words.

Our deadline for the hotel was 3pm and by 2pm I had attempted to eat some lunch and Emma had wished me luck. She was staying at home with the children and it was time to go when my friend Tony Britten arrived to take me to the hotel. He discreetly sat outside for ten minutes as the family gave each other final kisses and hugs. There were tears everywhere and little Jack sat on one of my cases, as if he somehow knew I was going out of his life. Within ten minutes of our emotion-charged farewells I was on the phone to Emma: I had forgotten my England blazer, shirt and tie, hanging from a hook behind the bedroom door. I was barely a mile from home and had got as far as the Apollo Hotel. Emma came to the rescue and within the hour I was checking in at our hotel.

Only later did I discover another horrific mistake. Malaria tablets are an essential part of our equipment when we travel to the sub-Continent and mine were at home in Basingstoke. Again, a panicky call to home and this time Jon Hardy, the former Hampshire, Gloucestershire and Somerset batsman, made the trek to the hotel and, at last, I was up together and ready. There was a team meal, we suffered for Michael Vaughan as Sheffield Wednesday struggled on television and then, early next day, we were off.

Selected

Islamabad seemed a world away when we touched down in the early hours. A certain musty smell hits the nostrils. By 9.30 we were in the hotel swimming pool as the prelude to a routine we adopted later of a 20-minute swim every morning at 7.30, time enough for some water polo and a dozen lengths. By the end of the tour I was a much-improved swimmer. Freddie and Steve Harmison came out a week later than the rest of us and on the day Freddie arrived there was a loud knock on my door. As I opened it, Freddie and Harmy loomed in front of me, two very large men on a mission. "Congratulations," they said. Freddie's hand enveloped mine and his pat on the back would have knocked most men sideways. "You're coming to dinner with us," he ordered. I will never forget that Freddie moment either. "When I first went on tour, nobody took me under their wing," he explained later. "I know what it is like to be a newcomer, not knowing anybody else closely enough." From then on we became firm pals. Freddie has this way of making everyone feel important to the squad and at ease with each other. It is a great gift and he is one of those people who does not have to work at being genuinely funny. There is no way anyone can out-banter Freddie, he is so sharp-witted and quick but without ever being derogatory. People say he has calmed down since meeting and marrying Rachael but I will always be grateful for the way he so effortlessly helped me adjust and settle.

Harmy is different, a little more introverted perhaps and prone to bouts of homesickness, but great friends with Freddie and good for morale. We used to eat together a lot, our favourite restaurant being a Japanese in Lahore, expensive but top quality. Harmy brought with him a huge stack of DVDs and he would giggle away for hours at endless re-runs of 'Only Fools and Horse', 'Max and Paddy' and 'Shameless'. The rest of us were glad he brought them because we, too, whiled away the hours by sharing his stash of films. Play stations came to our rescue also since it was so hard to get a drink or socialise in the way we knew in a 'dry' country. Collingwood, Giles, Vaughan and Trescothick formed a Football League between them because, cricket and training aside, there was not a vast amount to do after stumps.

Having played in Pakistan in 1995-96 with England A I knew how impossible it was to lay your hands on any beer so it was a major surprise when Ian Botham, now a Sky TV commentator, always seemed to conjure up a bottle or two of wine when it mattered. How he got hold of them we will never know but I still have a wonderful picture of the great man fast asleep on his sofa, slightly the worse for drink, bottle by his side and me, Freddie and Harmy staring into the camera, thumbs up. Going a long time without alcohol can have adverse affects, as I found out during the second Test. I'm not sure how, but we came across a decent quantity of red and white wine and some syrupy local lager which we drank in Freddie's room. On an empty stomach I put away rather a lot of all of those and it was not until 9.20pm that some Chinese food arrived, too late to soak up the drink. Uneasy on my feet, I tripped over Freddie's play station wires and toppled into his cupboard, sending his clothes and belongings flying all over the room. "You all right, Shaggy?" said Freddie. I was not. I retreated to my room where I fell asleep fully clothed until 7am, some six hours after even Freddie admitted defeat.

Chapter 2

Heat And Dust

ON THE EVE of the first Test in dusty, industrial Multan, Marcus Trescothick sat in front of us, piece of paper in hand. Ahead of him lay an attentive and nervous England squad, every one among us hoping our names were on that scrap of paper. None were more desperate than me. Trescothick, as captain in place of the injured Vaughan, had the task of telling us who had been chosen to face the Pakistanis and my prospects were distinctly good, or so people kept telling me. Giles was still struggling with his hip injury and was moving with increasing discomfort and nothing was going right for Vaughan. Multan may not have been the most beautiful city in Pakistan, with its mud huts, mules and choking traffic, but the cricket stadium was impressive and the facilities fit to be compared with any across the world. The England players were not so impressed by the wicket when we went to make our inspection the day before the match: Flat, dull and probably lifeless, just the sort of 'shirt-front' on which to make a debut. The Pakistanis had massive quality all the way down the order and this wicket was seemingly an open invitation to them to rack up colossal scores. Not that I could afford to worry about that. If I wanted to be a Test cricketer I had to be prepared to pit my wits against the world's best players on any kind of surface and not complain about it. And, my word, I really did want to be a Test cricketer.

The first indication that I might, just might, be close to playing came in the nets the day before the match. My bowling was going well enough but it was not my bowling which was the first clue to my possible selection. It was my batting. Duncan Fletcher had decided that the openers should net first and others got their chance in probable batting order. "Get your pads on, Shaggy, you're at nine," came the order. It was then, for the first time, I allowed myself the luxury of beginning to believe my long, long journey to overnight stardom might have a successful ending. Even then I was determined to keep such thoughts to the back of my mind because my hopes and ambitions had been dashed so many times before. I thought back to how close I had got to playing in Tests against Australia, South Africa and the West Indies and how each time the prize had been snatched away from me at the last minute. Was this going to be yet another close failure and yet another disappointment? The growing expectation was fuelled by the English press, mingling among players and officials and looking for an early 'steer' as to what the team might be. Let's face it, an England player making his debut at 36 was a very good newspaper story. Many reporters seemed to think I was in, as if they had been privy to a secret, and other players further encouraged me by saying they thought we would play with two spinners, partly because the wicket might offer a bit of turn and partly as insurance for the ailing Giles. In my heart of hearts, I, too, felt this was going to be my big chance, but until my name was pinned up on a board somewhere I could not afford to take anything for granted.

That evening at around 6pm the selection committee of Vaughan, his replacement captain Trescothick, Freddie Flintoff and Duncan Fletcher met to decide our fate. Some of us were going to be gutted, others were going to be elated and I began to think what would be my reaction if I was again left out. The rest of the squad, still basking in the Ashes glory, had either become well established as internationals like Strauss, Freddie and KP, or had at least played at that level and had in their lockers an England cap and a jumper with three lions on it. I was the exception, and my time was running out. As the committee deliberated, there was a distinct edge of nervousness among the players and I only hope my jitters were not too apparent when, around 30 minutes later, we were called in by the selectors like errant kids summoned before the headmaster, and even then our misery was prolonged. As we fretted and became lost in our own thoughts, we were forced to stare at a movie screen as the highlights of the Ashes were shown to us as a reminder of what could be achieved against the odds and then the conversation turned to Pakistan. Fletcher and Tim Boon had prepared a sort of dossier on their weaknesses, helpful hints on how to get them out. Always throw the ball to Inzamam's end when he's running, was one such edict, based on the Pakistani captain's dismal reputation for run-outs. Don't forget to shower Mohammad Yousuf with bouncers when he first takes strike, was another. Judging by Yousuf's record-breaking sequence of scores in 2006, that theory of weakness may no longer have much credibility, but it was worth saying. All the while I kept thinking what I would do if I was again overlooked. Could I just shrug it off and say to myself, there are two more Tests? Or would my rejection numb me into silence?

The tension was close to unbearable as Marcus at last prepared to announce the eleven. "It's a great honour to be captain of England and I will do my best to lead the team as outstandingly as Michael Vaughan did earlier this summer," he said. "I know I will be under the microscope but after beating the Aussies we must do it against Pakistan." On he went; they won't be easy, outstanding players, great respect for them etc, etc...and then he picked up the team sheet. By this stage I was looking at the ground, my heart racing, not daring to look at our new captain as he reeled off the names in what I took to be batting order. "Trescothick, Strauss, Bell, Collingwood, Pietersen, Flintoff, Jones, Giles... (there was a slight pause, I thought) ...Udal...Hoggard, Harmison. It was all over in 20 seconds. Trescothick rounded it all off, "Sorry to those who missed out but you are all still very much part of the team. Very good luck to Shaggy." Freddie embraced me in one of those great rib-crushing hugs, the others quickly offered hands and messages of congratulations, Duncan Fletcher, not a man of many words or obvious emotions, limited himself to," Good luck, young man," a comment I now realise was slightly ironic bearing in mind how much my advanced cricketing years had attracted such attention. In fact the warmth and the profusion of the goodwill was almost too much to take in at once and, in danger of being overwhelmed, I had to ask for five minutes to myself to gather my thoughts and my emotions. I went out into the car park, looked up to the sky, expelled a breath of relief, pleasure, surprise, elation all mixed in together and, with a shaking hand, fumbled my mobile into action. First call, home. Second call, mum and dad. Then my brother Gary. Emma and the children were almost hysterical with delight, their voices in autumnal Basingstoke loud and clear in a Multan hotel car park. Dad, for whom this must also have been a seminal moment in his life, put it in crisp perspective. "It does not get any better. You're playing for England."

My Turn To Spin

The press were not told until the next day, although the papers were full of stories about my probable first appearance, and when the team was finally announced to the outside world, there were yet more messages of good luck from all over the world. My great childhood hero, Ian Botham, as firm of handshake as ever, was among the first to congratulate me. I was walking on air. That night before the match began, I slept well, lulled into fitful unconsciousness as I chuckled at Harmy's DVDs, although I could not help thinking back to the years when international recognition eluded me again and again; at times, admittedly, on the basis that I had simply not deserved it. I came to the conclusion that my selection was a big plus for the English championship. I suppose I had developed into what is described as a good county pro, better than average but not quite good enough to play for England in Test cricket. Every county had a player or two like me, all of us able to make a decent living from something we loved doing, with the prospect of a tax-free lucrative benefit somewhere along the line. Some, like me, had tasted international cricket in the shape of a tour, perhaps, or some limited overs internationals, but the big prize, the ultimate challenge of Test cricket had, by and large, eluded us. For most of my career I had harboured the belief that I was the best finger spinner in the country and that my time would come but, as time wore on and the call never came, I had accepted and come to terms with what I thought was my fate. I had at least played in ten limited overs internationals, so I was almost there, and I was content in my own mind that my career had been productive with more than 1,000 wickets in all competitions for Hampshire and therefore some domestic fame and acknowledgement. If I was to analyse myself, as I did often enough, I would have conceded that I had not taken those England chances which had come my way a decade earlier when I believed there would be plenty more. This was very definitely my final, final opportunity and I intended to take it.

On the morning of the match, Emma and Katherine were up at 4.30am to catch the opening overs from Multan before the English day had dawned on Sky TV. "Great news for the Udal family," said the commentator, as if he knew of their presence on the lounge sofa. Tres lost the toss, Pakistan predictably consigned us to the field and I had this surreal experience of walking out for the start of the match with all these big names, household names in fact since the Ashes had been reclaimed so wonderfully. Only Vaughan and Simon Jones were missing and I felt like a football supporter who had won a lottery prize and been allowed to play in a Premiership match with his heroes. In the heat I wanted a cap, an England cap. After all, I had waited long enough for it but no one seemed to want to give it me. "Wait until the team huddle," said Phil Neale, spotting my impatience. Tres, as captain, duly handed it over and, yes, it did not fit. By lunch on the first day, Pakistan were an increasingly commanding 103-1 and it was 30 minutes into the afternoon before Tres suddenly said to me, "next over," a short sentence but one for which I had waited the best part of 20 years.

Before my departure from England, the children had given me a special present, a leather wristband, which they told me to kiss as a signal of recognition before I began bowling. This I did, fleetingly imagining them at home pointing to the television set as I kept my part of the bargain. I don't remember being nervous, but here in front of me were Salman Butt and Younis Khan, both well set and eager to test the credentials of the ageing county rookie. Salman Butt was on strike and my first ball came out perfectly, and disappeared just as perfectly over long off for four. Welcome to Test cricket was the message written all over it. Butt is wristy and loose, a typical product of the sub-continental pitches and, with well over 50 already gathered, he looked hungry for more runs. I'm pleased to say the rest of the over was fine in terms of length and line and there was no obvious wobble in my delivery. My plan, and there was a plan, was to contain Butt for four balls and then get him driving at a wider fifth delivery. In the seventh over that tactic, employed often enough in county cricket against anyone prepared to attack me, paid off handsomely, although in a manner which still brings a smile to the face. Four balls came and went and Butt, on 74, could do nothing but repel them. The fifth drifted wide of the off stump as I had hoped and Butt could not resist, propelling himself at it in almost blind fury. The ball flew towards Tres at first slip off the edge but our captain could only raise his hands, as if intending to surrender, while it struck him, comically and almost in slow motion, on the head. The rebound looped in the air just long enough for the sharp-witted Geraint Jones to dive back and grab it. "Catch," I screamed, and as Jones indicated his success, ran off heaven knows where in sheer, unfettered delight.

As Butt departed, the pleasure of removing the dangerous opener was tempered by much mirth aimed at Trescothick. Inzamam promptly hit me for an imperious six and a four as if to remind me what I had got myself into, but at the end of the day I was well pleased with my 16 overs for 40 odd. The pace of Test cricket was slower than I had expected but against so many class players, the margins for error were so small. Poor deliveries I might just have got away with in the county game were despatched with glee here. Harmy, Freddie and Matthew Hoggard took the other nine wickets and the papers reported that I had out-bowled Giles although, my wicket apart, our figures were similar when Pakistan were all out for a moderate 274. My final analysis was 17 overs, one for 47 and as Trescothick unleashed a fearsome 193, we built up a significant first innings lead of 144. I wish I could say I had been able to make a healthy contribution but, like many better batsmen before me, began with a nought, out fourth ball, lbw to Shoaib Akhtar. No complaints there. When Pakistan batted again, Harmison, Flintoff and Hoggard again took nine wickets between them with some magnificent bowling on a dead wicket, all life rolled out of it by the groundstaff to aid those bowlers on the Pakistan side who had the ability to skid deliveries through. My 12 overs failed to glean a wicket but at no stage did anyone get after me and I felt I bowled tidily without, I suppose, ever looking dangerous. Not that it greatly mattered. We needed 198 to win in a day and a bit and at the end of the fourth day England were 24-1 and, so we thought, on the way to victory. How wrong we were.

We even got to 64-1 with the target shrinking by the minute when Shoaib's searing pace became allied to a bit of turn that Danish Kaneira suddenly found in the wicket. From a position of power, we were 117-7 when I walked out with the team in trouble and me on a 'pair'. While the wickets tumbled, I worked out a strategy I hoped would spare me the embarrassment of beginning - and perhaps ending - my Test career with two noughts. To avoid gifting Shoaib another cheap lbw, I resolved to take a leg stump guard and make sure my backlift was shorter. But it is all very well making plans to counter a world class bowler performing at full pelt, it is another thing altogether to put it into practice. At this stage we were 82 short and Pakistan sensed they were into the tail, but this is the sort of situation I relish and I was in no mood to let what could have been my last England innings slip away without a fight. Shoaib hurtled in, the crowd baying for blood, and I got an edge. Half expecting a catch I turned instead to see the ball running away for a comfortable single and the pressure eased, so much so that I straight drove Shoaib almost immediately for four. At lunch Geraint Jones and I had taken the score to 138-7 and the Pakistanis were not quite as chirpy as they had been, nor were the crowd quite so triumphant. Duncan Fletcher praised the pair of us at lunch. We were 60 away from a famous win and I remember saying to Geraint that I fancied our chances.

Those chances grew by the minute as we took the score to 166, just 32 away, without any great worries and Shoaib was noticeably tiring. Inzamam gave him one last over. Had we held on through that I feel certain we would have gone on and won, but Geraint edged into his stumps after we had put on 49 and now the initiative was back with the celebrating Pakistanis. The match was all but concluded in the next over when Kaneira bowled me with a googly and we were all out soon afterwards for 175, my contribution to a 22-run defeat being 18, a reasonable innings spread over an hour, but in the end not good enough. Having got back into the match and having had such a significant first innings lead we should have won easily. It was a badly missed opportunity, a sad end to a match we had dominated. Had we gone one up in the three-match series, I feel sure we would have gone on to win it all. Shoaib was the hero despite the fact that he and Shabbir Ahmed were reported by the umpires for suspect bowling actions. At 95 mph he is a frightening prospect to have to face and you don't get time from 22 yards away to see if his arm is straight or not, but it is the development of his slower ball which is just as deadly and slightly underestimated. When Shoaib bowls at you, the ball is either around your head or spearing in at your toes; there is precious little to hit. Needless to say, we had hoped that the two bowlers would be suspended for the next match in Faisalabad but the ICC match referee, Roshan Mahanama, allowed them to continue on the basis that their actions were still being properly analysed.

Duncan Fletcher has a reputation for being economical with comments, good or bad, so when he told me I had done well in Multan and would be playing in Faisalabad I shook him by the hand, even more enthusiastically when he said I would be staying on for the one-day series after the Tests. It was a decade since I had last played in one-day internationals and if I have a gripe it is that I should have played in many more than my final tally of eleven. Robin Smith, kindly, said I should have played nearer 100, while my own belief is that 40 or 50 would have been nearer the mark, a more reasonable representation of my own conviction that I was England's best one-day bowler in the late 90s and the early 2000s. It's a belief backed by facts in terms of runs scored and wickets taken in domestic competitions for Hampshire, better than those either ahead of me in the England team or those competing for a place. I was a more mature person and player than when I actually played for England in the mid 90s at a time when my star appeared to be in the ascendancy. The biggest blow to my pride was when Martyn Ball of Gloucestershire was chosen in front of me for an England tour of India in 2000-01, I imagine on the basis that Gloucestershire were sweeping the board in one-day competitions around that time. I have absolutely nothing against Martyn but his figures don't compare with mine in any way. Indeed, I have taken twice as many wickets and I like to feel I am a far better batsman and fielder. At that time I was only 31 and in the form of my life, so that age and ability would not have been issues. I think also that if I had got in the England team then, as I should have done, I would have been in the team for the next four or five years, giving me ten to 20 Tests and nearer the 50 internationals I felt I was due.

Faisalabad was another flat wicket, a small ground with disconcertingly tiny boundaries. Pakistan's already-powerful batting was bolstered by the talented all-rounder Shahid Afridi and I knew that Ashley Giles and I would have to work for any success. I wish Afridi had not played because he hit me for the biggest six of my bowling life over the pavilion and into the distance. It was an astonishing strike although its sheer brutality was marred to some extent on the second day when he was seen scuffing the wicket with his boots and subsequently banned for three matches. It was while Pakistan were compiling 462 after winning the toss that Michael Vaughan turned to me, the Test match novice, at mid-on to ask me what to do next. We were struggling at the time and not much was working in our favour. I suppose I need not have been quite so surprised. I had led Hampshire to the C & G Trophy at Lord's a couple of months before and in other matches often enough to have an opinion worth listening to. I told him to give Harmison another spell and almost immediately Harmy got us a wicket. My 13 overs cost 60 without a wicket but there was not much in the pitch for the spinners, as Kaneria found out when it was his turn to try and extract some life. Ian Bell and Kevin Pietersen each hit centuries, but when last man Harmy joined me we were 399-9 and well adrift. I decided to be positive from the start because there was little point in playing for a not out, especially as Harmison is not a noted batsman. Shoaib was hurtling in with all his power and determined to finish us off, but I made up my mind to hit him as hard as I could. Luckily he dropped it short and with the sweetest of timing, I pulled him over square leg for one of the most satisfying sixes of my career and partial revenge for what Afridi had done to me. I also drove him elegantly through the covers for four. The great man was not used to such treatment, least of all on his home grounds. Harmy was run out 47 runs after we came together, stranding me on 33 when I nurtured genuine hopes of a half century.

I was not kidding myself. For all my useful batting defiance I needed a wicket or two to quieten those among our travelling commentators and experts who believed I was out of my class, or at least struggling to make an impact. I have the controversial Darrell Hair to thank for my second Test wicket. I was bowling to Salman Butt and doing what I could to contain him when Hair invoked law 42.14b.ii as Butt ran on the wicket for the second time while batting and following a warning. Butt was clearly upset at being sent back and denied a single in such unusual circumstances and, with his concentration disturbed, I fired in my wicket-taking quicker delivery next ball and had him lbw. Inzamam took a long time to come in next, as if to suggest he was not happy with the manner of Butt's dismissal and perhaps sowing the seeds of their row at the Oval in 2006. Inzamam scored a century in each innings but my tight figures of one for 31 off 14 overs might have been better had Andrew Strauss clung on to a catch offered by the Pakistan captain at mid-wicket. Left with 60 overs to get 285, we soon lost Trescothick and Vaughan but held on for a draw, six wickets down and 120 behind. Fletcher went to the trouble to thank me and Harmy for our batting in the first innings, pointing out that not only had we scored important runs to limit the Pakistan lead, we had also eaten up valuable overs.

I have to say that I did not expect to be playing in the final Test in Lahore. The policy of playing two spinners, Giles and myself, had not worked. The pace bowlers had done most of the work and taken most of the wickets and I think I would have stood down had Giles's persistent injury not finally got the better of him. As the only spinner, therefore, I had to play. It was around this time that Willis attacked me, and England, for selecting me, and I was aware from what people were saying at home that my continued presence in the Test side was not as popular as it might have been. As a professional cricketer I had to accept this criticism and get on with life, but that is not easy when it has never happened to you before. If you play for England, you have to take it in your stride, maintain your self-belief and be determined to prove your critics wrong. This is, of course, not so simple against high class players whose natural inclination was to attack my type of spin.

At Lahore, home ground of Shoaib, we took a heavy beating at the hands of the local hero. Collingwood hit 96 in our 288 but Inzamam, Kamran Akmal and the prolific Mohammed Yousuf, treating our bouncers with impunity, compiled huge scores before they were all out for 636. I had the satisfaction of having Yousuf caught in the deep by Pietersen but not before he had scored 223, and I fear those prejudices against me were to some extent reinforced by my figures of one for 92. In my defence, I don't think I bowled badly, and nor did those within the England hierarchy, but I can understand that England supporters, perhaps believing we were the best team in the world after beating Australia, were disappointed at my contribution and Willis was possibly not alone among the press in dismissing me as a county pretender. Shoaib ran through us in the second innings with five for 71 but I held him up with an innings of 25 batting at nine. During that innings, Shoaib hit me painfully on the hand and when the physio came to examine the injury, he was convinced I had a broken bone. No way was I going off. I stayed on, doing what I could before we slumped to defeat by an innings and 100 runs, a bad setback by any standards.

As the one-day squad arrived and took shape, my hand merely bruised, I was left to reflect on three very expensive wickets, a 2-0 series defeat and the realisation of just how difficult Test cricket could be. None of that had been expected by me when we left Heathrow seven weeks earlier. What I had expected was a Test or two, a much closer contest and less personal criticism. While the stats were disappointing, undeniably, I felt I had made a contribution with bat and ball and in all other respects connected to the team. Fletcher offered solace when he said to me: "I know how difficult it was on those pitches," and he was not the sort of man to say anything he did not mean. Duncan was a surprise at times, saying nothing to me or the others for days on end and then tap unexpectedly into my experience and ask for my views on how, for instance, to get the best out of my county colleague, Chris Tremlett. I came to like him as a sincere person and respect him for his quiet diligence and his integrity. I'm not sure he was a great man-manager and the fact that he was wary of the press made him appear more aloof and dictatorial than he was. But he liked a glass of wine after stumps without ever mixing socially for long and yet was always polite and honest. Where he excelled was on technical coaching, a part of the game in which he had a fantastic knowledge and appreciation. He liked the scientific side of cricket and surrounded himself with a big backroom staff of similar-minded men. There was also, I discovered, an inner circle of players in whom he confided and in whom he placed his trust. I was not naïve enough to believe that I could ever be among them.

Struck down by a stomach bug, the last three weeks dragged and I dreamed only of going home in time for Christmas. I am not sure how I got the virus, possibly the air conditioning, and while it lasted only 24 hours, it made training hard and time hung all the more heavily. Everything was done to make sure we avoided such problems with a carefully considered diet. Nigel Stockill, our physiologist, insisted we had good, nourishing familiar food wherever we went. We had omelettes and porridge, beans on toast and cereal for breakfast, a lunch of grilled chicken, mashed potato and beans or some curry, naan bread and toast, supplemented with energy bars. Our urine was tested every session for evidence of dehydration, there was plenty of bottled water and our weight was checked every morning. In the evenings, hidden from the privations outside in our five-star hotels, I found there to be a massive improvement in the standard of food available compared to the days of my previous tour with England A ten years before. There was international class Indian, Chinese and European cuisine and even burger and chips if we were so inclined. In Lahore there were plenty of good restaurants.

But for all that, it was not always possible to avoid a stomach upset and for the first four one-dayers I was a not very interested spectator, pounding the internet for news of home and occupying the long dark evenings with emails and phone calls. I watched as Harmy sat with Peter Hayter of the Mail on Sunday, the News of the World's Dave Norrie ghosted KP and John Etheridge of the Sun recorded the thoughts of Freddie for his paper, each fulfilling lucrative contract columns. I sat quietly in the corner with my laptop writing my weekly thoughts for the Basingstoke Gazette! Freddie was the centre of attention when he won the BBC Sports Personality of the Year, his manager Neil Fairbrother flying out to help officiate, but for all the diversions, the novelty had worn off and I longed to see the family again. I had missed Jack crawling, Becky's birthday, Saturday mornings when I took the children dancing and swimming, wet leaves on the road and incessant, dismal rain and I don't think anyone in the squad was as badly affected by the mounting sense of dislocation and homesickness.

My only game was in Rawalpindi where we won and where I was out first ball and was only playing because of a late injury to Kabir Ali, having been listed as a supersub for Freddie. Bell dropped a catch off me and while I did get a wicket later, I could not think beyond catching the plane home that might. At the first available opportunity, all the players were in the bar, most of us shaking off ten long, hard weeks. We stopped at Dubai where I rang Emma to say I was on my way and at Heathrow, my bag was last off the plane. Most of the squad had emerged from baggage control and customs by the time I came through and caught sight of Emma and the children out of the corner of my eye. "Daddy," they shouted and soon we were kissing and hugging and, I admit, shedding another tear or two. All I wanted was a bacon sandwich and although the cold was a shock, I was home within an hour and a bacon sandwich quickly despatched.

It was December 22 and the anticipation of Christmas had never been greater. Emma and I had a meal out that evening at a club where the DJ announced my presence, such was my new-found celebrity. Christmas was spent catching up with mum and dad and mum was still my greatest fan despite my relative lack of success in Pakistan. We had a family lunch on Christmas Eve before setting off to my in-laws so that all the family could see our children and on New Year's Eve, Emma, the children and I went to a black tie party in Kent at the home of Tony and Lillian Marsden, parents of Claire, Emma's brother

Chris's fiancée. They certainly knew how to throw a party and at 3.15am, after a cracking evening and long after the champagne had been drained and 'Auld Lang Syne' rendered for another year, the phone rang. It was Freddie. "Shaggy? Just to wish you and your family a great New Year and hope to see you in February on the plane to India." For an astonishing drinking machine that he is, he sounded remarkably sober and how nice it was of him to call and remember little old me, bringing to a bizarre end an extraordinary episode in my life.

Chapter 3

Indian Summer

AS THE HAZY sun rose through the smog and above the packed stands of Mumbai's famous Wankhede Stadium, the England players cut a silent path out on to the pitch and I had never felt so low or alone. This was my last, last chance to show I was worthy to be called a Test cricketer and, deep down, I feared I was about to blow it. The previous evening, nothing had gone right. I was riddled with nerves, my hands were sweaty and shaky and I tossed up a heap of rubbish, sometimes too short, sometimes over-pitching, other times begging to be hit and feeling all the time that I was bowling from the wrong end. I could not even hold the ball properly. Four overs for 25 was my final analysis at the end of the day and it might have been worse, so poor was my performance. That evening I was inconsolable, staring into space, not speaking to my teammates and wondering what I had to do to change my luck. I could feel the purpose of my entire career slipping through those greasy palms, all that I had worked for destroyed in one hopeless session. I rang my friend and spin mentor, Shane Warne in a desperate bid to find a solution. "Never stop believing," he said. "One ball can change everything." Troy Cooley, England's bowling coach, sensing my unhappiness, took me aside. "What would Warne do? This is your last opportunity, don't mess it up." But he did give me a glimmer of hope. "You are in the England team because you have earned it." Even my old pal, Robin Smith, in Mumbai as host to one of his 'Judge's Tours' for cricket-loving holidaymakers, tried to cheer me up without much success. 'Judge' was as positive as he could be. "You are the best spinner England have got," he said, but I did not feel like it. In fact, I felt more like the worst.

But from the deepest of despair one incredible twist revitalised my life and set me on the road to becoming a temporary national hero. As we walked out on to that pitch, and for no obvious reason, I suddenly thought about another of my mentors, my grandfather Geoffrey, long dead but one of the great early influences on my determination at the age of ten to become a cricketer. Geoffrey Uvedale Udal was a character, an independent spirit who once turned down the chance to play for Middlesex because he preferred to go racing and who was once described in the Evening Standard as being as fast a bowler as Harold Larwood. Geoffrey was a gambler, an ex Army man who did eventually play one match for Middlesex and two more for Leicestershire in 1946. There is no doubt, had he so chosen, my grandfather could have made a life out of cricket, but while he enjoyed playing at club level, it was evident the county game held no great attraction. The race track was too much of a lure. What Geoffrey had done for me was fire my enthusiasm for the game. As a near neighbour in Cove, Hampshire he had taught me the high bowling action, which had stood me in good stead over the years, the basics of batting and of throwing. The strange thing is that he only ever saw me play once for my school but he always praised, always made me feel good about my cricket.

How I needed him now. I looked skywards as I walked, closed my eyes and thought about him, the old boy with his massive enthusiasm for me and my cricket and suddenly, suddenly all my fears and tension evaporated as if they had never existed. I am not a religious person, indeed I think organised religion is responsible for many of the world's problems, but this was akin to a religious experience. An aura of tranquility descended upon me and I felt a tremendous inward calm as if he was up there somewhere, saying "don't worry, your day has come". One minute I was being eaten away by self-doubt and turmoil and the next my determination had returned and a clear picture of what I had to do emerged in front of me.

I cannot to this day explain the transformation but I like to think grandfather Geoffrey had something to do with it. Everything changed for the better virtually from the moment play resumed. The grip on the ball became firm, the sweat dried up and I became focused on my job, as if it was just another day at the Rose Bowl. It was not, of course, this was quite probably my last Test and all I wanted was for teammates to say I had contributed equally to the England cause, my abiding horror being that I might somehow be regarded as a passenger.

After what had happened the previous evening I suspected Freddie might not bother with me again, but he did, and my next 12 overs were nice and relaxed and cost me only a further 28. Along the way I removed Irfan Pathan in an intriguing passage of play. Having deceived him twice, he tried to heave me out of the ground next ball and lofted a catch instead to Hoggard at mid-on. I should have got Dhoni even before that but failed to hang on to a sharp return catch and at last I felt as though I was indeed contributing. I remember thinking that I now understood the job Ashley Giles had been doing for England, a job for which he was not always appreciated. I know he was disparagingly referred to as a wheelie bin by one commentator but I could see how valuable he was by adopting his methods, settling into a groove, keeping the score down, allowing faster bowlers to rest and chipping in with the occasional wicket or two. Having stood in for him and played alongside Ashley, I know what he did for the England team and while they all knew his purpose, I am not sure the public realised his importance.

India were all out for 279 in response to our 400 (to which I had contributed nine) and my whole mood and demeanour had changed for the positive in 24 dramatic hours. This threatened to change yet again when Duncan Fletcher asked me to be nightwatchman and, while that was in itself a vote of confidence, I had not bargained for us being 21-2 with Strauss and Bell out in no time at all. If I was honest I was hoping I would not be needed as my record for Hampshire as nightwatchman was very poor. I had been out hooking twice when the opposition had two fielders back on the fence for that very shot, not the sort of thing you are supposed to do when the sole objective is survival. Suddenly I was being pushed out of the dressing room door, metaphorically-speaking, and told to make sure I did not get out between now and third evening stumps. Duncan told me it was a chance to make a Test 50, but nought seemed more likely as I flailed away at everything the Indian attack put in front of me. I have no idea how I survived those last few overs and when I came off, happily unbeaten, Fletcher said it was the worst 20 minutes batting he had ever seen by a nightwatchman. Sreesanth thought he had got me to a catch behind but Darrell Hair turned it down, as he did when Sreensanth thought I was plumb lbw. I was swishing wildly at anything within reach and to this day I don't know why. I all but played on after that and Sreesanth and I exchanged a few words about my apparent good fortune as we passed in the middle. I have to say he had a case. Harbhajan appealed for a ball that pitched a foot outside leg stump and from Sreensanth's last ball of the day, Yuvraj spilled a simple catch at second slip. No wonder Fletcher was mystified at how I had got away with it and baffled by my needlessly aggressive attitude.

The match was entering a crucial stage. The first Test in Nagpur had been drawn and the second in Mohali had been won comprehensively (by nine wickets) by India. Through illness I had played no part in either, so this match was as big for England as it was for me personally. We needed to win to level the series and I needed an overdue performance to establish my Test credentials. The Indians obviously felt aggrieved that I had not been dismissed the previous night and next morning, after I had blocked a ball from Pathan, he threw the ball at my pads in exasperation and earned a warning from the other umpire, Simon Taufel. Batting in an altogether more orthodox fashion, I made 14 in a total of 85 minutes, doing my bit to blunt the Indian pace attack before edging to second slip. I had been starting to feel comfortable and relaxed and paid the price. The heat was so intense during that opening hour or so that sweat dripped from my helmet - and no one else found it any easier. We were all out for 191, leaving India a full day of 90 overs to make 313, and there was a strong sense among us that we were going to be the more likely winners. I recall saying to Freddie while he had a drink that fourth evening with Robin Smith's customers on his tour that with a whole day we could become the first England side to win a Test in India for 21 years. I said to Robin and my friends, Tony and Lilian Marsden, that there would be a party if we did go on and win.

Sleeping well that night until 7am, I went for a swim on waking and found the India manager, Greg Chappell and his assistant also in the pool, looking pensive. It was then that I was approached by Fletcher and Cooley. Fletcher did not waste his words. "The pitch is turning. You have to come to the party." The message could hardly have been more bluntly put: It's up to you to win us the Test match. For all my other faults, I was not the sort of person to shrink from such a challenge. I relish it when I carry the extra burden of responsibility when others may not. I know I had played only three Test matches and none at all in India, but here was an opportunity I could only have prayed for. Throughout my county career I looked forward to last-day pitches when the ball was liable to turn from worn foot-holes and from cracks on the surface. There is not a spin bowler of any variety worthy of the name who did not dream of such pitches all summer long. I imagine Fletcher and Cooley must have said the same to young Monty Panesar, but at least I had the benefit of years of experience. Monty was still new to cricket at first class level, let alone Tests, and for all his prodigious promise, this was expecting perhaps too much of him. I could hardly wait. And wait I did until ten minutes before lunch, by which time India were only three down and heading carefully towards the draw they needed with the formidable Tendulkar and Dravid apparently in control. Monty had been brought into the attack before me and I have to say he looked nervous, bowling short and feeding the Indian strengths.

When I played for Hampshire, I made a habit of always knowing where my father was seated and here in Mumbai I was looking out for those in the large crowd I knew, Tony and Lilian and my brother Gary among many, as if to give myself reassurance by their presence and their familiarity. Gary was the only family member to make the trip and did not miss a ball despite feeling ill. I was particularly pleased to have him watching. Apart from a first-ball loosener which Tendular surprisingly missed, my little spell before lunch was just as I had hoped it would be, accurate, easy out of the hand and landing in the right spots. I was absolutely confident at lunch that if Freddie persevered with me in the afternoon I could do some damage. So I went to the England captain at the interval and told him I was desperate to continue, pleading for my opportunity. Freddie said he was undecided but in any case he had other things on his mind, namely our now famous rendition of Johnny Cash's anthem, 'Ring of Fire'. I'm not even sure how it started but for some completely unknown reason every England player joined in, singing at the top of their voices and clapping in time, so that before long we had a full choir, belting out every line as if the outcome of the match depended on it.

During a tour of India, ring of fire has different connotations from those envisaged by the great country and western star, but our impromptu sing-song raised spirits, left our opponents bemused and a little shocked by its sheer ferocity and finished, I think coincidentally, as the umpires came out for the start of afternoon play. We still needed seven wickets and from our relaxed attitude, the crowd must have thought we had given up hope and become sort of demob-happy. But we were far from that, there being a real belief among us that we could win. Freddie turned to me and said: "You and me start the bowling." That was what I wanted to hear, but in his first over after the break, Freddie got rid of Dravid, and while there was of course general delight, I feared he might alter his plans as a result. He did not, and for that I shall be eternally grateful.

I told Freddie I wanted an attacking field with a third close catcher and for a moment I thought he was going to turn my request down, but I think I had convinced him - if he needed convincing - there was only ever going to be one way to win this match and that was to attack. "Don't worry," I told him jokingly, looking down the wicket at Tendulkar in his crease at the other end, "I'm going to get him bat-pad." Tendulkar is one of the greatest batsmen of all time and he never likes to get out in Mumbai, where he is treated as deity. But he had batted with strange unease on his way to an uncharacteristically subdued and tentative 34 when he provided me with my greatest moment in cricket. Even as I write about it, I can feel every sensation and see The Ball Which Turned a Test as if in slow motion. Tendulkar had clearly been confused and had padded away anything I offered him outside the off stump. I was surprised by his indecision before lunch and was encouraged by his lack of aggression, so with my third ball I bowled fractionally straighter so that he had no room to manoeuvre. Tendulkar fell into the classic off spinner's trap, nudging without conviction into his pads and straight into the hands of Ian Bell at short leg. I did not wait for the umpire to give him out. Instead I took off on an ecstatic and jubilant 50-yard dash, arm raised in triumph, part-shocked and part-overwhelmed, towards Owais Shah somewhere in the outfield. I didn't care where. If there is a greater 'high' than that, I would love to know what it would be, because it would be hard to imagine, like scoring the winner in a World Cup final or volleying the winning shot in a Wimbledon final. Tendulkar made a sad return back to the pavilion, the massed ranks of his supporters as silent as the England fans were celebratory. The Barmy Army could sense an unlikely win.

By now I was bowling a much tighter line and for the first time since I became a Test player I was crowding batsmen, which just shows what confidence can do, as someone like Warne had been doing all his career. The Indian wicketkeeper Dhoni had obviously decided the game was up and decided to take me on during one of the most bizarre passages of play I had ever been involved in. Attempting to smash me for a straight six, Dhoni lifted the ball instead high to mid-on where James Anderson and Monty Panesar converged to take the catch. Monty was the closest and I knew from the moment it began to descend that Monty was in no position to get it. The ball plopped harmlessly on the ground next to him, the hapless Monty made to look foolish by his misjudgement. People say the look on my face was one of fury, but I think 'shocked' was a better description. In fact I was totally gobsmacked. I don't think I had ever seen a fielder at that level get it so comprehensively wrong. The worst thing a bowler or his captain can do in such circumstances is move the culprit out of the firing line so we left Monty in the same position. Little did he imagine that two balls later he would get the chance to atone as Dhoni went for another wild swing. The ball before he had played gently back down the pitch to me, but years of experience had taught me that he was going to have another dart so I pitched it a little wider and, sure enough, Dhoni heaved high in the air towards Monty again. I said aloud 'please, please, please' as Monty kept his eyes on the ball and, to the relief of himself above all others, held on grimly like a drowning man to a life-line. Freddie jumped on my back, temporarily winding me. "Get off", I recall saying, but there was no halting the jubilation.

The Indians were in fast retreat and I knew there were some easy pickings to be had from the tail. Sure enough, Harbhajan Singh pulled me somewhat disconsolately to deep square leg and suddenly I had three wickets for next-to-nothing. As we waited for last man Patel to come to the crease, I looked at my watch, hoping the children had delayed their departure to school to witness my finest hour as an England player. For them, as much as myself, I was desperate to get four wickets, and as Freddie began his over, I was disloyal enough to not want him to get the last wicket so that I might get another chance. All the while KP kept saying to me, "You are astonishing." And who was I to disagree. Once Freddie had failed to dislodge the last pair, it was my turn and, with the match nearly won, I had six balls to remove Patel. I knew in a lost cause he would hit out since there was no point in defending. Sure enough, Patel drove me high and a curious timelessness fell upon the stadium as Hoggard at deep square leg completed the catch, my four wicket haul and England's first win in India for a generation.

For a player with my largely parochial background, to hear the Barmy Army light up a 40,000 crowd with shouts of "Shaggy, Shaggy" was an incredible moment and still sends shivers down the spine. Freddie said: "I so hoped you would do well today, you old git," while KP had the foresight to get me a stump, now signed and a treasured memento, before our captain got us in a huddle, still on the pitch, and told us, "You were all remarkable. Everyone has contributed. We have drawn the series after everyone wrote us off. Now we are going to party." As we left the pitch for the last time, Freddie generously pushed me forward to receive the acclaim of the crowd first and the Barmy Army responded in style. It was like a dream, a wonderful reward for years of toil on the county circuit, often performed in front of the proverbial two men and a dog. Now here I was listening to my name being chanted around one of the game's great stadia. Duncan Fletcher, a derided figure a year later after losing the Ashes, was a hero then but he was quick to recognise my part in India's astonishing early-afternoon collapse. "I have waited 20 years for this," I said to him. As a former coach to Glamorgan, he knew what I meant. "You deserved it," he said. We did a lap of honour and Dean Jones, the commentator, singled me out for special praise. "A young man of his time," he told his viewers. Freddie was rightly named man of the match for his far greater all-round contribution, but it was me receiving the congratulations for actually winning the match, my four for 14 will be forever etched on my memory.

Shane Warne was among the first to get in touch by text and by phone. Apparently he was in the Australian nets when the result came through and he asked another player who had got the wickets. "Your mate," was the reply. "I'm over the moon for you," he said, when he eventually got through since the phone was so busy. "I hope it is the start of a long England career," little realising it was in fact the end. All kinds of people were kind enough to leave messages of support, old school friends, my old Hampshire captain Mark Nicholas and later, by letter, Charlie Mortimore, the schoolmaster who saw something in me as a child cricketer worth nurturing.

Mumbai, being something of a tourist city, had attracted plenty of friends and relations from England so the celebrations began on a chartered boat for players and their families. Later there was dinner with some familiar faces on Robin's tour; Nick and Linda Budge, Nick and Gilly Twine, Pat and Tony Atkinson, Lyn Dyson, Pete Vickery, Steve Brookwell and, of course, my brother Gary. Mark Dennis had given up football for a few weeks to come out, and my lifelong friend Chris Evans and his girlfriend Olga had flown in from Moscow, where he worked, to see my finest hour. It was gratifying to have won a Test, if I'm not being immodest, in front of them. My one regret was that my family was not with me that night. That would have capped everything, but I stared into the Mumbai sky and thanked grandad for getting me through. After midnight, for about three hours, I sat by the hotel pool with Tony and Lillian Marsden mulling over the day when KP's agent, Adam, approached me, offered his congratulations and said that if ever there was anything he could for me, to let him know. Jokingly I took him on. "Yes, there is, you can get me on Question of Sport." Reaching for his mobile, he pressed a few numbers, had the briefest of conversations and then said: "You're on." And I was. All this from a Mumbai poolside at 3am local time. I went to bed happy and contented but was looking forward to going home.

The next day, before we flew home on the same evening, was one of the most weird of my life, holding a press conference in the morning to re-live my match-winning performance in greater detail, packing as fast as I could to get to the airport where I ran into a departure lounge territory row with some Germans. The Germans had graciously allowed me a tiny space to put my gear on seats close to them, but they were less than pleased when I ushered Monty, Alistair Cook, Shah's wife, Geraint Jones's girlfriend and ECB official Andy Walpole into the same confined area. "You were OK, but not the others," they said to me, and an argument threatened to develop until common sense prevailed.

On the plane home I shared a bottle of wine with Atherton and Derek Pringle before my mum and dad met me at Heathrow, exhausted but triumphant, my mind set not on a bacon sandwich this time but on a bargain bucket of Kentucky Fried Chicken, my absolute favourite. Dad is not a man given easily to shows of emotion but he was quite moved and it was as much as he could do to shake me by the hand, words struggling to be said. I had barely collected my bags and my wits when Sky TV leapt forward asking me yet again to go through my 15 proverbial minutes of fame. The ECB sent a driver to take me home and as I loaded up the car, he said: "You did all right yesterday." My good mate Darren Ryder had sent me a text picture of the Sun showing my name in headlines. I have to say I had not expected this extended fuss and I was glad to stop and get my KFC down the road in some anonymity. In truth, anonymity was not possible for a few heady days, nor did I mind. Pietersen's friend, Simon Turner, got us in the famous London restaurant 'The Ivy' for dinner when it might otherwise have been difficult, and we indulged on pink champagne. In the streets of the capital I was three times stopped, thanked and had my hands shaken in gratitude. Outside Lillywhite's, an elderly man said, "Mr Udal, really well done."

And so to Question of Sport. I doubt if anyone would admit it, but all sportsmen and women fancy their chances on this programme and I was no different. Three programmes were recorded each day, so we had to wait our turn and watch others being recorded. I was on with Dean Macey, the decathelete, a woman weightlifter, the footballer Dennis Rommedhal, and the two captains, Ally McCoist and Matt Dawson. Sue Barker introduced me as "a veteran of the game who is enjoying an Indian summer." To my lasting shame, a picture appeared of Steve Harmison as my question and I had not got a clue who it was. "Don't know," I said sheepishly. "This might embarrass you, Shaun," replied Sue, and it did. However, I did partially redeem myself by guessing Matthew Pinsent and one other but I don't think I shall ever quite live down my failure to spot Harmy. The BBC organised a car and driver and a little group of us comprising my parents, Rob Ashley, Nigel Butler and Tony Britten stopped off at three pubs on the way home. My 15 minutes had become a sort of happy hour.

None of this would have happened had the selectors not kept faith with me when it would have been easy to drop me after Pakistan, or had I not recovered from severe stomach trouble which threatened to ruin my tour before it had begun. My tour report from Pakistan had been a good one, far better than what I had actually achieved, but there was an anxious wait as the press pushed for Monty Panesar, Alex Loudon and Gary Keedy as options, while Ian Blackwell's extra batting ability was considered as a means of bolstering the late middle order. So it was with some relief when David Graveney told me I would be going to India, partly I'm sure, because Ashley Giles was still nowhere near fit. "Nothing has changed. We know how tough it was in Pakistan," he said, adding that I would not be in the one-day squad. Graveney had worried me until that call because he had always 'talked up' Panesar - and with good reason. Although Blackwell did get his chance, Monty, of course, came out later for what I am positive was the start of a long international career. Monty is a great talent who needs to be nurtured and cherished until such time as he is a mature and experienced Test player. There is no doubt he needs to work hard on his batting and his fielding, because they are not yet up to standard, but his bowling can become a spinning weapon every bit as potent as any in world cricket. The first thing you notice about him are his massive hands and fingers. My fingers are long, as are those of most spin bowlers, but his must be an inch longer and he lives, eats and breathes the game with an insatiable appetite to learn more about his craft. There is room only for one other interest in his life: cars, he loves them.

I felt I would do much better in India than in Pakistan because the pitches were likely to favour me, but I nearly never got that far, even after Graveney had assured me of my selection. A few days before we were due to go to Loughborough for the pre-tour fitness tests, I went up to the footballing Old Trafford for a benefit dinner for Freddie. Freddie gave us a top table place next to Sir Alex Ferguson and it was a great night for everyone except me. I did not feel particularly well going north and worse still catching the plane home. I felt shaky and sick and headed for my bed for what proved to be a week. I missed the first meeting at Loughborough after being advised to rest and only went to the second because I was determined to go at any price. I drank as much water as I could but it was obvious to our fitness expert, Nigel Stockill, that I had come back too soon. Even so, I got on that plane to India feeling lousy while believing I would soon get better. How wrong I was. A week before the first Test I became seriously ill again with sickness, diarrhoea and a temperature soaring above 100 degrees. Driven on by a fierce inner desire to play every single minute of this tour, I got to the ground before our first provincial match but it was obvious I was in no fit state to play, my stomach was terribly painful and Duncan Fletcher said he did not want my problems passed among the rest of the party. I was taken by ambulance with Peter Gregory, our team doctor, and a security guard to hospital where scans and x-rays revealed a severe bowel infection, maybe picked up from food or air conditioning and maybe lingering in my body since Pakistan. Antibiotics and fluids were prescribed and even though I was allowed out of hospital after a couple of hours, I felt dizzy and out of breathe. My recovery was at best slow and I faced, in dark moments, the prospect, so I thought, of being sent home early for what would have been the third time in four major tours. We got to the first Test in Nagpur and Fletcher asked me if I was fit enough to be considered and I knew, deep down and reluctantly, that I was not. I had to tell him in fairness to all concerned, not least myself, that I could not cope with a five-day Test in India's intense heat and he told me later that on medical advice I had been ruled out. In came Monty, and I feared I might not play in any of the Tests if he did as well as was anticipated. Monty did not disappoint.

This was also Freddie's first match as replacement England captain after I had had an early insight into the tragic mental problems that burden Marcus Trescothick. Trescothick had gone home, variously because his father-in-law had fallen off a ladder or because of a virus. But we, the players, knew better than that without ever being furnished with the real reason or given a proper explanation. In the match before the first Test, Marcus was captain and I was doing 12th man duties as well as my illness would allow. On the third morning of the match we met in the lift and all seemed well. He asked me how I felt. As play got under way, Marcus was out and sat in the dressing room, his head in his hands. It soon became obvious to me that Marcus was sobbing and I told Fletcher. Any players in the vicinity were told to stay out of the dressing room as the tour management moved in to talk to him. That evening, Monty, Blackwell and myself as the tour fines committee sat in the hotel foyer as Tres came out through reception on his way to the airport. It was as much as he could do to say goodbye and we remained mystified until we were informed later he had gone home for "personal reasons". That was as close as we got to the truth. I first came across Trescothick as a would-be bowling all-rounder in Somerset 2nd XI but I got to know him as the most professional man in the England team in terms of preparation and dedication, poring over videos of opponents and batting with great attention to technical detail in the nets. While he was always approachable and happy to give advice, his fixation with cricket used to lead to the occasional cry of "get a life, Tres" from those of his teammates who thought he should be less immersed in his game. On the pitch, he was a quiet man, sledging was far removed from his nature, but there was never anything to suggest he was suffering in any way from depression.

As to the drawn Test, Monty said it was a privilege to be bowling to his hero, Tendulkar, and his celebrations were lavish when he got him out, but I found it frustrating not to be able to play as India chased 180 in roughly 30 overs since that was just the sort of situation I thrived on, but a draw it was. Liam Plunkett was chosen for the second Test in Mohali ahead of me, even though I was by now fully fit and anxious to make up for lost time. From my point of view it was memorable only for close friends Dave and Rina Muir coming out from Camberley to support me only then to discover I was not playing, and for the first sighting of KP's new girlfriend, Jessica Taylor of the band Liberty X. Paul Collingwood was playing some of her band's music in the dressing room when Jessica was first introduced to us. I feel certain she and KP thought it was some kind of wind-up. To be honest, it was. We lost the match and with no other first class fixture in between, I headed for Mumbai and the third Test not having played a single match since Pakistan.

I could be forgiven for feeling a bit low in the circumstances, but I actually felt physically and mentally in top form. Mark Dennis, the former footballer, and my brother Gary had travelled to be with me, and the Barmy Army were there in force. In total there were about 15 or 20 people from Hampshire I knew who had come out expecting me to play and I remember saying to Freddie: "I will do something for you this Test", to which he replied, "It's about time you did." Freddie and I took part in the 'Magic Bus Foundation' in Mumbai's hectic and horrendous back streets, where kids with no clothes and rotted teeth pretended to be Tendulkar, batting without bats amid an unbelievable stench and the poverty inflicted by three-storey shacks and shared water boxes. Later, Freddie, KP, Robin Smith and friends Nick and Linda Bridge attempted to go shopping, but even with the burly aid of two security men, we had to head back to the hotel because our presence attracted a huge following. That never happened in Basingstoke. They say that local boy Tendulkar has a gleaming red Ferrari but he never gets to use it because the roads are always so busy and he only has to step outside his house for crowds to form. It is also said that Tendulkar emerges only at night so that he can drive his glorious Ferrari unhindered. Duncan Fletcher told me the day before the match I would be playing and while I quickly told Gary the secret, I was sorry my parents and family were not going to be there. I was probably in my last week as an England player and my 37th birthday was spent with 12 friends in a Chinese restaurant. I promised them something special and, sure enough, I delivered - with just a little help from above, perhaps, from grandfather Geoffrey.

Chapter 4

From High To Low

WITHIN SIX months of returning from India a conquering hero I was ready to go into despondent retirement. From having my hand shaken by grateful England cricket supporters in the streets and appearing on 'Question of Sport', enjoying my Indian summer, by the end of the 2006 domestic season I had had enough and was seriously contemplating quitting cricket for good. Only now, with the benefit of rest and a return to normality, do I think I made the right decision to continue with Hampshire for as long as we need each other. Call it anti-climax, call it rejection, I am not sure what triggered almost my worst full season ever. As likely was the terrible discovery that our beloved boy Jack had autism. All of that gave me serious grounds to calling a halt to my cricket career and starting afresh in something completely different. As the season drew to a close and I considered my meagre haul of 15 first class wickets at 43 each - hardly Test calibre figures - I spoke to our coaches, Paul Terry and Giles White, about the possibility of giving up, even though I had a year to run on my contract and physically I was in great shape. Their advice was straightforward enough: "Don't do anything you don't want to do." I had to decide whether I really wanted to play cricket or would be better off moving on to the next phase of my life. They assured me I had a part to play, that I had not become a bad player overnight and reaffirmed the old adage about being a long time retired. At 37, with 710 first class wickets, more than 1100 in all competitions and so recently a national icon (for a few heady days at least), I resolved to carry on.

The discovery of Jack's autism was one of the great shocks of my life and came at a time when I thought I could do no wrong and that nothing could go wrong. I will be forever grateful to Emma for keeping her fears about Jack to herself while I was in India, allowing me to play cricket freed from the constraints of domestic worry. She deliberately hid her concerns about his possible condition from me. Had I known, had she told me, I don't know to this day what I would have done. Would I have come home and missed Mumbai? Would I have stayed on and felt bad about not being at home where a proper parent should have been? It is hard to know exactly. At that stage, as the India tour unfolded, they were merely fears she felt about him and had no proof of anything sinister. It was only after I got home and life started to return to normal, and I was sifting through the newspaper cuttings she had so kindly kept for me, that I noticed Emma was spending a lot of time on the internet, scouring for information on autism. It was then that she told me of her concerns that Jack was not developing in quite the way a two-year old should be.

My feelings of post-tour euphoria, and they were euphoric in many respects, changed the instant I realised there might be something seriously wrong with our little boy. To begin with, I simply could not comprehend that a child of mine, a child of ours, could possibly be afflicted in such a way. I was a sportsman for a living and Emma was fit, gym-loving and in the prime of life. How could it have happened to us? Then other emotions kicked in, guilt of a sort, self-pity (what had we done to deserve this?), anger, disbelief. I felt them all as Jack exhibited some of the signs associated with autism, the apparent failure to pick up any language, the flapping of the hands, the rocking of the head. It was there in one form or another. The problem is that a swift diagnosis is not possible, it's not like going to a doctor, telling your symptoms and going away with a handful of pills and expecting to be better in a few days. Autism can be treated and treated very well, but it's for life and inevitably requires constant monitoring. While Emma was stoical, having had a little longer to think about it, for me it was a thunderous shock.

Jack was in any case a late and very welcome addition to the family. There is a sizeable age gap between him and our two daughters and even behind his arrival there is a story. A year or two before he was born, Emma, on a whim, visited a psychic at a fair who said he could 'see' a baby boy. In September 2003, Emma announced with great happiness that she was pregnant, only to miscarry a month later. We thought that was the end of it until we went on holiday to Barbados with Robin and

Kathy Smith and we noticed Emma was on soft drinks. It was then, in some triumph, she told us: "I'm pregnant again." Months later a wonderful bonus, our much-loved Jack was born. I'm a family man and my wife and children matter more to me than anything else in the world. If Jack's welfare had meant me giving up cricket there and then I would. But we had to wait until August 2006 to receive confirmation that he was indeed on what is known as the autistic spectrum and November before we knew the extent of his disability.

I can honestly say that the discovery of his autism changed my entire outlook on life overnight. It rocked us all. For those unaware of autism, the internet information Emma found spoke of abnormal functioning in at least one of three criteria, social interaction, language and imaginative play. It is only when children reach the age of two or three, as Jack had done, that these failures become apparent. Jack would flap his hands and although he did make eye contact, there was no sign of him picking up words, as children of that age start to do. He also tended to throw his toys after a period of playing with them. Not unnaturally, Emma and I were frightened, frightened that he would need special education and frightened that in the long term he would not be able to fend for himself as an adult.

Cricket was therefore something of an escape and, after a short break, I was back in the Hampshire nets with the twin aim: to stay in the England team and to stay in the Hampshire side. Neither was going to be easy. England were obviously looking at Panesar as the long term number one spinner, Ashley Giles was showing signs of returning to fitness and my age, my bloody age, was sure to count against me. Had I been 27 I am convinced my England place would already have been cemented after what had happened in Mumbai, but I was 37, a veteran by any standard, and as you get older your performances are scrutinised more closely, less is forgiven and the need to keep performing is absolutely essential for fear of exhibiting signs of decline. Had I been at any other county, as a current international, I would have been number one spin bowler without question, but at Hampshire our captain and main spinner was Shane Warne, the best of his type in the history of the game. So I could not even be sure of my club place. There was the strange possibility, before the season started, that I could be England's spin bowler without being able to get into the Hampshire side.

From High To Low

One factor worked heavily in my favour and that was Warne's late arrival in England from his Australian duties. That meant I began the season in the Hampshire team, where England's selectors could monitor my form, and, as much to the point, I was also captain. In fact, I thought I led the side well in Ireland where we began the defence of our C& G Trophy title (albeit now in league form) with a sociable, eight-wicket win in chilly late April. Unfortunately, under my leadership and minus the inspiration Warne normally provides in such abundance, we were bowled out by Mushtaq Ahmed in a championship match at the Rose Bowl. The fact that Mushtaq was to do the same to numerous other counties throughout the summer as Sussex went on to the do the 'double' failed to stop an inquest taking place in our dressing room where we noted a lack of energy and where we resolved not to wait for Warne to rescue us. With the Sri Lankans arriving any day, I was pleased with my own form, taking four wickets in the Sussex match (for 39) at a time of year and on pitches not much help to the spinners.

The debate about the constitution of the England team started earlier than usual, since there were Tests also to fit in against Pakistan and I have to say that I had one eye on the selection procedure and the other on life at Hampshire. We were playing Middlesex, Warne had taken over the captaincy, and the papers were saying that it was between Panesar and myself for the spinner's spot in the England team for the first Test. By chance, I met the knowledgeable Steve James at the Rose Bowl and asked him if he knew Fletcher's thinking, as he often did, not that Fletcher alone selected the international team. "From what I know, you're in," he told me. Not surprisingly, spirits were restored at the prospect of a home Test, and in particular a Test at Lord's. There is not a professional cricketer anywhere in the world who does not dream of playing in a Lord's Test match, and now it was tantalisingly within my grasp. Indeed, the day before the Test side was due to be announced, the papers appeared to be backing me to play at Lord's almost unanimously and I told Emma that I reckoned I would be selected.

We were playing Middlesex again, this time at Uxbridge in the C & G Trophy on the Sunday, and I had a nervous night awaiting the call from Graveney. He had only ever imparted good news before and I really felt he would do this time, but when it came, at 8am, there was an apologetic tone to his message. "We don't need two spinners at Lord's and we have decided to go with Monty." That short conversation signalled the end of my international career, and I think I knew it. There could be no way back. I had set my heart on a Lord's Test to crown my career and there was an awful numbness as I digested and analysed our brief conversation. I rang Emma, as I always did, but there was nothing she could say or do to ease the devastation of my loss. I kept thinking how it was that I was being abandoned two months after winning a Test in India. How many times in the past had a match-winner, in my case five wickets at 13 each, been dropped for the next match? Shock gave way to annoyance and fury and now there was a match to be played on the same day as I had been so ruthlessly discarded. Shane Warne could see I was upset and, having been through as many downs as ups in his own fantastic career, gave me some great advice. "If anyone asks, congratulate Monty on his selection. Don't say what you really feel, just say you will do your best to get back into the England team." They did ask, of course. The papers came on, sensing that I might have been the victim of an injustice, but I followed Warney's advice, backing Monty to succeed and promising to fight back with consistent success for Hampshire.

How I got through that match, I don't know. I went into a sort of overdrive and took one for 34 and scored 32 in a 13-run defeat. But at the end my anger was so intense I remember almost smashing the stumps out of the ground. Two months after my best day in cricket, I experienced one of the worst at tiny, leafy Uxbridge. As for Monty, I never had a problem with him. I admired and liked him and he quickly justified his selection ahead of me by twice taking five wickets in an innings over the summer. Would I have been able to do the same? We will never know. Later I was able to piece together the thinking and the voting of the England selection panel. Not that he was a selector, I knew Freddie Flintoff, again standing in for Michael Vaughan as captain, would have been happy had I been chosen ahead of, or with, Monty. Freddie even thought I was in the team when we met for a drink in Kensington after he had spoken to Duncan Fletcher about the composition of the team. Soon afterwards I joined Warney on an incredible journey to watch the FA Cup final in Cardiff, having begged a ticket in his wake because West Ham were my favourite Premiership side. Shane's job was to deliver the match ball on behalf of Mitre to the stadium and from our London hotel we travelled by car, helicopter and speedboat through Cardiff docks to the Millennium Stadium. That is the sort of thing that happens to you when you are as famous as Shane and it's a day I'm not likely to forget either, even if West Ham lost.

So where did I go wrong? The simple answer, I think, is that Graveney and Geoff Miller, the former off spinner on the panel, were against me and that is what swayed the decision. Ultimately it was two against one and I was out and Monty was in. I like to think I have no axe to grind here, but I cannot say that even now their decision rests comfortably with me. It still rankles on the basis that had I been ten years younger my place in the England team would not have been a matter for debate. Graveney tried to be conciliatory, tried to keep me interested by ringing me before the second Test at Edgbaston to tell me that two spinners were wanted for a pitch likely to turn but ruined it by saying that he thought I might be contesting the spot alongside Monty with Alex Loudon. Had he said Batty, Keedy, anybody else but Loudon, I would have understood. While I have absolutely nothing against him as a person or a player, I did not consider Loudon one of England's better spinners. Loudon can bat, I agree, but I have never thought of him to be in the frontline of the county championship spin bowlers and I was disappointed we were being compared. It was all the more baffling when Loudon was also left out of the squad. By unhappy coincidence, BBC's teletext service rang me at around that time to ask me if I thought I would be playing at Edgbaston. I answered honestly, bearing in mind the chat I had shared with Graveney, that I thought I would. Later I discovered, after I had again been overlooked, that Geoff Miller had been upset by my assumptions, making public comments about selection about which I could have had no knowledge.

So Edgbaston came and went and it was increasingly clear that even lingering hopes were now extinguished. It was all the more baffling that Loudon also never played. By early June, with Warne now back firmly in control, I had taken nine wickets and was playing well. We crushed Nottinghamshire at the Rose Bowl but, as our championship challenge gained momentum, my own performances began to fall away to an alarming extent. Between that match and the end of the season, more than three months, I managed six championship wickets. In my defence, there were occasions and wickets when it was possible only to choose one spinner and that was always going to be Warne, but if I had been a Test contender, you would never have known it by my swift fall from grace. And it was swift.

In early August, after a fallow period in which I was confined mostly to one-day matches, I was selected by Hampshire - by now something of a bonus - for the championship match at Canterbury. My friends Tony and Lillian Marsden, as Hampshire supporters, laid on a big evening party for the team. There was pizza for Shane, because it is pretty much all he eats, and Canterbury is normally a pleasant place to enjoy cricket. But on August 1st I learned the horrible truth. After extensive tests, it was revealed that Jack was suffering from autism. Our worst fears had been confirmed. When I got the news I went for a walk at our hotel in Ashford to gather my thoughts and emotions. I thought I was alone, but Shane Warne was in the lobby by chance as I burst into tears, unable any longer to contain the terrible consequences of our family tragedy. Warne is a good man, a softer soul than is the public perception, and he loves his children as deeply as I love mine. I think he too must have been struggling to subdue his feelings when he said: "I could not bear it if anything happened to my kids. That is the only thing that has not happened to me." He said how sorry he was, but there is precious little anyone else can do and when I told Paul Terry he advised me to go home if I thought it would help. I stayed on, took one wicket in the match for 93 and my season was never the same again. I am not sure even now if I am fully restored to the Shaun Udal of old. How could I be?

On top of all that, the crisis surrounding Jack and my rejection by England, I developed one or two technical faults with my bowling. I am not sure how this happened, possibly because my thoughts had wandered from cricket, but the ball was not coming out right, my feet were in the wrong position too often for comfort and I became expensive. I like to think that over my career, even when I have not been taking wickets, I have been economical. But not now. August and September, for instance, are normally profitable months for spinners as the wickets dry and bounce after a summer of sunshine. I have always reaped a rich harvest in those months but August and September 2006 might just as well have been November and December in terms of success. I took one wicket in that fateful match at Canterbury and just four more in the three matches for which I was selected between early August and the end of the season. I was left out altogether for the final two championship matches against Durham and Lancashire. That is when my thoughts turned more firmly towards retirement as I sat pretty much alone on the balcony doing the 12th man's tasks.

I still played in the one-day matches but I knew I was not concentrating properly when we were fielding because, for the first time in my life, I was volunteering to hide from the action at fine leg and third man, just to get out of the way. For 20 years or whatever, if I had not been bowling, I liked to be in the thick of it among the close catching positions or somewhere the ball was going to be. But now, outside influences were affecting me far more than I imagined they ever would and concentration was hard, so hard that I acknowledge that the last couple of months were a write-off. Our own season, as a team, fell away badly towards the end, the C & G Trophy slipped away all too easily and although third place in the championship would be considered good by most clubs, Shane Warne had got us believing that only the title itself was worth achieving. What made it worse was the fact that had I been able to get on top of my feelings I might just have been able to influence a match or two as the season came to its conclusion. The conditions were all in place but my head was not. Warne was playing as the lone spinner at a time when he could have expected me - a recent Test match winner and experienced bowler - to have helped him, but when he and Hampshire needed me most I was found wanting. I knew it was not good enough because I had fallen from the high standards I had always attempted to set myself.

Hampshire's summer finished with a whimper, although it would be fair to say my own had never really started. It was hard to believe that six months beforehand, my name was being chanted all around Mumbai by the jubilant Barmy Army. Luckily, Paul Terry and Shane Warne and our chairman, Rod Bransgrove, knew of my personal circumstances and made allowances, but I am not the sort of person who wants to have allowances made for him or to make excuses. They realised my mind was often elsewhere and those matches I actually played in were often happening around me, not because of me. A year ago almost exactly I had just bowled myself into the England Test team and now I could not on merit even get into the Hampshire side.

I can only apologise. I did not bowl well or contribute in the way I should have done and as the bails were lifted for the last time, I thought of a life beyond cricket. After all, it is only a game.

Quite how Shane Warne copes with the off-field pressures created by his personal life, I have no idea, but he does so it's just as well he is comfortable with the attention he gets. Shane has this wonderful capacity to immerse himself in his cricket, almost as a release, so that once he is on a cricket field, nothing else matters. His constant cigarette is a prop of sorts and his diet, while not the sort to please the purists, is typical of the way he needs everything to be in its place when he plays his cricket. His main meal is margherita (cheese and tomato topping) pizza and chips. Sometimes, by way of variation, he will indulge in a spot of lasagne or, if we eat Mexican food, he will tuck into cheese nachos. For lunch, he asks only for a cheese baguette and chips with salt and vinegar. I dare say many people in the game have tried to get him on something a little healthier but he has resisted their advice in the same way that he carries on smoking. His reasoning is that he likes to feel good when he is on the cricket pitch and if all of those things contribute to his sense of well-being, then who is to say he is wrong. The little matter of 708 Test wickets would appear to say he got it right.

But then, he must get his energy from somewhere because he lives life at 100mph in a way others would find incredible. On his days off, Shane is to be found in London or at any of the multitude of events and functions he attends. I spent a day with him once at his manager's office and he was a one-man cyclone, pausing only from signing the numerous contracts which come his way to place his moniker on bat after bat for commercial or charitable causes. It is just as well he loves being the centre of attention and has this wonderful ability to project himself in the media because nothing seems to ruffle him, he is never disrespectful and is always fair. I was left to admire his drive and saw a glimpse of the same desire to succeed at whatever he is doing as he showed in becoming the best of bowlers. I will never forget either his patience or his enthusiasm at Whitgift School where we had been playing Surrey. There was a massive crowd in the picturesque little ground and it seemed every one of them wanted Shane's autograph. For an hour and a quarter he lined them up, one after another, and signed every single piece of paper, shirt, arms, legs, you name it, and always with a genuine cheery smile. And that is not an isolated incident, he does that all the time and when he rejoins us in the dressing-room it is clear he has enjoyed himself doing it. It is never a chore.

You read of film and music stars who say they hate the attention of the public yet never shun the limelight if it is there to be basked in. Shane conducts himself brilliantly in the limelight and he thoroughly deserves all the attention he gets. What may not be apparent to outsiders, all of whom seem to have an opinion on him, is the incredible generosity of spirit of the man. There is his charity work through the Shane Warne Foundation in Australia, set up to benefit children, but more than that there are his little acts of kindness, which others may never see. If, for instance, he was due to pick me up on the way to a match, he would always insist on driving to my home on the outskirts of Basingstoke rather than an easier meeting point. I also know that when he joined the club he was sensitive to how I must have felt, a Hampshire man through and through and undisputed number one long-serving spinner, at being usurped by a superstar. He was clever enough to realise how much Hampshire meant to me and went out of his way to make sure I was asked to contribute and became comfortable about him being there. That is one of the reasons why, I think, he was so pleased for me when I finally made it into Test cricket. Somewhere along the line he had played a part. There is a gentler, caring side to Shane Warne, which was not always evident from the seemingly brash, in-your-face bowler who terrorised international batsmen the world over for 16 years or more. We at Hampshire have been lucky to have him because he has been a massive influence on us all in terms of attitude, application, setting of goals, professionalism and unflagging ambition. The young players adore him and the older ones are as much in awe. All of us like as well as admire him as a person. I know how much he wants to win the county championship before he finally quits altogether and we all want to win it for him. That would be a great end to his English career.

On the pitch, Shane never stops thinking, never stops manipulating, never stops teasing and testing and has a fantastic cricket brain. Off the field, he hates being alone and was always glad when I, among many, used his house as an overnight stopover and he's a great host. Many a night a group of us would be huddled around a table at his home playing poker and sending out for pizzas. Dimitri Mascarenhas and John Crawley are as close to him as I am but when it comes to poker, he plays the card game in the way he plays his cricket: all or nothing. Chris Benham, whom he once anointed as Hampshire's captain-in-waiting, Michael Brown, James Tomlinson and Nic Pothas are regulars at the Warne poker table. He speaks every day to his ex-wife Simone and I am not alone in thinking there is still a love between them, which might be re-ignited. Simone and family are over with Shane for the whole of the summer of 2007 and I sincerely hope they can rekindle the undoubted love they have.

I only wish I had been able to help him more in 2006 but while he took 58 wickets in 13 first class matches. My 15 from ten left me 104th in the national averages of those who bowled for a living so that my star fell as rapidly as it had risen. As for Jack, his presence on the autistic spectrum was confirmed in November and he is now receiving the very best of specialist treatment and there is every hope he will be able to cope fully with life as he grows up. In England terms, my chance has come and gone and I have to be grateful that I did get that opportunity, which I like to think I took. I am truly pleased at Monty's development and that Ashley Giles made enough of a recovery to play for England again. The resentment I felt at missing the Lord's Test is still there but fading with time and I guess there is no easy way to tell a player he is not in the team. I did myself and Hampshire no favours in 2006 but it was an amazing year of highs and lows and now I must look forward, not back.

Chapter 5

Spin By Chance

I WISH I could remember the name of the umpire who converted me from an aspiring but not particularly successful medium pace bowler into an off spinner. I was Hampshire under 14s captain and we were playing Somerset and I was so enthusiastic at that stage of my youthful development that I would have bowled at both ends if I could have done. What I do remember is that Somerset were seven wickets down and we were rapidly running out of time to win the match. My medium pace was getting nowhere and the eighth wicket pair were well entrenched. As captain, I was at a loss as to what to do next and it was then that the umpire, who was in charge of the Hampshire team, turned to me and said: "Don't bowl medium pace, try a bit of spin." To be honest, spin bowling had not much appealed to me before and I had to ask him how it was done. "Stick your fingers across the seam and give it a tweak." As the match threatened to stall I would have probably bowled underarm if I thought it would make a difference, so I did as he said. Two overs later, I had taken all three of the Somerset wickets and a spin bowler was born. I gave dad a call with the news and his response was, "Why bowl that medium pace rubbish anyway?" So, on the spot, I resolved to become a full time off spinner.

I think I can say it turned out to be a good move but the arbitrary way in which I embraced a whole new discipline would probably horrify those who now run academies. One chance remark by an umpire set me on the road ultimately to a county and international career which might never have happened had I stuck to my medium pace 'rubbish'. Even now I am not sure I am the biggest spinner of the ball, perhaps the wrist is not always in the best position, but having long fingers helped and while I would never dare mention my name in the same breath as Shane Warne, I believe I stand comparison with any of my English contemporaries.

My Turn To Spin

Cricket has always been in the blood with a long family history of relations who have dabbled with the game over the years, some more seriously than others. Who knows what my grandfather Geoffrey might have achieved had he treated his chances with Middlesex and Leicestershire a little more reverently. Geoffrey Francis Uvedale Udal lived near us in Cove, but we have dropped the Uvedale bit because it means much the same as Udal, derived as it is from yew and dale with its origins in Dorset. Udal is not a common name but over the years people have come up to me at grounds all around the country with a similar surname and wondering if we might be related. Geoffrey came from Walton-on-Thames and family research by my uncle Geoff, another of his sons, shows that he joined the forces and excelled at cricket, boxing and swimming. All his medals ended up at the pawnbrokers because his dead certs were more dead than certs, said my uncle. He had a distinguished war with the expeditionary forces in France and Belgium, had his ribs broken in the Leicestershire nets on demob and ended his working life as a runner to the bookies for a bricklayer.

The rest of the Udal clan from Cove include my cousin Donna, who is like the sister I never had. We are only a year apart in age and have been close since early school days, going to the same schools and enjoying each other's company. In fact, we went to a George Michael concert together a few months back. She isn't a lady to cross and is known in our family for speaking her mind and not worrying about the consequences, but we have always got on and I'm sure that will be the case forever. My other cousins, Kim and Glen, are probably the quieter ones, both strong family people.

Cove is only three miles from the Surrey border and Camberley, the club of my father, brother and myself, play in the Surrey League. I consider myself very much a Hampshire man, although I did spend a year at under 17 level with Surrey where Graham Thorpe and Martin Bicknell, later of course also to play for England, were colleagues. At that point I had played all my cricket for Hampshire from under 11 onwards but for some reason, Hampshire did not have an under 17 side and had I not been committed or determined to become a professional cricketer I might well have fallen by the wayside through lack of opportunity, having left school at 16 and started work as a printer at Mirage Graphics on £36 per week, a tenner of which I gave mum. My father Robin was

64

something of a Camberley stalwart having clocked up a record 40,000 runs, 2000 of them in one season, and a prodigious number of wickets with his off breaks delivered off six paces. Dad played for Surrey Colts while doing his printing apprenticeship in Aldershot, but it was at a time in the 1950s when Surrey's first team, containing the likes of Peter May, Alec Bedser, Jim Laker and Tony Lock, were immensely powerful and won the county championship seven times in the decade.

I was playing for Camberley during my Surrey sabbatical and I suppose if it had gone well that summer I might have been lost to Hampshire. I was batting at four for Camberley with dad as captain, getting runs and bowling my spin at first change to such good effect that I got 100 wickets. But with Surrey, it did not work out for me. I bowled only occasionally, batted mostly at eight and was 12th man more than once. While Martin Bicknell had already developed his smooth action and was tall and quick, the real star of the side was inevitably Thorpe. In fact, Martin Bicknell, who, like me, played in four Tests for England, had once scored past me in my goalkeeping days when we were 14. It was the only one of many cup finals my school team lost. But it was Thorpe who dominated as a bowler and batsman and stood out even then as a cricketer with incredible potential. We were playing Middlesex at Guildford and a certain Mark Ramprakash stood in our way but Thorpe nominated the delivery by which he would get him out, "Caught at cover off my slower ball." And he was. Surrey's coaching staff were already aware of him then, as with Bicknell, while James Boiling was, I suspect, rated more highly as a spin bowler than me and it was he who was later offered the contract.

While Boiling did make the grade, he did not last as long as I did and it is odd that Surrey have had to rely heavily on imported spinners ever since in the shape of people like Ian Salisbury, Anil Kumble, Harbhajan Singh and Saqlain Mushtaq. It is odd, too, that I have always reserved my top performances for when we at Hampshire have played against Surrey, for instance in the pulsating run chase to beat them in the 2005 C&G Trophy quarter final at the Oval, while both my career-best batting and bowling limited overs figures have also been achieved against them. I wonder if there is not some kind of sub-conscious seeking of revenge for the way they snubbed me, but in truth I had always preferred playing for Hampshire as a kid and it was not that much of a blow when Surrey did not pursue their interest beyond that one season.

But then grandad Geoffrey and my father were not the only Udals to create a wave or two within cricket. My great-great grandfather, John Symonds Udal, educated at Oxford University and an MCC player between 1871 and 1875, was credited with introducing the game to Fiji in his capacity as attorney-general. Later he went to New Zealand and then on to the Leeward Islands where he promoted the game among the local populace. I am sure those cricketers on the receiving end of such Leeward greats as Viv Richards, Andy Roberts and Curtly Ambrose will wish he had minded his own business. John's son, Nicholas Robin Udal, earned a cricket Blue at Oxford and when, as a youngster, I played for Hampshire at the Parks I spotted his name on a board of honour. My teammates were baffled how anyone related to me could possibly have gone to Oxford University but all I can confirm is that the genes have not been passed down.

Academically I was not very good at Cove Secondary, although I was passable at mathematics and far better at sport. For that, I was definitely at the right school because our deputy headmaster was Charlie Mortimore, a Cove cricketer of high pedigree and brother of the former footballer and manager John, and a man with a lengthy record of finding and nurturing sporting talent. Our year at school had plenty of that for him to work on. I was a centre forward at football, but when a lad by the name of Nicky O'Brien arrived, it was obvious that he was far better than me so I went in goal on the basis that if I was not allowed to score goals, I could at least try to stop them. Not for me the anonymity of midfield. It was here that I got to enjoy the challenge of winning games, which is something in England we have perhaps lost or not always relished, and I discovered I liked the pressure created by playing in crucial positions.

Over the years I have found out that there are far too many players with great ability who look for excuses. I remember Phil Tufnell failing to rise to the occasion at Brisbane on my Ashes tour as Warne was turning the ball miles, and there was no better left arm spinner in England at the time. He just did not relish confrontation and putting himself on the line. You can see it in the eyes, those who like a battle and those who do not. A perfect example was Matthew Keech, a batsman who had all the talent in the world but never got the best out of himself or fulfilled the world class potential Mike Gatting saw in him at Middlesex. We thought we had made a top signing when he came to Hampshire but there was a mental weakness and he always seemed to develop an injury when it mattered, once pulling out at the last minute just before the start of a match after a session in the nets, saying "I can't play". As Robin Smith said to me, and I found it to be true, the higher you go, the more cricket is played in the mind, though I suppose the same might be said about all sports. Graham Gooch and Mike Atherton had ordinary techniques as batsmen, in my opinion, but they were mentally extremely strong in a way that Keech, and others dotted around the counties, never were.

Charlie Mortimore taught us the value of competing, lessons I took with me into professional sport, although I would rather have stayed at centre forward, given the choice. But he said,"Nicky O'Brien is the district centre forward, so you will have to play elsewhere." I was, I think, all right as goalkeeper, good enough to become the district number two, but our team was strong, winning numerous cups against competition from all over Hampshire. Allen Tankard, who had a long career at Southampton, Wigan and Port Vale, was a mainstay of the school defence and O'Brien was taken on by Portsmouth without reaching first team level. I fancied my own chances of playing football for a living and when my pal, Neil Roberts, was taken on by Aldershot as an apprentice in 1985, I wrote to then manager Ron Harris, the former Chelsea defender, for a trial. But sadly, my embryonic football career was cut off at the knees by 'Chopper' Harris in the same ruthless manner he had cut off a generation of centre forwards. He did not even bother to reply. Neil never made the step up either and went on to own a window cleaning business. Charlie imbued us with his love of cricket, too, and O'Brien, myself and a lad called Andy Armstrong became the key players in our school team, although by then I was part of the Hampshire Schools set-up.

At Cove we won every inter-school competition and I only wish I had been able to show the same enthusiasm for the academic side, leaving with eight CSEs, as they were then called, two in grade 3 and five in grade 4. Religious Knowledge was a weakness and I was told off a lot for staring out of the window, probably dreaming of the cricket pitch. By now, all I wanted to do was play cricket as high up the ladder as possible. My first recollection of competitive cricket ended, as many others were to do later, as a victim of the weather. Aldershot versus Basingstoke at Frimley was called off because it rained and I was led to believe by a mischievous teacher when it was replayed in boiling heat that it would be called off again because of the heat. Being so young, I thought he was serious. I batted at five, hit the second ball through the covers for four, got a single and then got out. Dad stood motionless on the side, his silence being evidence of his displeasure at my wastefulness. In those days before my grandfather ironed out my action I bowled off the wrong foot at the end of a funny little skip but I got a wicket at first change, so the afternoon was partially redeemed. That was the day I really got the cricket bug.

As I grew, tall and thin with a mop of ginger hair, I was the obvious victim of the school micky-takers, but I gave as good as I got and was respected for my sporting ability. I was in and out of the head's office and as the time to leave school drew closer, Oxford University (or any further educational establishment for that matter) did not beckon. By then I had started to arouse some interest at county professional level. Charlie Mortimore was a respected man of influence and recommended me to Hampshire to attend their district coaching trials at Basingstoke Sports Centre, where Tim Tremlett, Bob Parks and John Rice, all established Hampshire players, were in charge of developing teenagers of above-average potential. Dad took me along when I was 12 and I was shaking with nerves because I had no idea how good or bad my contemporaries might be. The first time I went, I wore my school uniform with a jumper knitted by my grandmother which made me stand out for all the wrong reasons among the track suits and 1980s designer sports gear. Julian Wood, a powerful left-handed youth who could hit the ball a long way, and a long-haired fast bowler called Kevin Shine, were evident immediately. Shine was a frightening prospect for someone of my age, thundering in wildly from 20 yards and I admit I committed the cardinal sin of backing away from him as he galloped towards the stumps, especially as I could never be certain where the ball might go. Both later became colleagues on the county staff and Shine, of course, rose to the eminence of England bowling coach.

As a boy, Tony Greig had been my first hero, followed later by my main icon, Ian Botham. I suppose I was only about seven at the time but Greig was a golden vision as England captain and I adopted his rocking run-up from the same 14 or 15 paces and I tried, like him I thought, to hit every ball for six, but the great 'Both' soon transplanted him in my affections from the moment he bowled Greg Chappell in an Ashes Test. I have come to know Botham well over the years since playing against him for Hampshire, but I have never completely lost my awe of him, springing from my childhood adulation. I remember watching Botham's every move in the morning warm-up, only to discover there was not much of it. But it is just about my proudest boast that I have his mobile number lodged in my own phone, as carefully tended as if it was an autograph. I first met him when his son Liam joined us at Hampshire for a few years, eclipsing his famous father on his debut when he dismissed Mike Gatting - something Ian never did - when he ran through the Middlesex batting at Portsmouth. If Ian likes you, he will do anything for you, but if you cross him then I imagine he could be a bad enemy. I love being in his company and it was somehow typical that in Pakistan he should somehow procure a bottle or two of wine and be generous enough to share it, because he is a kind and open man, too open for some people in authority who have been suspicious over the years of his honesty and capacity to speak his mind. He is still competitive, be it at golf, or when he's shooting and it was a privilege when at Robin Smith's behest, I attended a barbecue at his beautiful home in Yorkshire. I know it sounds trite, but I really was living a boyhood dream, me at Ian Botham's house and in his garden. I was always Ian Botham in my garden.

I fear Ian will never get closer to power than a Sky TV commentary seat, which reflects badly on England at a time when we could do with some of his inspiration after the Ashes debacle of 2006-7. What I think he would do best is act as a mentor, rather than as a collective team coach. I think he is the sort of person who could help restore individual confidence and morale among players, and in that respect there would be no shortage of work for him. I know from my own work with Sky TV that they view his commentary as controversial, which they like, because he says what he believes. Other big name commentators and ex players are less prepared to say what they feel for fear of offence. In that respect Botham and Shane Warne are strikingly similar personalities. Now that I have had the chance to see them both at close quarters, the same astonishing self-belief and personal confidence. They say what they are going to do and do it so that there is never any room for doubt.

Where Botham and David Gower grew in my estimation was in turning down lucrative offers to join the rebel tours to South Africa before the abandonment of the apartheid system and their readmission to Test cricket. Botham had this great loyalty to Viv Richards and would never have gone out of principle, but Gatting, Gooch and Emburey all sacrificed their integrity for money. At least Neil Foster had the good grace to admit as much. Robin Smith told me that the England dressing room during Test matches was openly full of talk of the rebel tour and the size of the pay packets they would be getting, which can hardly have been conducive to team morale. It is not known generally, I think, that Robin, born in South Africa but always desperate to play for England, turned down a massive offer in his prime to trial for baseball in America. That is proper loyalty, the sort you would expect from Robin or from Botham and I have always found it strange that the rebels should be so readily accepted into the establishment fold later in their careers. Gooch and Gatting went on to be selectors, which in my opinion should never have happened, while Beefy was rejected for that role. Loyalty, it seemed, counted for nothing.

As for Liam Botham, he was an outstanding young man when he joined us as a 16-year old, mature beyond his years, and the way he handled a packed press conference on his arrival at the County Ground will remain with me forever. It was an astonishing performance for its calmness and authority and reminiscent of his father in terms of confidence. That match at Portsmouth, where he announced himself properly to the cricketing world, had something of a twist to it in that he was a late selection, so late that he got to the United Services ground at the last minute and then, as his father did so often, took a wicket in his first over. People often ask me if he could have gone on to emulate his dad, but he was not getting many opportunities at Hampshire when he defected to rugby league and union and I think he made the right decision to escape his father's shadow. He deserves credit also for having played at first class level in three different sports, one more than Ian.

Having a pushy father was never a problem for me because dad was always fair, always encouraging me but never living his dreams through me. Gary was not as naturally talented as me but had the same aggressive streak and he loved his cricket the same. He has been a key figure at Camberley for a number of years. Not that I am convinced I was blessed with a great innate ability. I certainly was not in any way exceptional at school but my desire to keep testing myself at the next level had much to do with any development that I made. Hampshire had noted a steady progression and when I was 17, after my Surrey year, I got a letter from the club inviting me to attend nets at the County Ground to try out for the under 19 side. Unlike the school and college boys who made up the bulk of those also invited, I was a comparative man of the world, working for my living, stronger mentally and playing at a decent, competitive club level. I was also a little more selfish as a cricketer and starting to bat properly. Mark Nicholas, one of Hampshire's most successful captains and now a top class commentator, was batting in the nets next to ours, remodelling his game, when he noticed me bowling. Nicholas said later that he picked up on what he thought was my uncomplicated delivery and "lovely, natural off breaks" and invited me to bowl to him. Peter Sainsbury, our coach and a Hampshire stalwart, agreed and it was then, I think, that Nicholas marked me out as a future county player.

Two other long-serving ex-players in Jimmy Gray and Barry Reed ran the under 19 side and we had a tremendous summer in terms of results. Rupert Cox, a left handed batsman from Bradfield, Nicholas's old school, Julian Wood and the left arm spinner Ian Turner joined me in using the success of the Colts to promote our individual causes. Cox was a character who appeared not to take the game too seriously because of his constant smile and a youthful capacity for drink. I can see him now running down a line of car roofs in Oxford after one boozy evening but, like Wood, suffered from lack of opportunity caused by a settled and successful first team middle order in the late 80s and early 90s. Wood had the potential to have played at the highest level but failed, as many have done, to translate great ability into hard facts and figures and left the game, I believe, unfulfilled. It was a terrible waste of natural talent but confirmation of my own experience that not all the most natural cricketers make the grade.

Fearing I might still be a target for Surrey (they had phoned the County Ground to check my availability), Hampshire signed me in May 1987 on a summer contract, as much to hold my registration. Richard Stemp, a fiery spin bowler from Worcestershire, became involved in a sort of showdown in one Esso Oxford Festival game that summer. Stemp took four for 49 but I trumped him with seven and when I got him out, I was reprimanded by Jimmy Gray for celebrating. Jimmy had been the solid opening batsman foil to the flamboyant Roy Marshall during his own career in the 1950s and 1960s and he was not given to shows of emotion. Things had to be done right. I wonder what he thought of my Tendulkar wicket celebrations in Mumbai? Jimmy was kind enough to praise my development in 1987, saying that my batting had advanced while my bowling had been consistently good, which I think was fair comment. I regard it now, with the benefit of hindsight, as my big breakthrough year when I moved from youthful club player to first professional contract. I was lucky to have at Ravenswood Print, to where I had moved, a kindly boss in Roy Hornsby who gave me time off to play cricket, and there was an awful lot of it.

At Camberley I was forging a decent reputation by completing the 1000 runs, 100 wickets double for the first time in ten or 12 years since it had been last performed by a certain Robin Udal. Surrey would doubtless have noticed because it was all happening in the Surrey League, but by now I was committed to Hampshire and, by an astonishing coincidence, I was summoned to play for the 2nd XI against Surrey at the Oval in May 1987. I remember thinking 'oh, my god, the Oval' in awe when I was first told because at 18 and, from my humble background, to play at a Test ground, albeit a deserted one, was far more than I could ever have expected. We even got a meal allowance of six or seven pounds and £20 a day, more than I got in the print works, and after 30 minutes, as I surveyed the rows and rows of empty seats, I said to myself this was what I wanted to do with my life. From Camberley to the Oval is not far in terms of miles but in terms of a step up in class it was a world away. Darren Bicknell, brother of Martin, was the coming batsman at Surrey and he was among the opposition, as was Tony Gray, a massively built Trinidadian fast bowler, later to play five Tests and 25 internationals for the West Indies and who bounced the ball around your ears from 6ft 6 inches. I had never come across a bowler so fearsome and horrible. Tony Middleton, Cardigan Connor, the Dutchman Paul-Jan Bakker, Shine and Steve Andrew were in the Hampshire team, where I was known as the kid from Surrey, and none of us fancied taking on Gray, the Surrey overseas player in the days when every county had a West Indian and the faster the better. For an unknown kid from Surrey, I had a good match, finishing with match figures of seven for 106, dismissing Bicknell for 111 and Gray for two. In fact, I did not get a bowl until 3pm on the first day and had begun to think I never would and then later, as luck would have it, Andrew and I knocked off the winning runs chasing 218. We needed about 20 off the last four overs and I was unbeaten with five when we scrambled the last few runs to win by three wickets.

Spin By Chance

I played in two other 2nd XI matches that season, against Middlesex where we ran into Test players Norman Cowans and Angus Fraser, and Gloucestershire. Against Middlesex I found out for the first time how insecure a professional's life can be. Our side was augmented by one or two old pros, including Nigel Cowley, the club's number one off spinner, a position that had remained unchallenged for a number of years. Cowley was your archetypal county player who made up the backbone of most clubs, the sort who was never going to play Test cricket but who was more than useful a step below. The following year he was a key figure in Hampshire winning the Benson and Hedges Cup for the first time. But I now realise that as Hampshire captain that match he probably saw me as a threat, a cocky, chirpy replacement down the line. I did not get a bowl at all. In fairness, the weather ruined any chance of a positive result so that my opportunities were inevitably going to be limited, but he hardly spoke to me and I now see he must have been worried. While it might be a generalisation, the old pros tended not to offer advice, there being too much for them to lose. I like to think things have changed over the years and I make sure Greg Lamb, who is keen to develop his off spin, gets the benefit of any help I can give. At Gloucestershire I learned that mixing with county calibre players exposes the huge gap between that and club cricket, even a standard as decent as Camberley's. I made ten in my only innings, but there was never anything to hit and I can feel even now the impatience and desperation to impress threatening to get in the way. I failed also to take a wicket in six overs.

I bowled with greater success in the Warwick Pool Under 25 competition and in the Bain Clarkson Trophy, and even greater success in the Colts where I got wickets and runs against players more akin to my own age. We played in the Esso Oxford Festival and I finished the Colts season with 196 runs at an average of 24.50 and was top wicket-taker with 28 at 19. At the end of the tournament in Oxford (where we lost in the final to Yorkshire), our coach Peter Sainsbury congratulated me and said, "See you in the winter." That was the first hint that Hampshire saw in me a possible first class cricketer. 'Sains' was, I suppose, my first great professional influence, a coach of the old school with a formidable playing record and which in a less competitive era than the 50s and 60s might have got him a cap or two. Sainsbury did go on an England tour in his prime but, as a left arm spinner, had Tony Lock in front of him and so had nothing internationally to show for 20,176 runs, 1,316 wickets and 617 catches, often brilliantly taken at short leg. He is the only Hampshire player to have played in both the championship-winning sides of 1961 and 1973 and while, on his own admission, he was not blessed with outstanding natural skills, he knew what it took to be a cricketer. Sains and my dad shared the same philosophy, which was never to give in and always to fight. "Fight the f*****s" was his oft-quoted mantra and he expected us to do exactly that. Sains was not a technical coach in the sense that he analysed your game in detail, but he emphasised the value of the right attitude and the way to conduct myself as a county cricketer. He gave me advice, which stood me in good stead for the rest of my career.

Adrian Aymes, a Hampshire man who came up the hard way like myself, was a favourite of his because he saw in him many of the same qualities. Adie was probably not the most gifted wicketkeeper Hampshire ever produced but he was a fantastic fighter who never gave the opposition an inch whether he was batting or keeping. When I was in the Colts our keeper was Mark Lane, a hugely talented player who could have been Hampshire's gloveman for years. Who knows how far he could have gone. Mark was everything Sains was suspicious about in a player. He was overweight, liked a smoke and a drink and lacked the in-built desire and toughness Sains thought was essential for success. We Colts players all thought Mark would be offered a contract, but it never came and he was allowed to drift away having missed his vocation. It is true, Mark was probably not a man for a crisis and it was the failure of people like him to come through the system which emphasised the belief of Sainsbury that aptitude provided only the basis of what was needed to succeed. If you had a weak mentality, you would fail. So when Sainsbury said he would see me in the winter I had good reason to believe I had been given a major boost and seal of approval. All the more surprising then considering how Tim Tremlett remembers me from the Basingstoke coaching days: "Shaun was very keen and enthusiastic and you could see that he had a lot of talent. Although he was not a great spinner of the ball, he used his flight effectively. When he eventually joined the staff he was one of the best timers of the ball but was a compulsive hooker and Peter Sainsbury used to tear his hair out." A fair assessment, I would say.

Chapter 6

Learning My Trade

THE TELEPHONE has played a key role in far too many important decisions in my career. My mobile conversations with David Graveney will be remembered by me almost word for word. But one day in October 1987, Anthea Heslop, meticulous scorer for Camberley, was by chance at the Udal home and asked me if there had been any news from Hampshire. I was just about to tell her 'no' when the phone rang and I said to her it would be funny if that was Hampshire. It was. Peter Sainsbury was on the other end to say the committee had decided to offer me a one-year contract at the princely sum of £2,250. The contract ran from April until September and I was free to do what I wanted in the winter. It was almost too good to be true because it meant I could devote my summers to cricket and in the close season I could carry on learning the printing trade with Roy Hornsby. Even now, I cannot thank them enough for their tolerance and understanding because I am sure other employers would have been less keen to lose a worker for six months of the year and then welcome him back, as they did with me.

Hampshire sent me a list of exercises to be doing during the dark days and nights of winter and I cut a lonely figure as I ran round and round Cove Green, dreaming of the sunny days ahead. Ian Turner had also been offered his first contract and we each had strong similarities in that we were both sons of prominent local cricketers. My dad Robin had been prominent at Camberley for decades, although I am told his brother Ian, a left handed bat, was the more naturally talented. Uncle Ian had no desire to play cricket and instead got lots of goals in local football and devoted his time to his love of horses, a trait obviously inherited from my grandfather. Ian Turner's father, 'Topsy', had been a dominant figure at Hambledon, the village which is a shrine for all

75

cricket-lovers world-wide for its place in folklore as the cradle of the game. Topsy helped the club to the Village Knockout Cup at Lord's but Ian had gone a step further by being offered the chance to be a professional. Ian Turner and I shared a room in a house near the County Ground owned by the sister of Jon Ayling, the tall all-rounder from Portsmouth who was close to England selection until a collision with David Smith of Sussex damaged knee ligaments and cut him off in his prime and forced a premature retirement. We paid £20 a week each for our room and, like all teenagers away from home for the first time, ate copious amounts of fast food, all but living at the KFC in Portswood. I still love KFC.

On my first day at pre-season training I blundered again, sartorially. I thought I ought to look smart so I went to the upmarket tailors Austin Reed where they kitted me out in what I thought was appropriate, a blazer, tie, shirt and trousers. But at 10am, as the others rolled up for the start of the 1988 season, I discovered to my horror, they were all wearing t-shirts. Of course, the older pros just loved it and the mickey-taking (I could use a stronger expression) lasted for the rest of the day, and beyond. Such was my confidence that I felt if I was going to be a cricketer, I needed a bit of sponsorship. So I got in touch with kit-makers Duncan Fearnley to ask for a sponsored bat on the basis that my hero Botham was already sponsored by them. Mark Nicholas was kind enough to back me in my cheeky quest and, to my surprise, Fearnley's agreed to support me for a year. Not a bad coup for a complete novice.

In those, less sophisticated, days the key to early fitness was thought to be running and more running. It was easy enough for me, lean as a whippet and already fit from circling Cove Green. But for the heavier members of our staff like Chris Smith and P-J Bakker, this was part of the season they hated the most. In the Spring rains, we were obliged to run up the Avenue in Southampton to the traffic lights and back and while I coasted, Bakker and Smith trailed behind, gasping for breath. Smith, a high class batsman good enough to play for England, would never have called himself a great athlete. Indeed, on one such run, he gave up and caught the bus back and on another, as I was chatting away to him, he turned and wheezed, "Will you shut up. I can't talk and run." Raj Maru was another who struggled with the running. He was not one of the fittest squad members. Chris let his batting do the talking while P-J, our flaxen-haired Dutch pace bowler, was a more than competent player and a great character but struggled a little with injuries and hated flat pitches. P-J was always chuntering on about something or another. He loved flash restaurants and had a habit of ordering expensive wines for himself if we were out together as a team, and then insisting on splitting the bill.

Watching benignly over us all was our captain Mark Nicholas, a man to whom I owe so much. Having singled me out in the nets a year or two before, Nicholas kept a sort of paternal eye on my development and became an important influence well into my established career. I swear there was a lump in his throat when he rang me in Mumbai to congratulate me. "Shaun Udal, who would have believed it?" he said. I know Mark's public image beyond those who know him closely is at odds with the man we respect and admire. I understand there are those outside Hampshire who might see a foppish, theatrical public schoolboy with a silver tongue, hence nicknames of Elvis and Jardine, but he showed magnificent faith and trust in me from day one and there are others who will testify to his sharp cricket mind, his enthusiasm and his consideration for those who played for him. Under his intelligent guidance in the 80s and 90s Hampshire enjoyed an unprecedented period of sustained success, twice winning the Benson and Hedges, the NatWest Trophy in 1991 and the Sunday League. All that eluded Hampshire was a county championship title at a time when Malcolm Marshall was at his peak, but we were runners-up in 1985 and also finished third. Nicholas flattered me when he said that if I had been around in 1985 we would have won it.

If Nicholas was fortunate it was because he led an immensely powerful multi-national side, which included Marshall and the Smith brothers, Robin and Chris, who had come from South Africa to seek fame and fortune, Paul Terry, who also played twice for England, Cardigan Connor and two handy spinners in Maru and Cowley. Nicholas's own contribution is not to be underestimated, as I think it is sometimes, but a career record of 18,262 runs at 34, captain of England B, as it then was, and 102 not out against the 1989 Australians for Hampshire, indicate a highly capable cricketer. I think there was a time when he harboured ambitions of playing for England and I know that during one of England's habitual captaincy crises, he was hurt and disappointed when Chris Cowdrey was called in ahead of him in 1988 to lead the Test side against the West Indies. If he had a fault it was that he tried to give himself to everybody, spreading his favours thinly and trying to keep a squad of 22 professionals happy, a task I have come to realise is just not possible. Only eleven can play at any one time and there are bound to be those on the fringes who believe they should be in the team. But if trying to keep players happy is a fault, then it is not much of one. I prefer to remember the way he lifted me, a humble newcomer, by running across the County Ground car park, just as he was preparing to drive away, to rouse the spirits and banish any apprehension with the words, "Good luck, nipper. Keep spinning it." Mark always backed me to the hilt, his belief in me never once wavering. There must be players, particularly of my frail discipline, who have suffered elsewhere from a lack of the support that I always enjoyed so that their careers nose-dived. But while I was feeling my way in county cricket, succeeding some days, failing on others, Mark was always there to encourage and cajole. I have the utmost respect for him as a cricketer and as a person because he got the best out of me at a time when, in the wrong hands, I could have faded without trace like many other young spinners who failed to live up to early promise.

Ian Turner and I were pals from the moment we shared digs and tubs of KFC. His mother would come over to Southampton to prepare us meals because I don't think, as sloppy youngsters away from home, we ever did much cooking ourselves. Maru and Cowley were not getting any younger and we were the next generation of spin bowlers, me off spin and he left arm. There was a great chance for both of us to make the grade at the same time and to forge prolonged county careers. But Ian lasted only until the end of the 1993 season before going back into club cricket with a record of 54 wickets in 24 first class matches. There were moments when it looked as if he might make the next step, but there is a thin dividing line between success and failure in professional sport and it is harder, in my opinion, for a spinner to come through the system than for batsmen and pace bowlers. For a start, they need captains like Nicholas on their shoulders, telling them not to mind being hit around the field by class batsmen, eager to nurture tender sensibilities.

There is a fear factor in spinning which must be overcome if the bowler is to win the battle of minds, which is what it is. As a young spinner there is a tendency to panic if you get hammered, a feeling that you might end up in the record books alongside Malcolm Nash, the victim of Sir Gary Sobers' six sixes in an over. When I get hit now, as of course I do, I bowl the next ball slowly to get my feelings back on track and my head concentrating on the task of getting the batsman out. That may sound obvious, but again the tendency might be to contain rather than attack. I always attack even if the batsman is attacking me. A spinner has to be smarter than the man at the other end charging down the wicket at him, which is why I believe spinners make the best captains. We have to be thinking about our game more deeply.

I am by nature more extrovert and a more aggressive cricketer than Ian was and I think that helped me break through. Ian nearly made it, but not quite. Ian is godfather to my eldest daughter and after he left Hampshire, I got him to play for Camberley, a level where I think he was happier. I see him at Hampshire player reunions and we keep in touch, reliving those early days on the staff, but I am sorry he was unable to make the best of his chances. We might have bowled in tandem for years for Hampshire with greater luck. His assets as a spinner were his fantastic control and, from well over six feet tall, the bonus of bounce. But if things were not going for him, he could get angry and lose his way. He was also a little moody and temperamental, often unhappy and quiet and I think none of that helped him. I suspect he had drifted from his main purpose and had simply lost interest in county cricket as a career. Ian never lacked talent, every bit as talented as me, but someone at Hampshire said the difference was in attitude in that Ian did not want it enough. There was, however, an undeniable element of rivalry, since we were coming through the system together and provided with the same opportunities, but the better and more successful I became, the more it cannot be denied he went backwards.

We both envied Raj Maru, who held the left arm spinner's spot for a decade and who reaped a rich harvest while Marshall was in his pomp, bowling from the other end. I am in no way belittling Maru when I say Marshall got him an awful lot of wickets. A year younger than me and also from Basingstoke, was another left armer in Darren Flint, making his debut in the year Turner left but failing to last the course. Left arm spinners have a huge advantage in that their stock delivery is away from the right hand batsman and I feared this might count against me as Hampshire persisted with Turner and then Flint while they sought a long-term replacement for Maru. But Flint took only 34 wickets in 15 first class appearances and of the young spin generation, I was the only one ultimately who came through to hold down a regular place. The rivalry existed because, as I found out when Shane Warne arrived, it is not always possible to go into matches with two spinners, so that while Turner and Flint were friends and teammates, they could easily have forced me out at an early stage in my developing years with better bowling analyses.

My career, I think, can be broken up into three distinctive phases. There was the progression from staff rookie to my Ashes tour, a spell of decline thereafter caused I suppose by my first England rejection, and then the rebuilding process, which culminated in my call to arms in Pakistan and India. Towards the first part, 1988 was an important stepping stone in that while I did not play in the first team, I did appear in 13 of the 14 Second Eleven Championship matches without doing anything notable and ten of the limited overs Bain Clarkson Trophy games, where I fared a little better. Alan Mullally played for our 2nd XI that year and in championship matches my 16 wickets cost 38 each, redeemed only by a match-winning 57 not out at Canterbury, batting down the order. I feared at one juncture in the season that I was not doing enough to get another contract, but there was always plenty of encouragement, not least from Sains, our coach. It was the year Hampshire reached a limited overs final for the first time, beating Derbyshire at Lord's in the Benson and Hedges Cup. As junior professionals we were obliged to attend and each given two complimentary tickets. The nearest I got to the action was a place in the dressing room while we were fielding, watching Sains bang on the table while exclaiming, "you beauty", as our South African overseas player Steve Jefferies, who otherwise had an undistinguished year as Marshall's temporary replacement, ran through the Derbyshire batting with an inspired spell of swing bowling. Robin Smith's assured 38 was enough to get him into the Test side, proving the importance of being able to perform on the big occasion rather than shrink from it.

Peter Sainsbury was a hard man to please but he instilled in us a pride of performance, which he impressed on us had to be carried into our club cricket on Saturday afternoons when the county junior sides had no fixtures. For Camberley I was in cracking form. With Charlie

Mayes I helped set a club record of 236 for the first wicket against Streatham, and created another landmark with a club-best 202 not out against Byfleet, made in 40 overs. I needed a four off the last over to set the record. Was Sains pleased? No, not really. "That's more than you've got for me all season," he said. Sains would always ask us first thing Monday morning what we had done for our clubs and he did not tolerate failure, or praise success much. Sains wanted runs and wickets from us and if we had failed he demanded to know why. He wanted to know in what manner you had got out and if you ever had the courage to admit 'stumped' he would be furious. I cringe now at the bollocking he gave me for getting out, bowled having a slog, in a 2nd XI match against Middlesex - and I had no excuse. I had just hit the off spinner Andy Needham for six and thought I would try it again with inevitable results. I must now own up to the fact that we were trying to save the game and lost by an innings. "What were you doing? " he groaned. A double century for your club, therefore, meant not much at all. Only in the last week of the season was I told I would be getting another contract with a massive annual pay rise of £250.

"Spider" Mullally was a good friend of mine in 1988, a tall left arm pace bowler, born in Southend but raised in Western Australia and a long way from home when he came over to try his luck in English domestic cricket at the behest of Paul Terry, who had played grade cricket out there and discovered his eligibility. Spider was far too laid back for Sains, who struggled to get the best out of his obvious ability or to understand his attitude. He even played in one first team match against one of the universities, but I don't think there was much sorrow among the coaching staff when he did not come back for a second year. Spider did come back, of course, to take advantage of Leicestershire's green wickets, to help them win a championship and to get into the England side, and when he rejoined us in 2000 it was as an established star coming to the end of a highly successful career. My mum and dad looked after him when he first came over and he was among a small crowd when I got my double ton against Streatham. His second spell at Hampshire was not overall a great success, although he earned England caps while with us and in three of his five years he was still near his best. But his last two were beset by injuries and an inevitable decline and there was some animosity among our supporters and members when he was awarded a benefit in his final summer.

Spider was a good lad, more confident than in 1988, outspoken and amusing but earned a reputation for shooting from the lip.

Back at the printers for the winter, armed with a contract for 1989, I was able to indulge my passion for football, playing on Sunday mornings and watching my local team, Aldershot, when I could. West Ham are my favourite Premiership side, partly because I liked their claret and blue, partly because I liked the name and I think mostly because I watched on television when a rare header from Trevor Brooking won them the 1980 FA Cup final. But Aldershot were my first love, standing by a corner flag with my dad and cousin Clive and watching in the 80s some very good players like Joe Jopling, Wilf Dixon, Murray Brodie, Alex McGregor, the goalkeeper Glenn Johnson and Alan Wooler. But my real hero of that era was John Dungworth, a centre forward who year after year finished as top scorer. When Len Walker was manager, there was Bobby Barnes, Martin Foyle, Andy King, Tommy Langley, Ian Gillard, Colin Smith and Steve Wignall, all among my youthful world top stars. I feared for my life when I went with dad to watch Aldershot play at Swindon in the southern section semi final first leg of the 1986-87 Freight Rover Trophy. We got tickets among the Swindon fans and when Aldershot kept scoring in a 3-2 win, they turned on us as we leapt from our seats and cheered. Andy King was brilliant that day, but we were obliged to turn up our collars and get out of the ground as fast as possible at the final whistle. It was a sad day when a few years later Aldershot went out of business; it was as if part of my childhood had been taken away from me, but they reformed and are now in the Conference, bidding to reclaim their place in the Football League. Their former chairman Karl Prentice is a friend and I still watch them occasionally, as I do the Conference South clubs Basingstoke and Eastleigh, where Mark Dennis and Jason Dodd are big friends. In addition, I introduced another friend of mine, Chris Evans, to Eastleigh and he is now a director.

My first team debut came at the Parks on June 10,12 and 13 in 1989 when six first team players had been rested after beating Surrey at Basingstoke. Shine, Andrew and Connor were among the replacements and I recall being as excited as it was possible to be at the thought of making my first appearance. It was a big opportunity but, sad to relate, it was an inauspicious start: no wickets and no runs in a 127-run win. I was limited to eleven overs in both Oxford innings and did not get a bat. It was at Oxford, though, that I first came across massive Hampshire fans Ken and Jean Tichborne, who ran the Oxford Travel Agency and who hosted a box next to the dressing room. We went there every evening for a drink and they became friends, eventually helping me with my benefit, and Ken and I abused each other over the years with taunts of 'pig's arse' whenever we corresponded. Professor Tony Downes and his wife, Mary, habitually hosted a dinner in one of the colleges whenever Hampshire were in town and it was tradition that the youngsters or newcomers got up at the dinner and told a joke. One year Jason Laney stood and told the bluest of blue jokes and sat down again in total silence.

While I did not play in any more first class matches, I made my competitive debut against Nottinghamshire at Trent Bridge in the final Refuge Assurance Sunday League match on August 20, not finding out about my selection from Nicholas until the evening before, time enough though to alert my parents who drove up on the day. When people like Robin Smith are in the team, you don't expect to get a bat. His 131, aided by Julian Wood's maiden half century, took us to 254-4 and Nottinghamshire were 22-3 until Derek Randall led a recovery. I had never come across such an eccentric personality as Randall, although I had heard plenty about him. On his way to the crease he was muttering "Come on, Rags" and chatted away to himself throughout his innings. My first two overs went for a few runs but Randall became my first major scalp when he came down the wicket and skied a catch to the ever-reliable Terry. There was a squeal of delight among the crowd, I recall. It was mum. I finished with one for 36 off five overs in a 32-run win and a glowing feeling at getting out the great Randall. What a claim to fame.

Hampshire had eased me into the first team gradually during 1989. I played in the Seeboard Trophy at Hove, where we lost a high-scoring match to Sussex, and my averages in the second eleven improved in line with my greater experience. I played in all 17 of our Rapid Cricketline 2nd XI Championship matches, taking 35 wickets at 30 and scoring 332 runs at 23.71, by no means exceptional, but an indication of progress. Cowley was our captain for many of those matches in his last season on the staff and as our skipper he was far more encouraging and generous to me than he had been when I first broke into the side.

My Turn To Spin

It was customary, and still is, for many younger players to spend their winters abroad, broadening their knowledge. Many of them, for instance, had close season contracts with clubs in apartheid South Africa and I had reached the stage where I thought I ought to get away. Through Cardigan Connor, who was a regular visitor there, I got the chance to play in Newcastle, New South Wales for a club called Hamilton-Wickham. It proved to be an incredible experience for a whole variety of reasons. I was still only 20 and although I had lived in digs in Southampton, it was not far from the sanctity of home, so this was a big jump at a tender age. Hamilton-Wickham were looking for a batsman-spinner and I became nervous when I thought they might be expecting someone more advanced than me. I got out there, almost visibly shaking, stayed with a nice family and 12 days later I was on the plane back to England, the victim of homesickness.

The moment I touched down again at Heathrow I knew I had made a big mistake. I should have stayed and taken my time to come to terms with my new surroundings. Omega Printers kindly welcomed me back, but they knew I had blundered and let me work nights so that I could pay for an instant trip back to Australia. This time I was determined to stay. Two weeks later I was in Newcastle again and living with a family who have since become lifelong friends. The Shaw family - Brian, Marie, sons Stephen and Dennis and daughter Donna - went out of their way to make me feel at home. Stephen was my club's captain and Dennis was the smart kid on the block and knew all the in-places. To supplement my small earnings with my grade club I worked for a tiling company but then injured my back, which might have meant another early trip home. Luckily, the Shaw family paid for just about everything and dad sent out money when things got desperate. In many respects the winter of 1989-90 was a time I grew up as a person and as a player. With the responsibility of being the 'overseas' player', I developed fast. I had to. The standard was better than club cricket in England, the pitches were good and matches were played over two days. Gaining a lot of confidence the more I settled, I got a century against Belmont and I also helped the club's under 23 side reach a cup final. They enjoyed having me and I enjoyed being there, even if it was the second time of asking. There was inevitably a bit of anti-Pom sledging, but being able to handle it was a sure sign of a growing maturity.

Learning My Trade

My happy stay in Newcastle was memorable for two other incidents, which I will never be able to forget. The first was my own fault, but the second was a calamitous act of nature. The beer in Australia was stronger and colder than I had been used to in England and one evening I went off with Dennis to the pub. By the time I left, several boozy hours later, I was distinctly the worse for wear and could not see straight. Somehow I found my way to 998 Hunter Street, my digs, where I fell down the steps and lost my front door key. I was on all fours when Mrs Shaw let me in, but the drama was only just beginning. I was sick in my bedroom and then again violently along the landing as I made a desperate lunge for the bathroom. Mrs Shaw should have given me a stern lecture about the perils of drink, but instead she blamed Dennis and made him clean up the mess. It was my first experience of being drunk and, alas, not the last.

I shudder to recall the other incident, but the date of it, December 28th 1989, is etched on the memory. There was an earthquake in which between 30 and 40 people lost their lives. I was lucky not to be one of them. I was helping Dennis rolling a bowling green about a mile from the epicentre, we discovered later. Suddenly the roller began shaking and cracks opened in the ground. I am not ashamed to admit I panicked and ran towards an open field, but not before I had witnessed the most horrific sight. A pub, which I used often enough, was full of people and as some of them emerged from it in the mayhem, the top of a bed warehouse building opposite toppled and crashed down upon them, killing several instantly. It is an image that will live with me forever. All wires were down so that contact with the outside world was lost and for ten or 12 hours, my family, painfully aware of the news, could not contact me, or anyone in Newcastle. They had no idea if I was among the dead or if I had escaped. Mum even rang Australia House hoping they might be able to help, and when eventually she did get through to me, she was hysterical. "Shaun, is that you?" she screamed and I could sense the tears as the family gathered around the phone, relieved at my survival. And survival it was, because the city was devastated. Another pub, often used by Dennis and myself, was destroyed and had we been it at the time we would surely have been killed.

That winter in Australia, I turned from an eager lad from Basingstoke into a man of the world, seeing things I hope never to see again and growing up fast. I came back a better cricketer and a more rounded person. I came back also to discover Hampshire had signed David Gower, then just about the biggest name, with Ian Botham, in English cricket. His capture was a major coup for the club because we did not normally compete when such players became available. The presence on our staff of Robin Smith and Malcolm Marshall persuaded him to move south from Leicestershire. Smith, Marshall, Gower - all of them world class players - and to think, I now had every chance of being a teammate.

Chapter 7

Mixing With The Best

TWO OF THE great myths of cricket in the 1990s were that David Gower was a diffident, fey genius who could not have cared less about the game and that Graeme Hick was dour and humourless and easily intimidated by anyone bowling at more than gentle medium pace. I came to know them both at close quarters as I rose quickly through the system at Hampshire, making my county championship debut in 1990 and being selected for an Ashes tour four years later. Along the way, people like Hick and Gower, my heroes as I was growing up, became colleagues and opponents. Admittedly Gower did not play a great deal more for England after he came to Hampshire and I know his detractors felt he had only come south for a big pay day, but that was to underestimate him and his desire to fulfil completely one of England's greatest ever talents. There was still fire in the belly when he joined us, and a passion for the game, which his easy-going character tended to conceal to those who did not know him well. Gower chose Hampshire, not just because of the pretty countryside and the better weather, but because he felt we were a club with a big future and who could match his own ambition.

In retrospect, had he joined us two or three years earlier we might have swept the honours board. But we still had Robin Smith, albeit playing mostly for England, and Malcolm Marshall, now not quite as fast over long periods as he had been in his prime. Gower's presence gave us a whole new dimension, that much was apparent to me as a chirpy youngster just beginning to stick his nose into the first team dressing room in 1990. There were days admittedly when Gower, the flaxen curls of his youth now greying and thinning, appeared not to care, but when it mattered he always found his form, always brought his vast international experience to bear. I may have been new to county cricket but it was possible to see that opponents feared him, hoping they might catch him on one of those days when his attention was elsewhere but scared that he could mutilate their bowling in that elegant style of his if the mood took him.

There was nothing aloof or disdainful about Gower, although he might also have given that impression; he was instead very much a team player, a genuine superstar but never starry. There was a dry sense of humour, not the sort which is normal in the average dressing room, and which indicated a high intelligence, but what I liked about him was a complete absence of bitterness or rancour. I never once heard him say anything malicious or critical about anyone, not even Graham Gooch, at whose hands he had undoubtedly suffered. Gower would have prospered more for England if Gooch, as his captain, had been more flexible in his approach and more understanding. Not everyone is the same, not everyone needs to lap pitches to perform at their best. Gooch failed to understand Gower's mentality, I believe, and England were the losers. While Gower's international record is excellent, it could, with better handling, have been exceptional. And while I admit that some of the county out-grounds failed to capture his attention, Gower was competitive enough to take on those who stirred him or when the occasion demanded. Even now, he is still committed to Hampshire, contributing to Tony Middleton's benefit in 2006, and those who know him will never find a bad word to say about him.

There was a fun side to him, as I found out when in his Jaguar XJS, and I as a passenger, we raced from Southampton where we were playing the West Indies to Chelmsford in two and a quarter hours around the M25 in a blur of speed until we were stopped by police. That was somehow typical of Gower, but we all liked and respected him.

Graeme Hick was as prolific at county level as Gower was relatively unsuccessful. Where Gower reserved that sweet timing of his for crucial international matches, Hick's reputation as a flat track bully was not entirely undeserved. To have piled up the number of first class centuries Hick has done over two decades is a remarkable achievement, and many a time I have been on the receiving end of the broadest bat in county cricket. But in 1990, my breakthrough year, I got him out in a Scarborough Festival match and in a jubilant act of celebration, I jumped into the arms of our wicketkeeper, Adrian Aymes. The match was covered by Yorkshire TV and I have a tape of the incident in my collection. Later I came to know Hicky on the Ashes tour and got to know and understand him a little better without, it has to be said, getting close to him. I think he might have been a Test great, like Gower, if he had been able to make his England debut against someone of gentler pace than the West Indies. He would never have seen anything like their battery of fast bowlers, or encountered their incessant barrage of bouncers. Having fed on a diet of half volleys in county cricket, where each county had only one or two high class bowlers, he had to come to terms with four of the world's quickest, meanest bowlers all in the same attack and I think it scarred him.

Considering his inability to deal with fast, short-pitched bowling was an acknowledged weakness, I never once saw him practice facing it. On my tour, the Australians had Merv Hughes and Craig McDermott and he never got on top of them either, but I wondered why he never sought ways to counter them in the nets. I saw at first hand how his already frail ego took a battering in Sydney in January 1995 when Mike Atherton, the England captain, declared when he was on 98. Had he got a century, who knows what it might have done for his confidence. I was in the England dressing room that day when Atherton told him when he was 94 that he had ten minutes to get his century - and even then gave him an extra over as he laboured towards his target. Hick was devastated when he came back, absolutely shattered by Atherton's decision, but I think as captain he did the right thing. As it happened, the Australians saved the draw and Hick being sacrificed made no difference to the outcome but it had a huge affect on him. Hick took a while to speak to Atherton again on that tour, even after Atherton went to his hotel room in an attempt to explain why he had declared. At dinner that night a gathering that included Gary Lineker, Michael Parkinson and Mark Nicholas all agreed Atherton had no alternative.

Although he failed to see the funny side of that particular incident, Hick had a sense of humour, but I don't think Ray Illingworth or Keith Fletcher, the dominant selectorial figures at the time, ever saw him as their type of player. Graeme and Steve Rhodes, his Worcestershire county colleague, hired an apartment in Sydney for their families, which struck me as strange at the time, but that was not untypical of the way the whole tour splintered. All I know is that Hick has been just about the hardest man to get out during my county career when set and my friend Robin Smith always said Hick was a far better player than he was. He may well have been, but Robin averaged 43 in Tests and Hick a far from complimentary 31. Yet in terms of first class runs, Hick entered the 2007 season with almost 40,000, the vast majority scored outside Tests, at 52.68, which is an incredible total.

When it came to making my championship debut, I was preferred to Ian Turner at Arundel against Sussex in July 1990 when Mark Nicholas threw me the ball as our fifth bowler and told me to get on with it. What I had not expected him to do was keep me on for the best part of a day, bowling a mammoth 43 overs for my four for 144. I had never bowled so many overs in one innings and I can still recall the tiredness and the aching next day. I played in seven first class matches that year, taking 22 wickets at more than 40 apiece, and suddenly I was being expected to get out world-class players. I also got through another marathon stint in the second innings against the Sri Lankans on the basis that no one else apart from Maru wanted to bowl. Raj bowled 50 overs, I got through 40 and Aravinda De Silva took advantage of my inexperience and the lethargy of my fellow bowlers to help himself to an unbeaten double hundred, although I finished with a then career-best four for 139. The highlight of my second eleven season was an unbeaten 100 against Northamptonshire at Wellingborough School, thereby achieving an ambition to score a century at that level. I shared in a stand of 210 with Aymes, whose fighting qualities were much admired by Peter Sainsbury.

This was also the summer I met Emma, my future wife. It was about as close as you can get to love at first sight. I was playing for Camberley at Leatherhead when I spotted this attractive blonde in tight black leggings. We had a £5 bet among us players to see which one of us could get her phone number and I was more than pleased I won. I discovered her father, Graham, was chairman of Leatherhead and while chatting her up, I asked, "Which one is your old man then?", only to discover I was standing next to him. On a nervous first date Emma drove me from from Leatherhead to Farnborough and we hit it off straight away. I was immensely keen on her from the start and later, much later, I learned she thought on that first date she would marry me. Some 15 months later, on October 5, 1991, when I was 22 and she was 21, we wed. I would be lost now without her and she has been my rock in good times and bad. Emma knows straight away how well or badly I have done by the look on my face from the moment I enter the house but has learned it is wise never to comment on cricket, although she leaves nice messages if she knows of any success.

Basingstoke has been home for Emma, Katherine, Rebecca, Jack and me since 1994, although the Farnborough area, a few miles away, is where my extended family of cousins, uncles and grandmother lived. My cousin Clive, a policeman and two years older, was a good footballer who never took it on while my brother Gary, a pace bowler and middle order batsman has best figures of ten for 34 for Camberley. My mother, Mary came over from Ireland when she was 15 and made her home on the Hampshire-Surrey borders. She dotes on us and her grandchildren.

The following year, 1991, was about as bitter-sweet as it gets. Laid low by a hernia and allowed only to play in one-day matches, I ended the summer playing in a Lord's final. Along the way I attracted the attention of Godfrey Evans, who gave me my first man of the match award, Richie Benaud and the highly influential Ray Illingworth. My only first class match was a harrowing experience at the hands of the West Indies' tourists. Brian Lara was beginning to emerge, although Malcolm Marshall had tipped us off about his quality long before Lara announced himself to the outside world. But the West Indian player who I felt should have become one of the greats, on a level with Lara, was Carl Hooper. Like Hick in a way, Hooper should now be regarded as a top player but, brilliant though he was in flashes, he does not quite come into the 'great' category. Hooper was a fantastic player of spin, as I found out to my cost often enough, and had all the shots in a wonderful textbook style, so that it was a mystery to me why he did not make the step up. The mental aspect of cricket might once again be the reason, as it was with Hick, although it is hard to be sure. Hooper got runs at Southampton in that match but I also got him out, lifting a ball into the deep, and I dismissed Lara coming down the wicket to finish with two for 117. Normally I would not shout about those figures but the standard of opposition had to be taken into consideration.

Sadly, my career was restricted once the hernia had been diagnosed in mid-summer. When I came back from Australia for pre-season I felt a pain at the top of the groin but I had never suffered an injury like that before and plodded on. Only when a bulge appeared was a hernia suspected, all the more distressing because I had thought it was the sort of ailment from which only older people suffered. The pain was real enough, so bad at times that I needed a couple of tablets to play at all. I had the operation to repair the hernia three days after the NatWest Trophy final at Lord's, but the damage had been done. There is no doubt I would have played in a fair proportion of the championship matches but my loss was Ian Turner's gain. He played where I could not. We finished bottom of the Refuge Assurance League that summer - Nicholas and I were the only ever-presents - and in the Benson and Hedges Cup we got as far as the quarter finals before being turned over by Essex, so that for me at least, the NatWest Trophy became my focus. To win it is a treasured memory, but we almost never got beyond the first round.

Normally we would have been expected to see off Berkshire of the Minor Counties, but for a day and a half at Reading we sat and watched the rain come down. Our greater depth of talent would normally have overwhelmed the amateur club cricketers of Berkshire but suddenly there was a hint of panic when we were obliged to practice the art of bowling at one stump for a possible 'bowl-out'. This made it a lottery since professionals are encouraged not to bowl at the stumps but, in the main, just outside the off stump where it is more likely we might find an edge. Sounds curious, but for most bowlers to actually bowl at the stumps is not straightforward. Efforts were made to move the match to another venue to reward patient spectators and to avoid the dreaded bowl-out, but then the sun came out just long enough for a game to take place. Berkshire are neighbours and I think it was only because we enjoyed such a good relationship with them (Gordon Greenidge came to us via Berkshire Bantams for instance) that the game went ahead. They went out of their way to help us, although they might have won had the game gone to a bowl-out and, in the end, a 22-overs match was just about playable. I took two for 14 from five overs and Berkshire were restricted to 90-5, an undemanding score which Terry and Robin Smith knocked off with ten balls remaining. That act of kindness by Berkshire set us on our way. My little bowling spell, short but economical in the circumstances, caught the eye of the ex England wicketkeeper Evans, who adjudicated in my favour on my competition debut. Evans asked me how I pronounced my name, which is something not everyone has had the courtesy to do over the years, and to my occasional annoyance. Even people who have known me for a long time call me U-dal and not the single syllable Udal.

Lancashire were a powerful side in one-day cricket at the time with an array of decent batsmen and some quality bowling in depth, so to meet them in the next round was obviously going to be a demanding test. There was a big match atmosphere at Southampton, something I had not previously experienced, and among those watching on behalf of BBC Television were Benaud and Illingworth, two of the most respected men in the game. Lancashire made 261 and Nicholas, aware of my limitations, held me back until he felt I was ready at a time when our opponents were already well set. Almost immediately I got Gehan Mendis with my quicker one and followed that by dismissing Mike Watkinson and Graeme Fowler on my way to figures of three for 47 from a full quota of 12 overs. Benaud was heard to remark that I would be pleased with that, and I was. Illingworth, who knew a thing or two about off spin bowling, agreed with Benaud and, bearing in mind how he was to push my cause later when he was chairman of selectors, must have made a note.

Our batting in those days was immensely strong with Chris and Robin Smith and Gower, rising as he did so often to the big occasion, with 54 not out when we booked our place in the third round by an emphatic eight wickets. It was my first time on television and I also took a good catch in the deep to remove Neil Fairbrother. Illy said: "Udal has the best action I have seen in a young spinner in the last ten years." Benaud, another of the spinning greats, said: "He looks the part and is not afraid to give the ball plenty of air." I suppose one of the reasons I succeeded that day was because I was always ready to attack the batsman. Malcolm Marshall used to say to me to be patient and I know he was talking sense, but I was happier taking three for 47 than, say, a more defensive one for 25. I had got it into my mind not to worry about conceding runs and I think it might have been that attitude which so impressed Benaud and Illy.

Chris Smith's diligence and rock-solid temperament also won us the quarter final against Nottinghamshire at the County Ground. I failed to take a wicket in 12 overs, costing 54, as Nottinghamshire made a challenging 252-9, only for Chris Smith with 105 not out and his brother, making 67, to polish off the target with some ease. The match will be remembered for one curious incident after Paul Terry had been given run out while appearing to be obstructed by the bowler, a decision which so infuriated our captain that he marched from the dressing room out into the middle to discuss the incident with the umpire, Roy Palmer, and with his opposite number Tim Robinson. The run out decision was not reversed and it was just as well it did not prove to be crucial. All of this took us to a semi final at Edgbaston where Warwickshire would have started favourites on their own ground. But that most genial and amiable of bowlers, the underrated Cardigan Connor, enjoyed a day in the sun, taking three wickets in eight balls and four for 29 altogether as the home side fell away to 172 all out. My contribution was to have the captain, Andy Lloyd, stumped in taking one for 30 and our opponents' total never looked like being enough when Robin Smith started to smash Allan Donald to all parts.

Robin was by now an established England player and he relished contests such as this, taking apart just about the fastest bowler in the world on his own patch. Paul Terry was no less steadfast and he and Robin had unbeaten half centuries when we won by nine wickets with a massive ten overs to spare. There should have been wholesale, unfettered celebrations, but there were none, at least not at Edgbaston. The Hampshire players just packed up and went home, delighted to have reached the final of course but saving the champagne for some other time. I had been followed by a loyal batch of friends from Camberley all the way through the competition and there must have been 20 of them at Edgbaston. Mum and Dad came to see the match and drove me south, almost as if nothing had happened. I ended a long day back in the Camberley clubhouse drinking with my mates and watching the highlights on television. It hardly seemed probable that I could be on my way to Lord's. I think I always knew I was going to play in the final without being presumptuous on the basis that I had pulled my weight when bowling and had never given any indication of being overawed, even at my tender age.

The NatWest Trophy was the season's showcase, played over 60 overs a side and coming at the end of the season and assuming in cricket the prominent place the FA Cup final does in football. I only began to realise its importance when the demand for tickets began to grow. We were each given only four complimentary tickets and those were obviously going to be reserved for family, so obtaining extra ones became a full time job. Our build up to the big day was anything but perfect. Surrey, our cup final opponents, hammered us in two and a half days at the Oval in the championship match leading up to Lord's. The fixture was a coincidence, but they must have thought they had gained a big psychological advantage in disposing of us so easily. In addition, Mark Nicholas had had a knuckle broken by the Pakistan pace bowler Waqar Younis at the Oval and, much as he wanted to, was unable to lead us out at Lord's. We were lucky therefore to have as his replacement David Gower, a man who had led England and who would have relished such an opportunity, even if it came as the result of misfortune to another. By then, also, we had lost the resolute Chris Smith to Australia. I know Chris wanted to stay for the final but a new job with the Western Australia Cricket Association meant there could be no delay. As we sat in the dressing room at Edgbaston coming to terms with our achievement, Chris loaded up his cricket gear for the last time, waved goodbye from the dressing room door and walked out of our lives forever. Tony Middleton, a more than useful deputy, came in and made the opening spot his own to such an extent that he was to later play for England A in Australia. Tony was my roommate, a real ale drinker and soothing influence. Nothing seemed to worry him, not even having to take on the dreaded Waqar in front of a full house at Lord's.

Paul Gascoigne was never noted for his profound sayings but I read in his autobiography that he always ran out on to the pitch from the dressing room down the tunnel in third or fourth position among his teammates. That way he got the benefit of the crowd greeting, the full blast of their roar of welcome. He reckoned the first two running out often did so in near silence because they had caught the waiting crowd napping. By the time the player in third or fourth came out they had awoken to their team's arrival. That was Gascoigne's theory, anyway, and I was determined to see if he was right. In fact, it was one of the things I kept thinking about during a sleepless night at the Westmoreland Hotel across the road from Lord's where Hampshire were staying. Emma got lost looking for the hotel, which did not auger well, and I got up at 5.30 or 6.00 on the morning of the match wondering what on earth to do. Rather than mope around the hotel, constantly looking at my watch or making polite conversation, I decided the best antidote to my nerves was to cross the road and go to our dressing room, three hours before the start. Even at 8.20, there were Hampshire fans queuing on the pavement to get in, the shouts of "Good luck, Shaun," underlining how much the day itself and just being in a Lord's final meant to those supporters who must have left home before dawn. I only wish someone with greater experience had put a hand on my shoulder and told me to relax but, for want of something better to do, I sat on our balcony and watched the crowd and the noise build up, my hands shaking in a mixture of anticipation and stage-fright. Gower was calmness itself, as you might expect from a player who had seen it all, but the papers were all saying the outcome depended on the battle between Robin Smith and Waqar Younis. Both players were in their prime and would have been looking forward to this gladiatorial clash. Robin was just about the most aggressive batsman in England, maybe the world, while Waqar and his swinging yorkers was a weapon not easily countered.

Even in a crowd of 20,000 plus, I was able to pick out my family, which is as I have said, always important to me and seemed somehow to settle a few of the nerves threatening to engulf me. And then, yes, Gascoigne was right. The noise, which hit me as I ran out fourth behind Gower, was incredible, and the likes of it I had never before encountered. I did not bowl especially well, or with much luck, my nine overs going for 46 and without a wicket to show for it, but once again Connor, smiling as ever, produced an outstanding performance just when we needed it. Graham Thorpe, a teammate not much more than five years ago, made 93 and Alec Stewart scored 61 but Connor's miserly three for 39 off 12 overs had restricted Surrey to a very getable 240-5 and there was a feeling at the interval, when Hampshire fan Rory Bremner removed any tension with a cameo performance, that if we got off to a good start, we could and should win. A lot would depend on Robin Smith and his duel with Waqar.

Tony Middleton gave us a wonderful start, seeing off Waqar's opening burst on his way to a typically obdurate 78 before he was bowled, leaving our fate in the hands of Robin, our champion, with whom he had already added 70 precious runs. Robin was in no mood to let the occasion pass without making a major contribution. With a mixture of that typical swagger and fierce determination, Robin saw off another Waqar spell and started to build an innings based on formidable power and the tightest of defences. All the while the September evening light was beginning to fade and made it increasingly hard to follow the flight of the ball. From 186-2, Waqar came back and almost immediately we lost Gower and Smith to make us a more precarious 193-4 and, in the process, slowing the run rate. Robin's awesome innings of 78 ended in a run out, so after a promising and patient start, there were some jitters in our dressing room as Surrey sensed their chance.

With three overs left we needed 24. But at that point Tony Murphy's last over cost Surrey 14 with Jon Ayling smiting him over point for a superb six. In almost complete darkness, the lights in the stands shining brightly, I padded up ready to go in at number nine as Ayling and Aymes went into the last over of the match from Martin Bicknell requiring four runs. Aymes was run out off the first ball going for a second run, Raj Maru scuttled a single and then, with three balls left - and I still don't know how he did it in the gloom - Ayling produced the most important shot of his life, a four to deep square leg to win the match. By that stage, as next man in I could not have held a bat, let alone hit a ball, so bad were my nerves and there was conspicuously no volunteering from numbers ten and eleven to spare my inexperience by going in ahead of me at the death. But from the point of exhaustion there was this colossal release provided by a narrow four-wicket victory and the elation that went with it, an intoxicating mixture of extreme emotions squeezed into a few hectic minutes. Where once there had been silence in the dressing room, there was now shouting, the occasional scream of delight and joy tinged with a massive sense of relief.

Nicholas, deprived of his chance to lead the side by injury, joined the celebrations, fulsomely praising the captaincy of Gower. For an hour we wound down in the dressing room with committee members, family and friends and it was hard, as the team's youngest member, to come to terms with what had happened. One minute we were winning, the next we were shaking, the next we had won. Later that evening, we dined at a Chinese restaurant, something I had never done before, and I took an instant dislike to the seaweed. Not eating much, I made my exhausted way back to the Westmoreland, a winner's medal better off but completely knackered. It had been an immense day and I could not help thinking how many great cricketers were never to play in a Lord's final.

The rest of my season had been one of steady progress, where the hernia allowed. The 2nd XI reached the semi final of the Bain Clarkson where we lost to Surrey and in the second team championship my 27 wickets cost me 30.33 each. Peter Sainsbury, coach during Hampshire's two cup final wins to add to his playing achievements, retired at the end of that season and my own efforts were rewarded by being voted Young Hampshire Cricketer of the Year by the Hampshire Exiles. The Exiles were not alone in noting my development. With Tony Middleton and Robin Smith, I was selected for the national Whittingdale Cricket Plan, which provided us with personal fitness schedules during a six-week period in the winter, and we also had to report twice a week for coaching from leading fugures like Norman Gifford, Alan Knott and Bob Cottam at Cheltenham and Lilleshall. We were in an elite group of the 12 best up-and-coming players in England, a recognition I had hardly expected bearing in mind my injury.

Cricket took a back seat in October as Emma and I got married. My stag night was spent getting drunk at Ragamuffins night club in Camberley, creeping home at 4am just as the milkman was doing his deliveries. My brother Gary and Neil Roberts were best men and there was a reception for 180 at the Lakeside Country Club, a famous darts venue now, at Frimley and among the guests were Aymes, Maru, Bob Parks and Nicholas. At 22, with a cup final appearance behind me and newly married, life was falling nicely into place.

Chapter 8

Peerless Maco

MALCOLM MARSHALL had been a massive player for Hampshire for 13 years by the time the 1992 season started, but all he had to show for his fantastic efforts on our behalf was the John Player Special League title in 1986, paltry reward for a player of his quality. It is impossible to underestimate how good a fast bowler he was throughout the 1980s, running through high class batting orders around the world with a mixture of intimidation, raw pace and, later, a lot of cunning and guile. Marshall helped the West Indies dominate cricket in that decade in the same way the Australians do now as part of a quartet of fast bowlers, any one of whom would have been outstanding in any era. To have four available at the same time made Viv Richards' side irresistible on any wicket. Marshall never once took it easy while he was on county duty with Hampshire. We had signed him as a novice in 1978, unseen and unheralded, after playing in only one first class match for Barbados. As such he grew up with the Smith brothers, Nicholas, Terry and one or two others at Hampshire and it became very much his club.

There was nothing mercenary about Maco, and there was never any suggestion he was, as many had been around the counties, a hired overseas hand fulfilling a lucrative contract. Whenever he was called to play for the West Indies in England, we always struggled to find a replacement. Hampshire fans will recall Elvis Reifer, Shaun Graf and Linden Joseph, who were among those signed to fill the yawning chasm while he was away. The irony was that when Maco was playing for the West Indies in England, we did well without him. There was the 1988 Benson and Hedges Cup triumph when Steve Jefferies was the stopgap, and 1991 when we won the NatWest Trophy. On each occasion he was quick to congratulate us, but for all the success enjoyed by the West Indians, he would not have been human had he not felt somehow left out. Maco had after all given of himself unstintingly for the county. In 1982, for instance, he took an incredible 134 championship wickets and still Hampshire did not win the competition.

I was feeling my way, learning my trade when he was at his peak, but whenever Hampshire were talked about, Marshall's name was inevitably mentioned. With Robin Smith, to the outside world he was Hampshire. So in 1992 Marshall came back for another year and I think there was a feeling that we had to do something for him, win the championship at last or perhaps another of the big one-day trophies. By this stage he was 34 and his powers as a fast bowler were beginning to decline after ten years at the top. It was now or never. Some of the others who had served the club so well through the golden 80s were as close to the veteran stage and I was one of those who represented the future. Fearing that several of our big players would go out of the game together, Hampshire had to push through youngsters like myself to see if we could cope with the demands of regular first class cricket. It was one thing to drop occasionally into a good team, filled with experience, and another to become an integral part of it.

My hernia operation completely successful, I was now fit and expecting to start 1992 in the team, so although I was pleased I was not completely surprised when my mentor Nicholas told me I would play from the start. I cannot emphasise enough how important was his unflinching confidence in my ability. I am sure he was the reason I got among the wickets almost immediately and for my career taking off as it did. In less sympathetic hands, I could have disappeared quite quickly. I know he liked my natural gifts, but also what he perceived as my toughness and the fact that I was not scared of responsibility. I responded by taking 109 wickets that year, 58 in first class matches and 51 in the one-day games, more than anyone else in England in limited overs competitions. It helped, of course, having Marshall at the other end once in a while, not quite as quick as he was, but by reputation still scaring out the opposition and removing batsmen now by stealth as much as the blinding speed of his prime. Always at the back of our minds as the summer unfolded was the collective desire to get him a medal before it was too late and the team of his contemporaries finally broke up.

Peerless Maco

Paul Terry was a key opening batsman for us and later became the county's coach after emigrating to Australia and starting a coaching school, but it is he I blame for me acquiring my nickname of Shaggy in 1992. We were going through a spell of growing beards as a sort of dressing room contest and I had not shaved for three days. My efforts left a lot to be desired and it looked a bit patchy, to say the least. One morning I walked into the dressing room in a green jumper and light brown trousers. Terry took one look at me and said, "Look, it's Shaggy." The rest of the team convulsed in laughter when the resemblance to the cartoon character in Scooby Do was pointed out and I have to admit I was all too similar. From that day onwards it stuck to the extent that as many people know me as Shaggy as they do Shaun. My dad hates it, but it is far too late to do anything about it and Shaggy I will always be.

I actually took more wickets than any Hampshire player in 1992, more even than Marshall, and also scored a satisfactory 400 runs to confirm my belief that I could become a bowling all-rounder in due course, but one of the early matches, my seventh in fact in the championship, turned out to be one of the most bizarre of my career. Something is always likely to happen when we play Sussex and this was no exception. We were playing at Southampton and the four-day match was reduced to three by rain. Terry, Robin Smith and Middleton all got hundreds and we declared at 468-2. Sussex were 169-2 before reaching a contrived declaration of their own in the hope of chasing a reasonable target. Overnight they were 50-1 in the first innings so Nicholas decided to speed things up by getting our wicketkeeper Adrian Aymes and very occasional spinner Tony Middleton to lob up some easy runs. Aymes, as he would, took his bowling more seriously than Nicholas and after I had gone behind the stumps in his place I put down a snick. Adie was not best pleased.

The Sussex batsman David Smith had been a force in county cricket for years and had played for England in the West Indies where it was thought his resolute defensive qualities might blunt the Marshall-led attack. It did not work. However, Smith was an imposing figure who had a tempestuous reputation and was not a man to upset. Sussex duly rattled up 119 runs in 13 overs of 'declaration' bowling, but along the way Smith was out, caught and bowled by a delighted Aymes. Smith failed to see the funny side and after making a sullen way back to the dressing room to the background of Hampshire laughter, he smashed a tray of drinks with his bat in his fury. The noise of breaking glass reverberated around the County Ground. Forfeiting our second innings, Sussex were left to get 300 in four and a quarter hours. I was in the attack immediately, although I only stayed on after lunch so that one of our pace bowlers could change ends. In my second over I got rid of David Smith (his second dismissal in a matter of an hour or two) and Keith Greenfield in successive balls and although Alan Wells and Franklyn Stephenson tried to hammer me out of the attack, Nicholas persevered with me even though the wicket was turning only a little. I went on to complete a spell of 23-12-50-8 as Sussex were shot out with an hour to spare, giving Hampshire victory by 150 runs.

By the start of the 2007 season, some 15 years later, it remained my best bowling analysis. As we came off the pitch, delighted with our win and slightly shocked by my own success, I was approached by an interviewer from the BBC with a cameraman at his shoulder. It was the first time anyone had wanted to interview me and I fancied telling the outside world how well I had done. But I had barely got started when a loud voice interrupted. It was Mark Nicholas's and he bellowed, "What are you doing?" Thinking I was getting above myself, the interview was ended by our captain before it had begun. One of the traditions associated with a career-best performance is buying drinks for the rest of the team. The canny Peter Sainsbury once told me that if you are going to record your best figures early in your career, make sure it's a big one. That way the drink-buying was kept to a minimum.

We did not hold on to the NatWest Trophy for long, lasting only two matches, and while I had a particularly successful Sunday league season, the team did not. My 31 wickets, which included four for 64 against Durham in Bobby Parks's benefit match and four for 51 against Northamptonshire, was a county record, surpassing Sainsbury's 28 in a season. Allan Lamb, a great England batsman, was among those I dismissed that day to beat Sainsbury, although the removal of Tony Penberthy gave me my record. Later in the season our attempts to beat Yorkshire in the final of the Scarborough Festival were thwarted by rain, leaving the Benson and Hedges Cup as our only possible salvation. In that competition the early matches were played in groups. Ours included Lancashire, Northants and Essex, three sides always strong in one-day matches, and Scotland, the makeweights. It all went well, I took three for 27 to help us see off Essex by 41 runs and three for 40 to enable us to overcome Lancashire by 38 runs. Our last match in Glasgow was abandoned because of freezing and wet conditions, which was just as well because we were an uncomfortable 16-2 chasing Scotland's 151-5 when play was halted. I had taken two for 23, so that in reaching the quarter-finals I had collected eight quite cheap wickets and, more importantly, we were again two matches away from a Lord's final. Middlesex were our opponents at the County Ground and by now the groundswell of support for Marshall was growing and there was already a feeling that we were finally going to get him to a domestic showpiece.

Paul Downton, a former Middlesex player, made me man of the match in that quarter final for my four for 40 as Middlesex made only a moderate 206, which we knocked off with the loss of only four wickets. Marshall went off with a back spasm and for a few brief moments we wondered if it might be serious enough for him to miss the final, should we get that far. That took us to the semi final, again at home and against Somerset, who in one-day terms were certainly not the team of Botham, Richards and Garner in the 70s. We were expected to win and we did, handsomely. Graham Rose, a powerful right-handed batsman, took me on and I went for more runs than I would have liked. Somerset made 218-8 and my figures of one for 58 were nothing to write home about, but Nicholas trusted me enough to let me bowl at the end of the innings. Man-of-the-match Paul Terry guided us to another six-wicket win.

I can always remember the words Malcolm Marshall, who had won World Cups and Test series for a decade, told us about how much playing for Hampshire at Lord's meant to him. "This is as important to me as anything I ever did for the West Indies." I can also recall how breathtaking it was when he told us. I knew he was Hampshire through and through but I, for one, never imagined it could touch him so deeply or matter so much. I wish I had been in the same Hampshire team as Marshall when he was at his inspirational best but my arrival as a regular coincided with his gradual fading. But I was lucky enough to see him at his most destructive and lethal in one of my early games in 1990. We were playing away at Pontypridd and with two days to go, Glamorgan were about 20 ahead - on an admittedly dodgy pitch - and with seven second innings wickets in hand. Just before the start of play, Marshall rang Stoneham Golf Club in Southampton, where he was a member and low handicap player, to ask for a tee time at 4pm that day. I could hardly believe my ears and I turned to Tim Tremlett for confirmation of what I had just heard. Tim's a master of understatement and he said to me, "That's a very good sign." Maco put the phone down, turned to his captain and told him, "I'm bowling. It's going to be a good morning." With a game of golf as his incentive, Marshall produced a performance straight from his glorious heyday, ripping through the bewildered Welshmen in no time, taking six of the wickets for 47 and leaving us with 70 to win before lunch. We polished that off in no time. At 1.30pm, Maco was seen loading his cricket gear into his car and by 4pm, he was hitting a golf ball down the middle of the first hole at Stoneham, apologising for being three minutes late.

I count myself very fortunate to have been a teammate of both Marshall and Shane Warne, indisputably two of cricket's greatest players, and it says a lot for Hampshire that both were committed to the club in the long term.

And so to the final, my second at 23 and Marshall's first. Kent were our opponents and it would be hard to say which of us started as favourites. Where we had Marshall, they had Carl Hooper and there was experience all the way through their team. I was far more relaxed and less nervous than I had been the year before when I hardly knew where I was at times, so tense was I. Again we stayed at the Westmoreland, but I slept better the night before and crossed the road to the ground at a proper time. As a result I can remember the day, or days as it turned out to be, with greater clarity. One of the most conspicuous aspects was inevitably the behaviour of Marshall. Like Warne and all winners, he loved the big occasion and, in Hampshire terms, there was none bigger. Here he was, pumped up, enjoying the crowd and relishing the attention. The papers were full of 'Marshall's final' and he was determined to grace it with a performance befitting a champion.

We batted first after being put in and another champion, Robin Smith, made 90 in a decent, but not unbeatable total of 253-5 with Marshall getting a few runs at the conclusion. The great man was just warming to his task when bad light and then rain brought an early close, with Kent six without loss after 2.2 overs and the big crowd, many of whom had come to cheer Marshall to his winner's medal,

England at last - posing for a photo with the flag after my selection for the tour of the sub-continent.

Above: Out-Montying Monty. I celebrate the wicket of Tendulkar at Mumbai.

Left: Another celebration as the Test match is won.

Above: Where it all began - Aldershot vs Farnborough under 11s.

Right: My surprise championship debut vs Sussex at Arundel in 1989, where I had match figures of 6-156 off 48 overs.

The Winter I grew up. Above: With Denis Shaw in Sydney in
1990 before regrettably flying home.

Below, 'The Billys' of Hamilton-Wickham, the most attractive
team in Newcastle, New South Wales.

Right: 1990, the Summer
I met Emma.

Below: Our engagement
party at Camberley CC
later that year.

Above: With Emma, six weeks before the birth of Katherine, after victory in the 1992 Benson & Hedges Cup Final.

Left: "Maco", whose contribution to Hampshire cricket and that 1992 triumph was immense.

Above: With Beefy, Dave Muir, Ian Garden and Peter Lake at Camberley CC in 1994. Beefy, my cricketing hero, flew down to speak after one aborted attempt.

Below: With the boss, Rod Bransgrove, in younger days.

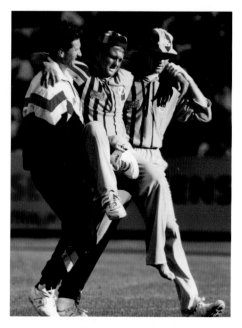

Three views of the Ashes 1994/95.
Above left: With Neil 'Harvey' Fairbrother in pensive mood.
Above right: Carrying Goughie off at the MCG.
Below: After being told I was flying home early.

Above: In mine and McGrath's room on the Pakistan 'A' tour in 1995. Nick Knight and Keith Piper are enjoying our hospitality of sponsors' beer.
Below: On the same tour after being told I had been left out of the one day team.

Above: Me, Robin Smith, Mark Nicholas and unidentified horse toast the site of the new Rose Bowl in 1996. Without Mark's careful nurturing in my early days, who knows what may have happened to me.

Left: Walking off the field milking the applause after my only century and a 235-run partnership with Matthew Hayden against Warwickshire.

Right: Recovering from the broken ankle I got "falling off a kerb" in 1999.

Below: With Rod Cousens, who did so much in my Benefit year - a true friend.

Above: Kath Smith, Me, Robin and Warney relaxing at a polo match at Kenny Jones's Hurtwood Club.

Below: Celebrating Warney's 100th Test match in Cape Town in 2002. Rod Bransgrove (centre in blue shirt) and I flew out for it. My arm is on the shoulder of Keith Warne, Shane's dad, who I thought was a smashing bloke.

Above: I love this picture -
Me and Judge in happy
times.

Right: Major Ronald
Ferguson and his wife
Susan. He played a selfless
role in my Benefit season
and was one of life's great
men. I miss him a lot.

Above: Left, Dad and two sons. Right, Grandad and Nan.
It was in their back garden that I started my cricketing
journey. Grandad threw balls at me even up to his dying day.

Below: Mum and Dad and me with my son Jack the day he
came home in August 2004 before we knew the problems
he would face.

Above: Katherine and Becky ready for battle and together with Jack - the three things that mean more to me than anything in the world.

Above: The whole family together before I went to Pakistan in October 2005. I'd recently had my head shaved for charity and raised £2,000.

Lifting the C&G Trophy at Lord's in September 2005
- a moment that will stay with me forever.

drifting home disappointed at the soggy anti-climax. The Duke of Kent, due to meet the teams on the pitch in the interval, was invited to the dressing rooms instead. Once it became clear that more play was not possible that day, it was difficult to know what to do. We could not celebrate a job half done, nor slink away to drown our sorrows. Instead we went off for a Chinese meal on a barge on the Thames but left at 11pm for our beds, wondering if the match could be continued at all next day.

The morning was just about dry enough to resume, but no one had told the crowd. Except for a few diehards there was hardly enough people to call them a crowd, with big open spaces on the terraces and an eerie quietness about the half-full stadium. But none of that daunted the determined Marshall who got a couple of early wickets to set the tone for the rest of the innings. Hooper and Mark Benson briefly threatened to take the game away from us, Benson hitting out at Kevan James and Hooper getting after me. Just when it seemed Hooper might win it on his own, he chopped a delivery of mine into his stumps and Kent fell away. Kent were always just behind the required run rate and were eventually all out for 212 with two and a half overs remaining. Once again Nicholas trusted me to bowl some of the last few overs, although my figures of three for 67 (my other victims were Steve Marsh and Martin McCague) were a little on the inconsistent side. It was, perhaps, fitting that Marshall should be bowling at the end and suddenly there was the great West Indian with the broadest smile in NW8, holding the cup aloft, his ambition fulfilled. I think there was a tear or two when he collected his medal and even Kent supporters did not begrudge him his finest hour as a Hampshire player. Bearing in mind how he was to die seven years later at the age of 41, barely into middle age, I am just so pleased we were able to win him that final. I know how much it meant to him.

That aside, and after no great celebrations, we drove off home, though not before Gary Lineker had again somehow shown up in our dressing room to see his pal, Gower. There was a handy little bonus of between £3,000 and £4,000 as tangible evidence of our latest success, money I knew would be more than welcome because Emma was about to give birth for the first time. On August 26th Katherine was born and I am pleased to say I was there to see it happen, one of the most moving events of my life. Emma was in labour for 26 hours at a time when we were due to play at the other end of the country in Durham. Mark Nicholas told me not to travel so I was able to take Emma to hospital and help her through the trauma of giving birth. Sadly, Katherine was the only one of my three children I saw enter the world since cricket had always got in the way. Even after Katherine's birth, I was off and away for ten days fulfilling cricket commitments.

Becoming a father for the first time was a great way to end a good personal season, but there was one setback. I felt I had a great chance of being named in the England A side to tour Australia and my credentials suggested I should have gone. I was 23, had appeared in two cup finals and won them both, taken 109 wickets in the season and set a new club record in the Sunday league. I had also been on the England coaching course, designed to fast-track the more promising young players, and had come away with good reports from the coaches. The A tour was therefore what I perceived to be the next step and I admit I was taken aback when the squad was announced and I was not in it. Ian Salisbury, a leg spinner, was chosen ahead of me and even when Salisbury was belatedly called into the main squad for India, there was still no reprieve. James Boiling, to my huge disappointment, was called in without having anything like the same claim as myself. Tony Middleton, who had batted so consistently for us at the top of the order, was chosen and rightly so on sheer weight of runs, but it was not a happy tour for him and signalled the start of a decline. I think it fair to say he was never quite the same force again on his return to Hampshire, and after working so hard to get on the tour it was the end of his international career and not the start as it might have been. My only compensation was another winter on the Whittingdale coaching scheme, but the main part of my off-season was spent back in the print industry, probably thinking about Australia.

My compensation, and in money terms it was a lucrative one, was to be awarded my county cap. At 23 I thought it might be a little early and I had to wait until the last match of the season when Nicholas stepped forward to present it to me. The prestige surrounding such an accolade is enormous and meant I was accepted as a fully-fledged county player with many years ahead of me.

If 1992 was a year of progression, 1993 was my biggest year yet. Ray Illingworth, soon to be chairman of England's selectors, was saying nice things about me and I responded by taking wickets in great numbers. Every time I bowled I got wickets, 74 alone in the championship and many more in the one-day competitions, building what I thought was an irresistible case for some kind of England recognition. It was Malcolm Marshall's last year as a Hampshire player and in retrospect it was one year too many. The old fire and pace had gone and the harder he tried, the worse it got. It was sad to see him labouring and striving as players he would have once eaten for breakfast got on the front foot and attempted to milk cheap runs. Maco finished the season with a meagre haul of 29 wickets, although in fairness he was as economical as ever, it was just that he did not get enough people out, and I was by far Hampshire's most successful bowler. Kevan James, with 36, was the nearest to me, and all of our four wins were away. One of those was at Swansea where the old spark was re-ignited in Marshall for the last time because of the presence on the other side of his old friend and rival Viv Richards. The years fell away and the eyes lit up as Maco tore into Richards in the first innings on his way to a season's best five for 62 (although it was Darren Flint who actually got Richards out) and then took another three in the second. Much to his obvious delight, Richards was one of them, caught behind for a single. It was the last of Marshall's many great triumphs.

Everything I touched, in contrast, turned to gold. Five times I took five wickets in an innings and twice ten in a match, ten for 171 at Trent Bridge and ten for 192 against Warwickshire. At Trent Bridge, Paul Terry, our captain, said, "I am going to declare. It's up to you to win the game for us." And I did. From being a tentative newcomer, feeling my way, I was now the spearhead of the Hampshire attack, the bowler most likely to take wickets. My batting also improved immeasurably with 509 runs, including half centuries, both at Portsmouth, 66 against Worcestershire and 79 not out against Sussex, so that I was one of the successes of the season in national terms. The Hampshire Cricket Society certainly thought so and made me the Hampshire Player of the Year, a much-appreciated award, but my ambitions were firmly set on one of the two England winter tours. I thought the main England tour to the West Indies might be beyond me at this stage of my career but there was also an A tour to South Africa and quite honestly I could not see how I would not be on it. There was no other spinner anywhere near me in terms of wickets and I had got runs as well. Maybe I had not got a tour the previous winter because the selectors wanted to see I could maintain my promise over a second full season. It's known as second-season syndrome and more than one shooting star has fallen to earth after a great start, flattering to deceive. But I had not. My progression was apparent for all to see and my reputation as one of the country's bright young prospects had gathered momentum by the day throughout the summer of 1993.

On the day the teams were to be announced I was at the County Ground in Southampton, fully expecting to hear my name read out when we gathered around the television in the squash and social club. The plan was to announce them live and there was an air of expectancy on my behalf among my Hampshire teammates. What more could I have done to get on a tour? The main England party to the West Indies was inevitably the first to be announced and I was not in it. In those days the West Indies was a good one to miss for all the delights of the Caribbean since many a career had foundered against their battery of fast bowlers and, in any case, the pitches did not suit spinners. The West Indies success had been based around their plentiful supply of quicker bowlers so that if they chose a spinner it was as an all-rounder, like Roger Harper and Carl Hooper. Fair enough, I thought, I had not seriously expected to jump straight into the full England squad.

Then came the A squad for South Africa and this was where my sights were set. But even now I can remember the shock, the humiliation, as one by one the names were read out and I was not among them. Robert Croft of Glamorgan and Essex's Peter Such got the spinning spots and I was totally gobsmacked, absolutely devastated. There were tears in my eyes as I fled to the sanctuary of the toilets where I sat and sobbed, my mind racing as I tried to come to terms with the hurt, the slight, the snub. There was no commonsense or logic to their choice. Croft was much the same age and there was no denying that he was a good player but my record over the summer had made me a cast-iron certainty, or so I thought. It was much better than his for a start. I could point to the little matter of 132 first class wickets over two years and just could not see how Croft could be preferred. What made it worse, in a way, was that I never heard a word subsequently from anyone in any kind of authority. Not so much as an encouraging phone call to say "keep at it". Our sympathetic captain, Mark Nicholas, saw how badly it affected me that day and sent me home where my mother was in as much of a state as I was.

What I do know is that the influential Graham Gooch was no fan of mine. I am pretty certain that he saw me as coming straight off the Happy Hampshire conveyor belt. Gooch was the ultra-professional and there was a feeling around some of the other counties, which I think he shared, that we were too busy enjoying ourselves to win the major honours that matched the depth of our talent. It was his belief, I am convinced, that we had been under-achievers in the 80s and 90s and I was not the sort of person to change that. True, we did enjoy a beer or two at the end of a day's play and, yes, there was always laughter in the Hampshire dressing-room, but that convivial atmosphere had been created deliberately by our captain who figured that a happy team was more likely to be a winning team. It was not that we did not take our cricket seriously. We did. But Gooch did not rate me and I wondered how much his opinion counted. In the last match of the season there was the perfect chance for me to prove a point to him. Essex were our opponents and Gooch was, as usual, the man we needed to get out. This I did, twice, but only after he had got a century in each innings, I have to admit. So determined was I that I got runs and I got wickets, seven of them to be exact, and I felt fully vindicated, though it was far too late to alter the tour selections.

As Croft packed his bags for South Africa, I headed back to Basingstoke and another winter at the printers. I had used my bonus money from our cup win to buy a shareholding in Omega Printers so, if England did not want me, there was plenty still to be done. I had always wanted to establish a business career because a professional cricketer's lifespan does not last long and injury can force you into retirement at any time before its natural conclusion. I was still hurting inside, there can be no denying, but I came to realise I should be counting my blessings rather than sulking. I was 24, I had a lovely wife and a year-old child and was now a company director, the best part of which was that my dad was now working for me. I was also an established county cricketer with every reason to suppose that my day would come. How many other people of my age had what I had? For all of that I had to be extremely grateful, and I was. Then early in 1994 there was some very good news indeed. There had been a change in the chairmanship of the England selectors. Ray Illingworth, a Yorkshireman of strong opinions and sound judgement based on a lifetime in the game, had got the job he craved. In the dark days of an English winter I knew Illy's elevation would give me a big, big chance and I could hardly wait for the new season.

Chapter 9

Catching The Eye

RAY ILLINGWORTH offered me my best chance of getting into the England side. From the moment he first saw me in action when he was commentating for television, he liked and encouraged me. In him I suddenly had a real ally in the selection process. In his newspaper columns, Illy made it clear he saw me, and Darren Gough of Yorkshire, as the basis for England's future. From what he wrote, he also rated Steve Rhodes, the Worcestershire wicketkeeper from Illy's home city of Bradford, while in his opinion, Gooch should continue to be the mainstay of the batting at 41 years old. What he wanted from me was runs. I got them in adversity at Southampton against Derbyshire after Philip DeFreitas had claimed a hat-trick. Chancing my luck, I hit the first ball I received for four and turned the course of the game in making 83. Illy liked the fact that I tended to get runs on just such occasions, when the team was struggling. I also got five wickets in the match in making an eye-catching start to the 1994 season, or so I hoped.

New Zealand in the Spring and, much later towards the end of the summer, South Africa were providing the oppositio. The first one-day Texaco Trophy game against the Kiwis was on May 19th at a time when county teams were still finding their rhythm. April and May are notoriously difficult for spin bowlers, the pitches are wet and green and there is little or no bounce. The pressure, therefore, was on. I had to get runs and wickets in conditions which did not suit me so that my name could be discussed at Illy's first selection meeting. As that meeting was about to take place, we were playing Sussex at Hove and Martin Speight hit me all around the ground, as if to remind me nothing should be assumed, until I got him lbw. I did an interview with the now defunct 'Today' newspaper in which I was asked, inevitably, if

My Turn To Spin

I thought I would be in the team. I had to be cautious but at the same time I think I felt my time had come at last.

That Saturday evening the Hampshire players went out for a meal and in those pre-mobile days there had been no call for me when I got back late to our hotel. I began to think I had been overlooked and sleep was fitful. Soon after breakfast on the Sunday, the phone rang at last. It was the Press Association, a news agency supplying all the national and regional newspapers, radio and television. The England selectors always pass on team news to them first so that all their news outlets receive the information simultaneously. An anonymous voice told me I was in the squad and he wanted my reaction. I was so shocked I put the phone down on him, thinking for a moment it might have been a prank of some kind since I never imagined that I would hear of my selection first from a journalist. No one from the England camp, nor the TCCB, as it then was, had bothered to get in touch first and I was later to discover I was by no means unique. Only many years later did the ECB, as it became, think it might be more professional to inform players personally when they had been chosen or, worse still, dropped rather than leave it to journalists. Some cricketers spoke of finding out their fate by teletext or from radio news bulletins and never, it seems, from those who actually did the selecting.

My own 'reaction' was instead shared with a handful of teammates and not the world at large. I turned to Tony Middleton and said, "I'm in" and there suddenly was Mark Nicholas, grinning, having heard my elation from the next room. Nicholas hugged me as I told him, "I owe you everything", and there was no doubt I did. Back in my neck of the woods, Mum ran down the road excitedly to my uncle to tell him how England had come calling. Emma, Katherine, Mum and Dad drove to Hove instantly to watch me and share the celebrations. At Hove cricket ground I was handed a faxed sheet from the TCCB congratulating me and listing a series of 'do's' and 'don'ts' in terms of preparing myself for the biggest matches of my career. It was all a bit formal and slightly unreal since there had still been no call. After play, the Hampshire lads joined me in Brown's restaurant where a magnum of champagne was ordered and drunk and signed by the team. I was on my way.

If there were any nerves at least I had Robin Smith as a calming influence and as a companion. There was also more interest in Gough than there was in me because he represented the fast bowling future, nevertheless it was still daunting, walking into that England dressing room and seeing all those household names, many of whom were established international players while I was still growing up. Gooch, for instance, was 16 year older than me while Hick, Alec Stewart and Gus Fraser seemed to me to have been around a long time at that level. Our first match was against New Zealand at Edgbaston and Emma drove me over to the Swann at Newbury to be picked up by Robin on our way north. "Right," he said, helping me load my gear into the back of his car outside the pub, "let's go and play for England."

The England players soon put me at ease, in fact they were more welcoming than I feared they might be, more inclusive than I dared hope and eager to help me settle. I felt like the new boy at school to some extent, or an interloper at an exclusive club. I was the only one who had not played for England at some level, many of them had for a very long time. My parochial claim to fame was that, if selected, I would be the first Hampshire-born Hampshire player to represent England since Trevor Jesty of Gosport left on Christmas Day 1982 to play in a handful of internationals in Australia. This did not say much for the conveyor belt of young talent in the county, something Tony Middleton is now attempting to put right in his role of academy director.

Training went well and that first evening I went out with Mike Atherton and Alec Stewart to TGI's, dining with the stars, so to speak, and hoping to learn something between courses of what was required to play for England. No one gave more for the England cause in the 90s than Atherton and Stewart, so if I had to choose dining partners, they were definitely the right people. The next day, the last before the start of the Texaco Trophy, was decidedly odd. We practiced in the morning and then went off to a wine bar at lunchtime before being given the rest of the afternoon off. The hotel was nice enough and we each had single rooms but time dragged and I sat on the bed watching television, thinking it all a bit bizarre. Was this how England prepared for all big games? My boredom was relieved when we went down for a team meal in the evening, and I could not let the event pass without getting the full squad to sign the menu for me. In retrospect, this was very much Illingworth's squad but another selector, Brian Bolus, the former Yorkshire and Nottinghamshire batsman, did not attend our first meal because he went off to earn some money at a speaking engagement elsewhere in Birmingham, which I felt was not the most tactful of starts for a selector.

I slept well, not knowing if I was in the team, just happy to be part of the international set-up and thinking I probably had years of this ahead of me. There was none of the desperation and anxiety I was to feel 12 years down the line when I came back out of the wilderness for my one, last chance.

I had hoped my parents would travel to Edgbaston for the occasion, even if my participation was not guaranteed, but mum said she was too nervous and Dad and Gary made the journey instead. That morning, as they drove up, Atherton called us together and read out the team. With the sublime casualness of comparative youth, I cannot recall being especially worried, nor feeling unduly elated, when my name was called out ninth. In fact, Robin later admitted how nervous he had been for me, which was typically kind and sensitive of him, and the only time I felt any kind of tension was just before the start when I prayed we would field first so that I could be involved in the action immediately. Those hopes increased when Ken Rutherford, the Kiwi captain, won the toss, only then deciding England should bat. The England team that day was Atherton, Stewart, Smith, Gooch, Hick, Reeve, Rhodes, Lewis, Udal, Gough and Fraser, which was an experienced line-up except for me, Gough and Dermot Reeve. Atherton made 81 and I had an increasingly agitated wait before I got my chance, Chris Lewis and I putting on 25 at the end and me finishing with three not out.

To my great surprise, when we bowled Atherton threw me the ball first change after Fraser and Gough had got us started. Adam Parore hit me for a four early on but he became my first international wicket when I tossed up a slower delivery and bowled him through the gate. I greeted his dismissal with a clenched-fist salute and Judge was the first to congratulate me, knowing how much it would have meant. All the way through the whole series I was glad Robin was with me, talking me through the match and helping maintain morale even when the opposition attempted to get after me, as Parore had done. I wonder how much help he got as a newcomer when England first called on him after his success for Hampshire at Lord's in the Benson and Hedges Cup, but here he guided me through, step by step. Rutherford came in near to tea and my first ball to him was quick and accurate, a perfect delivery, and it struck him on the ankle. Nigel Plews, the umpire, gave him out, bless him. In many ways it was close to being a dream start but my final figures of 11-0-39-2 were tarnished somewhat by an assault by Stephen Fleming, who hit me for a four or two. There should have been a third wicket and today there would have been. Bryan Young was stumped by Rhodes, as television replays showed, but since those replays were not then available to the umpires, he got the benefit of the doubt.

Lord's was the venue for the next match, or at least it should have been. Unfortunately it was washed out without a ball being bowled, the first time it had happened on home soil and all the more annoying because Emma, family and friends had travelled to headquarters to see me play, as I am sure I would have done. I have said how much it affected me in 2006 when I failed to gain selection for the Lord's Test with Sri Lanka because I knew it was my last chance to play for my country on the great ground, but here in 1994 there was not quite the same sense of loss. There would be other days, or so I thought. We went shopping in the afternoon with Robin Smith as the rain teemed down and, at a time when he might have expected to be hammering the Kiwi attack to all corners of Lord's, Robin was forking out £600 for a Hugo Boss suit and I nearly collapsed when I saw the price tag. Yet that little incident was somehow typical of the way the players were left to fend for themselves, there being little sense of a team together at work and play.

It has often been said that England teams have been more a group of individuals than a sporting entity over the years as a perception of weakness, and I was surprised at the way we were allowed to drift off into London once the no play ruling had been made. I was to discover that a sense of dislocation accompanied us at home and was not that much better in Australia a few months later. In this particular series, for instance, we spent hours and days apart from each other as players, often eating alone or in little groups, driving to the grounds alone or in twos and not coming together for a communal meal until just prior to the game. It had noticeably improved when I 'rejoined' England a decade or so later, even if, disappointingly, results have not improved much overall. This was another reason why I was lucky to have Robin with me. At least we hung around together and kept each other company, and I often wondered what it would have been like had I been Hampshire's only representative. When play was ruled out on the second, reserve, day I was allowed to go and play for Hampshire, where the weather was better, against Middlesex in a Sunday league match. When I got home to pick up my kit, I discovered my blue uniform was in the wash and by the time it was serviceable, I only just made the start with about 30 minutes to spare.

Hansie Cronje's fall from grace and subsequent death in a mountain-side plane crash were well-documented tragedies in the 90s, but he was a good cricketer and, oddly for a South African, particularly capable against spin. At the time, and it may be a generalisation, the South Africans had recently come out of apartheid-induced isolation not having seen much spin or worked out how to counter it. This weakness was something I hoped to exploit when I was chosen to face them in two one-day internationals in August. For 20 years, from their expulsion from world cricket, the South Africans had lived in a cricketing cocoon where pace bowling ruled, and when they eventually emerged blinking into the daylight, it took them some time to realise that there were other forms of attack and they needed to adapt and catch up. Cronje was different, he used his feet and his shot selection indicated a control other batsmen appeared to lack.

The season all but completed, there was still the Texaco Cup series and I was named in the squad to face the South Africans at Edgbaston on August 25th. Fairbrother, Thorpe, DeFreitas and Cork had been brought into the side and the full team was Atherton, Stewart, Hick, Thorpe, Fairbrother, Rhodes, Lewis, DeFreitas, Cork, Udal and Gough. My part in a six-wicket win was comparatively pedestrian, no wickets for 34 from eleven overs and, chasing 215-7, Hick got 81 and we won with an over the spare. It rained in Manchester, now there's a surprise, so that the next match against the South Africans in the following week needed two days to be resolved. Once again we won easily enough and my contribution to a four-wicket win was altogether more telling. After Atherton put them in, I took one for 17 from a full quota of eleven overs, the most economic of the match and one of the most economical of my career to that point. I was relaxed enough to have a few drinks the night before and I did not feel any the worse for it next day when it was clear the South Africans had no real idea how to score off me other than to slog. Brian McMillan was itching to get at me, his mission to knock me out of the attack, but I saw him coming, pushed one down the leg side and Bumpy Rhodes stumped him. Rhodes and Thorpe each got half centuries and we won with 6.4 overs in hand, the match going into a second day with us poised at 80-4 half way through our innings.

There was something else about Hansie Cronje which caught the eye. He was the first player at the end of a day's play to run around the pitch to warm down. As such he was an object of curiosity in the England dressing room as we watched his metronomic lapping. These days, the whole squad goes back out on to the pitch to do a few supervised exercises, which are accepted as beneficial and necessary to maintain fitness and aid recovery, but Cronje can claim to be something of a pioneer. By the end of the one-day series, I felt happy and comfortable with my performances and any awe at being among so many big names had long since evaporated. Illy singled me out for a little chat. Yes, not many runs given away, no, not enough wickets. "Seven out of ten" was his verdict - and he was about right. But, considering I had never played at international level before, I thought I had made a reasonable start and the experience gained had done nothing to disturb my belief that I could be an England candidate for years to come.

For Hampshire I had another excellent summer, 684 runs including four half centuries, and only Cardigan Connor with 72 wickets took more than my 69 in first class matches. I missed two matches because of England commitments and I am sure I would have beaten my best of 74 if I had played in those. Seven times I took five or more wickets in an innings and finished with ten for 163 against Surrey in the match at Southampton. I also came within a whisker of my first century, but after hitting 94 against Glamorgan at the County Ground, chasing a bonus point and with a declaration in the offing, I was caught on the ropes at mid-wicket going for the six which would have given me my ton. I also got 59 against Essex, the 83 I have already mentioned against Derbyshire and 64 from the Warwickshire attack. With the Tests against South Africa coming up I took five for 63 in the tour match at Southampton (including three in seven balls) in what proved to be a stormy match, almost ending in a fight. Perhaps the South Africans had not been used to any kind of on-field banter - I hesitate to use the word sledging - after so long away from international cricket, but Kepler Wessels and McMillan took exception to some remarks made by the mild-mannered Kevan James and at the end of a day's play came to our dressing room looking, I believe, for retribution. Luckily for Kevan, he was away in a corporate hospitality tent talking to some commercial clients and was unaware that two large men (Wessels had boxing experience) were waiting to sort him out.

Adie Aymes, a good man to have on your side in such circumstances, got involved, advising the South Africans to go away, and it took some time and a lot of words before the situation was resolved amicably. That evening Wessels and James attended the same barbecue and I understand got on well together. None of which altered my view of the South Africans. Those cricket fans who remembered them just before their worldwide ban came into force in the early 70s speak sadly of the lost generation of Barry Richards, Mike Procter, Graeme Pollock and Eddie Barlow, to name but a few, cut off in their prime and destined to spend their careers outside the international spotlight their talents deserved. But 20 years or so down the line they were a comparatively dull, one-dimensional and predictable side, only the extraordinary Jonty Rhodes offering anything different with his incredible fielding and occasionally spectacular batting, although Allan Donald's pace was outstanding by any standards and McMillan was an aggressive batsman.

When the side was selected for the first Test at Lord's, there were 12 names, including mine, announced, but I think it fair to say I can blame my friend Shane Warne for not making my debut. Warne was not long on the international scene and was already demolishing strong batting line-ups across the world. Not so long before the South Africans came to England, Warne had strangled them to death by taking 15 wickets in three Tests and the feeling among the selectors was that the South Africans therefore had a weakness against leg spin. In truth, as most sides were to discover over the next 13 years, they just had a weakness against Warne. But rather than choose me, England went for Ian Salisbury, just about the only home-produced leg spinner in county cricket. To say I was annoyed would be an understatement and the nearest I got to the action was as 12th man, fretting at a lost opportunity. The plan backfired spectacularly with Salisbury taking only one wicket in the match for 121 and South Africa winning by a colossal 356 runs.

The match at Lord's will be remembered for the Atherton dust-in-the-pocket incident, allegedly to use it to tamper with the ball. I wish I could shed some light on it but at 10.30 on the first day, when it was decided I would not be in the starting eleven, I was despatched to Worcestershire to play instead for my county, so I missed all the fun. Having been told I was not required by England, I had to drag three cases of cricket gear from the Pavilion End to my car at the Nursery End. I was not allowed on the pitch, obviously, so I had to force my way through the gathering crowds in gangways behind the stands. I lost count of the number of times England fans stopped me and said, "Oh, you're not playing then." I would have thought it self-evident as I staggered past them laden with cases and clothes, but it was as if they had made an exciting discovery. I am not sure what I was supposed to reply.

For the next Test at Headingley, traditionally a seamers' wicket, I was not even in the 12, although I had just taken 14 wickets in four innings for Hampshire and presented what I thought was an irresistible case for inclusion. At least Illingworth had the good grace to tell me I was not even in the squad, which showed some sensitivity, but I was not best pleased to see Phil Tufnell restored yet again as the safer option for his only appearance of the series in a draw. No one doubted Tufnell's ability to spin the ball quite sharply at times but he was a genuine number eleven and not the best of fielders, so I had cause to feel slightly aggrieved when he suddenly reappeared. But it was the end of my Test hopes for the season.

For the third Test at the Oval I was nowhere to be seen, a forgotten man. Indeed, no front line spinner was chosen - Hick bowled a total of seven overs - and the match will be best remembered for Devon "'You guys are history" Malcolm's match-winning nine for 57. My omission was therefore completely justified. No matter how well I had done for Hampshire, and I had to maintain my level of consistency in the championship, I drifted out of contention without ever having had the chance to show what I could do. If I had been given a Test and flopped I could have understood it, much more acceptable than being called up, then ignored and finally discarded. All I could do was keep reminding the selectors that I was thriving on the south coast, and I was. I took six for 79 at Old Trafford, six for 85 at Worcester, five against Gloucestershire and Northants and, of course, the ten against Surrey, the team I might have joined eight years earlier.

My Turn To Spin

As the season drew to a close, all the talk was about the composition of the touring party in yet another attempt to win back the Ashes. The papers were full of it, dropping in names like confetti, and although the consensus of opinion was that pace was more likely to win it, spin was obviously going to be an important factor, as the emerging Warne was constantly proving. My credentials were impeccable, so I believed, with three productive years in the championship and in the one-day competitions. I had got runs when it mattered and was a keen, capable and enthusiastic fielder. Not all the same things could be said about my rivals for the spinning spot. There was Tufnell, Salisbury, Such and Croft. Croft and I were without much in the way of international experience, and from my point of view it did not help that Hick, who was sure to be chosen for his batting, could also be employed as an occasional off spinner, as he had been in victory at the Oval. For all of that, I felt I should go.

Once more it was going to be trial by television. The squad was going to be announced live on TV and there could be no hiding place, no sliding off to the toilets or using any other escape route. We were at Edgbaston and I had a drink or two the night before the Ashes squad was to be made public, but alcohol failed to calm the nerves. My hands were shaking as, one by one, the names were read out. There was some mild muttering when the Surrey quickie Joey Benjamin was called. Benjamin had made a successful debut on his home ground at the Oval in the thrashing of South Africa but was 33 and relatively untried. There were a few nods, too, when old warhorses Gatting and Gooch were summoned once more. The mouth was dry, the hands sweaty as 14 of the 16 players were confirmed alphabetically and then finally, sensationally, Udal and Craig White. Mike (MJK) Smith chosen as tour manager and although Keith Fletcher was still coach, he was relieved of his team manager's role after the Ashes tour. I am not sure Fletcher rated me, I think he preferred Croft, but Illy was still supportive and may have swung the voting in my favour. The full squad was Atherton, Stewart, Benjamin, Crawley, DeFreitas, Gatting, Gooch, Gough, Hick, McCague, Malcolm, Rhodes, Thorpe, Tufnell, Udal and White.

I can remember a huge release of emotion when my name was read out, although I don't know how I would have behaved had I been left out, and I rang home to share my glory. I struggled to contain my tears and it took a long, long time before I was able to say to myself: "I'm going to Australia to play for England." My hands, shaky at one stage, were now being shaken in some numbers by delighted teammates and well-wishers. As I found out when others from Hampshire were chosen to play at international level, it somehow reflected well on you as a team and as a club. But, as the news sank in and I had the chance to digest the details of the tour party, I came to realise my old friend Robin Smith had been omitted, not in itself a surprise I suppose since he had been left out for the South Africa Test series. Ray Illingworth may have liked me but he did not like Robin and was the man suspected to be responsible, a year or so later, for ending Robin's England career prematurely. Illy was known to have this puritanical streak and was unimpressed by the way he perceived Judge had enjoyed himself too much when on tour.

As I pointed out earlier, when comparing his record to that of Hick, Robin had a Test average of 43 and barely six months earlier had stood up to the ferocious West Indian fast bowlers (Ambrose, Walsh and Kenny and Winston Benjamin) with immense bravery and skill when they peppered his body with one bouncer after another. His 175 in the heat of battle in Antigua will be remembered by those who saw it as one of the great contemporary Test innings. Now England had dropped him without so much as a thank-you. I felt as sorry for Judge as I did happy for myself, and while I do not dispute the claims of those chosen above him, I could not come to terms with Robin Smith being shunned at the age of 30. It was a bitter blow for him and he showed great dignity in keeping his hurt private when those of us close to him realised how badly affected he was. Rumours of the way he unwound in the Caribbean had obviously got back to Illy. Robin liked to party and enjoyed a few drinks and jokes. His tourist groups demanded some of his time, so that there were those connected to England who felt his priorities were wrong. But his main focus was always England and when it mattered he stood up to be counted, as he had done in Antigua so recently. Robin once missed the team bus during the West Indian tour, and he and Matthew Maynard were seen to become regular drinking companions. There was a drink-fuelled incident when Robin and Maynard put tomato sauce on a pillowcase, feigning serious injury next door to the room belonging to a decidedly unamused Michael Atherton. Athers did not think it behaviour appropriate to Test cricketers and the story is sure to have travelled home with him, or so Robin was later convinced. In all the years I knew him at Hampshire, and in the little international cricket we shared, no one practiced more than Robin; no one was more professional.

Perhaps there was some resentment about his South African background, but on the basis of foreign birth or upbringing, at least five of the Ashes party should have been excluded. All I know is that Robin cared deeply about playing for England, he made his home here and should have played in many more Tests than he did so that he could have taken his rightful place among the all-time greats. There was, of course, a recall for the home series with the West Indies and tour of South Africa in 1995/96, but it proved to be only a temporary reprieve and his international career was over at 32, long before it should have been. Illy was at the heart of that and I am sure he had his reasons. For a year or two after 1996 and the South African tour, Robin nurtured the belief that having made one comeback, he could make another, but it gradually became clear that his international days were over. England's loss was definitely Hampshire's gain. As far as I am concerned, he is comfortably Hampshire's greatest player and my son Jack has a fantastic godfather to look after him.

His absence from the Australian tour meant further chances for Gatting and Gooch, both of whom were older than Robin but, in fairness, had never let England down in the past. Gatting had even won the Ashes as captain in 1986/87, but the Australians were a side much improved from those days, as they had proved on English soil with such ruthless efficiency in 1989 and 1993. Without Robin's reassuring presence I wondered how I would cope on a long tour with elder statesmen like Gooch, Stewart and Gatting for company and I cannot pretend it was easy. As to the spinning department, Tufnell's left arm made him our number one, Craig White could bowl off spin if required, as could Hick, but on the face of it I was our only specialist off spinner. With Sydney renowned as a spin bowler's paradise, I thought this would be the venue for my Test debut. What a place to start. Next to Lord's, Sydney is about as good as it got. Tufnell may have been in pole position, but there was every reason to suppose that I would play in at least one of the Tests, maybe more. How wrong I was.

Chapter 10

Ashes To Dust

THE TOUR OF Australia in 1994-95 should have been the start of a long international career. Instead it was almost the end. Apart from a truncated A tour to Pakistan a year later, this was my lot for a decade, a decade in which the only time I went abroad was on holiday. Going to Australia that Autumn was a strange experience since it was nothing like I had expected in cricketing terms and, of course, it did not quite work out in the way I had hoped. Everyone seems to like Australia and my winter in Newcastle, New South Wales, had been a great introduction to the place, the hospitable people and to the way they played their cricket. I looked forward to it immensely, especially as Emma and our baby would be coming out later. But, in retrospect, the whole expedition was doomed from the start.

Mike Smith, an international in both cricket and rugby in his playing heyday, was the curious choice as manager. An eccentric man at the best of times, he was a poor organiser and his job was to organise. Our luggage, including all our cricket gear, disappeared somewhere between Brisbane and Sydney and all the bits and pieces which make a tour go smoothly, hardly ever did. There was a time in Sydney after Emma arrived that I asked him, if at all possible, if we could swap our tiny room for his palatial single because we had to accommodate Katherine's cot, but he refused. All was not well among our management, by no means all of it Smith's fault.

In addition to the manager's frequent absent-mindedness, Illingworth, as chairman of selectors, did not enjoy a smooth working relationship with Keith Fletcher, the team manager. Illingworth's greatest cause for concern seemed to be the teams chosen by Fletcher and Mike Atherton, which was a fairly basic sort of rift, while Atherton led us out to Australia still miffed by the squad chosen for him by the selectors. For all I know, I might have been one of those he did not want and no one is going to perform if they do not enjoy their leader's confidence. I do know that Atherton wanted the reliable Fraser from the start, but the Middlesex pace bowler, who might have expected plenty of bounce from Australian wickets, was passed over in favour of Joey Benjamin and Martin McCague, the raw-boned Kent bowler who had been born in Northern Ireland but raised in a remote part of Western Australia. Benjamin had been a success at Surrey but his selection for the Ashes tour was seen as something akin to a Ryder Cup wild card. He was either going to be a major discovery or a major disaster. McCague was a worrying proposition for batsmen when he was running down hill at Canterbury, but the facts show he got as many wickets away from Kent as he did at home. I must admit I thought Dominic Cork would have been with us, as many had tipped, but he was left out, and the disgruntlement was evident even before we left British shores. McCague did at least play in one Test, in the opening match in the series when Oval hero Devon Malcolm had chicken pox, and his two wickets cost 96 in total.

All of this was before an extraordinary catalogue of injuries destroyed our already frail self-confidence on the way to a 3-1 defeat, the match in Sydney being drawn. As the tour lurched on, Mark Ramprakash, Mark Ilott, Jack Russell and Fraser were sent out as replacements for the injured while Chris Lewis was recruited from Australian club cricket. Gough, Hick, Stewart and Malcolm missed a combined total of eight Tests at a time when we needed them most. It was a mess and the only man to emerge with any credit was Darren Gough, who took 20 wickets at 21 and looked to be a star for the future. Neil Fairbrother came out principally for the one-dayers but also got injured, and other key players like Stewart and Hick left the tour, all but passing their replacements at the airport so that it was hard to remember at times the composition of the original tour party. We were the victims of a poorly conceived schedule, a confused selection policy and a management which never presented a united front on anything.

The tour caught up with Gatting and Gooch, although, to his great credit, Gatting got 117 at Adelaide. But in five Tests, Gatting averaged only 20 and Gooch's 24 was not much better, especially as he managed only one minor half century. They were found out in the field, where the unrelenting sunshine drained players half their age, and at the crease, where Warne weaved his way through the England batting with astonishing ease. His 27 series wickets cost only 20 each, while Craig McDermott, in his pacy prime until injuries intruded, was even more successful with 32 wickets at 21. Gatting and Gooch, as our elder statesmen and possibly a little uncomfortable when their age and lack of athleticism was exposed time and again, spent a lot of time together off the pitch and the squad quickly broke up into cliques of the very sort England managements now go out of their way to discourage. Disharmony was created almost constantly, not least when on one occasion we all boarded the team bus only to watch the eminent Gooch driving off to the same destination in a hired car. There was never any sense of being together.

Sometimes constant adversity can help build team spirit, here it did nothing but undermine it. It was not the sort of atmosphere for a young player to blend and survive. At 25 and with a handful of one-day international behind me, I felt like an outsider as the unhappiness at the top percolated down to the juniors like myself. I would be less than fair if I did not point out how hard Gooch and Gatting worked at their game, or record how much they trained, never once shirking the physical aspect of preparation. It was ironic that Gooch, Gatting and Tufnell were the only players not to miss a match through injury and even our physiotherapist, Dave Roberts broke a finger in fielding practice. But for me the worse part was that Gatting and Gooch did not mix much with the youngsters, or seek to put us at our ease, as they could have done, and I found it hard to be comfortable around them or feel an equal. I never knew, for instance, if they rated me as a player or even if they cared if I was on the tour or not. One word of encouragement from them would have made a world of difference. I suppose I could have asked them for advice but, unsure how I would have been received, I left them alone and I can't remember actually having a prolonged conversation with either of them in the whole duration of the tour. Instead I sought solace in a group of the younger players, Gough, John Crawley, now a close friend at Hampshire but then at Lancashire, Craig White and Roberts the physio.

Gough proved to be the discovery of the tour with his wholehearted performances and his ability to trouble and remove the cream of the Aussie batting, Crawley played in three of the Tests with a top score of 72, while the Victorian-raised White, like me, did not play in a Test at all and returned home prematurely, injured. None of this helped Atherton mould a team or induce a shared sense of belief and responsibility, which might have seen us through. DeFreitas caused him problems, I recall, not being honest with his state of fitness. "I wanted youngsters," said an exasperated Atherton as he lamented the attitude of DeFreitas, who turned down the chance to play at Sydney. "I wish I was in his position," I said to our captain. There is no way I would have been found wanting in terms of fitness. I liked Athers. He could be fun, he had a great sense of humour and could enjoy himself, but he was weighed down by the burden of office and by trying to make the best of a squad he had not picked. There was a stubborn streak about Atherton, which he exhibited often enough when batting and here I think he needed it.

Ignored for all five Tests, as it turned out, my only first class appearances were in the tour matches against New South Wales before the first Test and Queensland between the first and the second. In those days the matches against the state sides were taken far more seriously than they appear to be now when they are not always rated as first class because of the new desire to play 12 players each side. Home players saw the state games as an opportunity to impress against the tourists and touring players saw them as a chance to nudge selectors in competitive conditions. Our match with New South Wales, coincidentally and happily, was played at Newcastle where I was reunited with the Shaw family with whom I had spent such a memorable winter. No earthquakes this time and in spite of a quantity of beer consumed when they laid on an evening party for me at the pub in which we had spent so much time, I was not sick.

New South Wales took the match in the proper manner with established Test stars Mark Waugh, Michael Slater and Mark Taylor all included. We lost, but I had my moments. I dropped Taylor off Tufnell and there were chants of 'useless' from the terracing where my ex-teammates from Hamilton-Wickham did not waste the opportunity to indulge in some sledging at my expense. Mark Waugh gave a return catch, but I suppose I did not produce enough in terms of wickets to warrant a closer examination from the selectors, nor did I impose myself on the strong Queensland batting. The match was played in what appeared to me to be a sort of Wild West town, Toowoomba, which calls itself Queensland's largest inland city. I had 'words' with Stuart Law during his innings but I got him out, little realising how much I would be playing against him in the years to come while he was with Essex and Lancashire.

I don't think my cause was helped either by the way it was clear the Australians liked to attack the off spinner. I wonder if Atherton and Illingworth came to the conclusion I could be 'milked' at Test level. Two matches against the state sides was as near as I got to playing for England for ten years, although I like to think I was not far away from selection at Brisbane and Sydney. The reason I nearly played at Brisbane had nothing to do with the state of the wicket or my form. It had everything to do with the mercurial Phil Tufnell.

The tour had begun poorly for me, breaking a finger while fielding at Lilac Hill in the traditional opening friendly so that I was in no position to claim a place, sitting out the four-day match with Western Australia and still nursing the injury when we played South Australia in Adelaide. It was a tortuous path, which took us from west to east for the first Test in Brisbane, thereby prompting criticism of the itinerary and allowing us no real chance to settle and develop. We always seemed to be on the move.

Tufnell was indisputably our number one spinner but his behaviour was at best erratic and I found myself in the unlikely role of his 'minder' as he struggled to cope with being away from his new wife. The 10,000-mile separation was obviously getting him down and painful calls home did nothing for his peace of mind. One week into the tour, when we were in Perth, Tufnell's distress finally got the better of him. Tuffers trashed his room and went AWOL. For two hours, England's great spinning hope was nowhere to be seen having vanished into the night air. Only later did we discover he had checked into the psychiatric unit of a local hospital for treatment and to sort his brain out. It's an ill wind, I suppose, but I have to admit that I could see the possibilities opening up for me. With him 'indisposed', I would have been England's main spin bowler unless, or until, they sent for a replacement for him. With the first Test a couple of weeks away, I fancied my chances. But just when my hopes were raised, they were dashed again when the unpredictable Tufnell walked through the door of our hotel, apparently none the worse for his experience, nonchalantly smoking a cigarette, as he often did, and rejoining us as if he had just come back from a stroll in the park.

My Turn To Spin

The management's solution to the Tufnell problem was to make me his baby-sitter. I am not sure exactly why, but while we were in Adelaide my task was to keep watch on him, never knowing if one phone call too many from home might set him off again. Venturing out one night in Adelaide to a casino, I left Tufnell behind in the room we shared, wondering if I had made the right decision to abandon him. Left on his own, there was no knowing what might greet me on my return. Creeping back into the darkened room at 2am, I did my best not to disturb him, hoping he might be sleeping peacefully, but I could see the glow of his cigarette as he lay on his bed. "That you, Shaggy?" he said. Then, out it poured, there had been more calls to and from home, more anxiety, more worry. Should he go back to England? Should he stay? As the prospect of taking his Test place at Brisbane loomed, I was in no unbiased position to comment. I must say this about Tufnell. When he is in a good mood I love his company because he is still one of the funniest guys I have ever met and great fun to be around.

When eventually we reached Brisbane at the end of November for the start of the series, Tuffers had regained some of his equilibrium and the more together he became, the poorer were my chances of making a Test debut. In fact, when Mark Taylor won the toss at the Gabba and chose to bat first, my tour had so far consisted of one warm-up friendly ruined by a broken finger, the four-day match with New South Wales and a permanent concern for the man I had hoped to usurp.

The Brisbane Test, being the first, tends to make or break an England tour. It broke England spectacularly in 2006/7, and it did so when I was there. Tufnell assured everyone he was fit, physically and mentally, and took his place in the team but failed to take a wicket in the first innings as Michael Slater and Mark Waugh each scored centuries in a total of 426. This figure quickly looked huge as local boy McDermott ran through us on his way to figures of six for 53. Tufnell failed to score and we were all out for an uncompetitive 167. At least he got four wickets in the second innings as Australia accelerated towards a declaration, but then Warne simply overwhelmed us, as he was still doing 12 years later. Warne took eight for 71 as Australia won by 184 runs to set the tone for the rest of the series.

It was at Brisbane that I first came across Shane while I was wheeling out the drinks when doing 12th man duties. Even though he was playing, Warne was doing the same job for the Aussies on this particular occasion. "G'day, Shaun," he said, and I must I admit I was surprised, even by this straightforward Aussie greeting, since I had no idea he knew my name. I knew his, of course, the whole of the cricketing world was aware of Shane Warne, but I was flattered he knew mine, a humble uncapped rookie from Hampshire. Later, after he had joined us at Hampshire, I came to realise this was typical of Warne. Part of his professionalism is to know about all players, good, bad and indifferent. By the time he became Hampshire captain, he had amassed an incredible store of knowledge about county and international opponents, their strengths and weaknesses, so that he could exploit them. Malcolm Marshall had much the same reputation for doing his homework, and one of the reasons why he and Shane became top performers is that they left nothing to chance, observing and probing even the most inept of county number elevens as minutely as they would an established international number one.

There was a month between the first and second Tests and the shame was that I could not use the state match in Toowoomba to push my claims. It was clear by now that the tour was beginning to disintegrate slowly, much to the fury of those enveloped in a dark winter at home. The Sun newspaper, always provocative, found out the fax number at Keith Fletcher's hotel while we were in Toowoomba and incited their readers to deluge him with hate mail. He awoke one day to discover heaps of paper outside his door and stuffed underneath it. By the time we got to Melbourne just before Christmas I had reached the conclusion I was not going to play there and, indeed, Tufnell was the only spinner picked. In a comparatively low-scoring match, Warne and McDermott bowled us out for 92 in the second innings to set up a morale-crushing victory for the Aussies by 295 runs. Two down and three to play, the Aussies only needed a draw in Sydney to retain the Ashes. They were as buoyant as we were downcast and I think there was an inevitability about the outcome of the series as we tried to enjoy the New Year celebrations.

I had dreamed of Sydney all the way backwards and forwards across the continent because I really felt it was my destiny to play there. The Australians had always picked two spinners and traditionally so had their opponents, therefore my optimism was well-founded and based on history. The day before the Test, New Year's Eve, I went down to Randwick, through the gates into the famous old stadium and made my way out to the middle. There I had expected to see a typically dry, bare, turning wicket, so I was shocked, horrified even, to see the sort of green, grassy and wet pitch I would normally have associated with England in mid-April. I stared at it in disbelief, completely helpless: There was no way England would play two spinners on this, and sure enough, they did not. Keith Fletcher and Atherton took one look and came to the same rapid conclusion, packing our eleven with pace and deciding the nearest I should get to the action was as 12th man. What made it worse was that I could not argue. If I had been in their position I would probably have done the same, but what made it galling for me, having had my chance snatched away by unseasonal rain, was the composition of the Australian team when it became available on the morning of the match. Rather than copy us and pick an extra pace bowler, the Australians had followed their instincts, which suggested eventual turn, and retained the off spinner Tim May to complement Warne, while there was also Michael Bevan and Mark Waugh to bowl their spin if needed.

As it happened, England got it right. Pace dominated. Warne took one wicket in the match, May, Waugh and Bevan none at all. Tufnell did not bowl in the Australian first innings and did not get a wicket in the second so that on the face of it, I was well out of it. But it cannot be denied that Sydney should have been my Test debut and in any other year it would have been. For all the discussions behind the scenes while selecting a team, it made no difference because the match was England-dominated but drawn. Gough took six wickets in the first innings, Fraser five in the second, and this was the match when Atherton declared on Hick. The Aussies, chasing an improbable 449, were 104 behind and seven wickets down when we ran out of time after centuries by Slater and Taylor had held us up at the start. So that was it, the Ashes gone again, rendering the last two Tests in Adelaide and Perth pointless.

Before Adelaide, I did at least get some action in the one-day Benson and Hedges World Series, but even then there was some disappointment because the tournament involved Australia A, an admittedly strong second team (they would say the second best in the world) and their matches were later ruled as not qualifying for international status. Zimbabwe and the Australian first team were our other opponents and I played in all six of our matches, five of them thrillingly in front of huge day-night crowds. To play, as I did, in front of 73,282 against

Australia at Melbourne was an incredible experience, the largest crowd of my life at the time. Gough got 45 but then got injured, Fairbrother damaged his shoulder, Hick and Gooch each bowled ten overs and we won. One-day matches tend to attract all sorts, some to watch the cricket, some not to watch it much and others who see it as an opportunity to get drunk. Play in one of our matches against Australia A, also at Melbourne, was stopped when the Aussies were batting because a few drunks started to pelt the England fielders with golf balls, beer cans, and, nearest to me, a water bottle. I was fielding on the boundary in front of the notorious Bay 13 and the perpetrators of these missiles were crafty, not making themselves obvious by standing up and hurling these things but waiting until the Mexican Wave came their way and, as others threw their arms in the air, used the 'cover' to hurl their weapons our way. It was a very scary feeling, knowing there were people behind me intent on doing me some serious damage.

It was while we were playing Zimbabwe that I did the injury which brought a sorry end to my tour. I remember how hot it was and how Andy Flower was trying to hit me out of the ground, even when there was some turn in the pitch. I thought I had pulled a muscle in my ribs and although I attempted to play through the one-day series, I was suffering increasing discomfort the more I bowled. Emma had gone home by now and not wanting to waste my England opportunities, I was reluctant to talk about the injury in case I was dropped. Not that I was able to make much of a difference and we failed, dispiritingly, to qualify for the finals. We had to beat Australia A to reach those finals and I was in at the end when we failed by five runs in an agonising slow death.

Eventually I spoke to Dave Roberts about the intercostal problem and I was sent for a scan, knowing that bad news would spell the end of my Australian summer. And bad news it was. The scan showed I had pulled a muscle, as I had feared, and the diagnosis was six weeks rest and recuperation and no cricket. My tour was over and there was nothing for it but to say my farewells and get on the next plane home with two Tests still to be played. As the rest of the squad headed for Adelaide, I jetted north to Basingstoke, arriving in cold, wet late January and while I was pleased to be with Emma and Katherine again, there was no denying the terrible sense of anti climax.

The irony was that England won in Adelaide, Gatting getting his last England century and Lewis and Malcolm blowing away the second innings resistance. How I wished I could have been there, celebrating in a minor sort of way, after failing to win back the Ashes and not even reaching the Benson and Hedges finals. It would have been a small compensation and, with so many players coming and going, there would have been a measure of relief for the beleaguered management. Hearing about it on the radio at home and watching snippets on television made it no easier to bear because I felt I should have been out there. I found it hard to sleep, hard to re-adjust and hard to slip back into a winter routine. I was down in the dumps in a big way and going out with my mates for a few drinks did nothing to ease the pain of being somewhere I did not want to be. Emma pulled me through, tolerating my unhappiness and letting me gradually come to terms with a slight feeling of failure, of not being able to last the course.

In many ways, England winning in Adelaide made it worse, not that I would have played and Tufnell, our only spinner, took only a solitary wicket while obeying orders to bowl defensively. There was at least some compensation in the shape of some media work with Sky TV, which I still enjoy now, and some radio, but I could not disguise my disappointment at not being in sunny South Australia. I don't think I would have played in the fifth Test at Perth either. The wicket there is one of the quickest in the world and there was never going to be much scope for an off spinner. Even Warne, as the only spinner on either side, took only two wickets and the match was won for Australia by McDermott and McGrath, with only Ramprakash, Rhodes and Lewis reaching double figures in a pathetic attempt to score 453 to win. We were all out for 123 and Australia, who were always the stronger, rightly claimed the series.

By now I was back at the printers, trying to immerse myself in a business about as far removed from cricket as it was possible to be. What haunted me was the feeling that I had not been able to do myself proper justice, which I now come to recognise was a strong motivational factor ten years later when I was chosen for Pakistan and India. I had gone to Australia as the junior member of the squad, with Gough, but while Gough had seized his chance with both hands, I had not. Conditions and circumstances were against me and, in mitigation, I was only ever likely to play at Sydney. Tufnell's mental problems almost let me in at Adelaide, but I was not sure overall if I had made enough of an impression on the people that mattered. Because of the broken hand suffered at Lilac Hill, I missed the two early state games and when I played against New South Wales and Queensland I would have played only the two first class matches in four months. There is no doubt I did suffer from a lack of cricket and the constant changes made to the squad were unsettling to those, like me, who had been selected from the start while there was no kind of continuity or cohesion.

The obvious antagonism between Illingworth and Keith Fletcher did not help either, and in such circumstances we were never going to beat Australia over five Tests because we were just not properly prepared. Being my first major tour - and tours are never bigger than when Australia are involved - I was surprised how poorly organised we were, emanating from Mike Smith's woolly-minded leadership, and how little team spirit seemed to matter. I had hoped over the intervening ten years that this would change, and I am pleased to say it had by the time I went to Pakistan in 2005. For England after the crushing defeats at home by the Australians in 1989 and 1993, this was a calamitous attempt to win back the Ashes. How they could have done with the stout-hearted Robin Smith, in his batting prime, for a start.

As the winter turned to Spring and the prospect of a new county season quickened the pulse a little, I was left to reflect on my Australian experience. I had played my part in the internationals but five wickets at an average of 69 in the two first class matches said everything I suppose. What I had to do now, having come to terms with returning home injured early, was to make a good start to the domestic season with Hampshire and force my way into the England side for the six-match series with the West Indies. There was everything to play for. I may have missed my opportunity in Australia, but at 26 I felt there would be many more and I looked forward eagerly to the summer of 1995. If only I had known.

Chapter 11

Down The Queue

MIKE WATKINSON was a capable cricketer, not outstanding, not a world-beater, but his elevation to the England side in 1995 when I should have been playing instead was the biggest blow I had ever suffered to my career. Watkinson was part of a good Lancashire side as a lower order batsman and a medium paced bowler before suddenly switching to spin. No one, I think it fair to say, had ever seen him as a potential Test player, and while he was effective in one-day matches, I had not pencilled him in as a potential rival. Watkinson was 33 and very much the sort of player who fitted the label 'good county player', and I don't mean that disparagingly because the same things were said about me further down the line. Watkinson came in from nowhere to play in the last three of a six-match Test series against the West Indies at a time when I was again enjoying a good season at Hampshire.

In many ways his selection was symptomatic of the way England sides were bedevilled by bias during the 90s when it came to picking international sides. No wonder we struggled to regain the ground lost to the Australians when patronising selectors were picking their pals on the flimsy evidence of trusting and knowing them at county level. This may sound like the fury of a spinner scorned, but look at the evidence. When Gooch of Essex was in charge, the likes of Neil Foster, Peter Such and Nasser Hussain got chances, although Foster, it has to be said, was already established; when Lancashire's Mike Atherton had a major influence on selection, Watkinson, Peter Martin, Ian Austin and Jason Gallian were given opportunities, some of them late in life, and when Ray Illingworth was chairman, Yorkshiremen Craig White, Steve Rhodes, Darren Gough and Richard Illingworth were all chosen by England. I am certainly not saying all of those players did not deserve their chances. Hussain and Gough, for instance, went on to have exceptional international careers and would have come through the system no matter who pulled the strings. But some of the others were probably not true England class and their flirtation with the big time was brief. I could never imagine the Australians doing the same thing and the constant switching of players, based on who they knew, did nothing for our cricketing image abroad, or of course for results.

I had a cracking 1995 as it turned out, plenty of runs and wickets for Hampshire, and being selected for the one-day internationals against the West Indies. Here I suspect I did not do enough to convince Ray Illingworth and the other England selectors that I had it about me to make the next step up to the Test side. I played in all three internationals at Trent Bridge, the Oval and Lord's and while I was economical enough (27 overs for 129 runs in total), except at Lord's where I went for 52, I did not take a wicket and I think this must have counted against me when the Test series followed. The West Indies were declining from their eminence of the 80s but they still had the remnants of a great side with Lara, Hooper, Richardson, Adams, Ambrose, Bishop and Walsh all formidable players, some of them still in their prime. We won the one-day series 2-1 and, while there was a nagging doubt about my lack of wickets, I still felt I would be in the mix for the Tests.

I could hardly have done more for Hampshire, that's for sure, to remind the selectors that I was worthy of consideration. In first class matches alone, I did the all-rounder's double (500 runs and 50 wickets) with 512 runs and 55 wickets for the fourth time, including 85 against Yorkshire at Southampton among three half centuries and five hauls of five wickets or more in an innings. Match figures of eleven for 170 were achieved on a Test ground at Trent Bridge, if it helped, but it appeared it did not because all the time, all the way through the summer they were picking other spin bowlers. I thought I might play in the Tests against the West Indies for a sound tactical reason in that they packed their side with left handed batsmen, making them potentially vulnerable to the off spinner. But for the first of them at Headingley, even allowing for its reputation for green tops, I still thought this was going to be my moment until, from almost nowhere, England called up the Bradford-born slow left armer Richard Illingworth from Worcestershire four years after his first cap. Even allowing for his successful start to the domestic season, I could not credit why the selectors had done this because his county record was nothing like as proficient as mine overall, and to some extent I was vindicated when he took only the one wicket in a heavy defeat, although in fairness conditions would hardly have suited him.

There were, however, suggestions that I was still not out of the equation when I was close to being in the squad for Lord's - once again a Lord's Test was tantalisingly close - only to end up rejected as Richard Illingworth went through without a wicket, overshadowed, as everyone was, by a sensational debut from Dominic Cork, who took seven for 43, the best ever by an England bowler on his debut, in a 72-run win. Bishop and Walsh knocked the stuffing out of England in the third Test at Edgbaston (Illingworth took one wicket) as the West Indies won by the huge margin of an innings and 64 runs. Changes had to be made for the fourth Test at Old Trafford and I confidently expected, as the spinner apparently next in line, that I would take over from him so I was certainly not ready for the day when Watkinson emerged from comparative anonymity to snatch a spin berth from under my nose. It was even more demoralising that John Emburey at 42 was called up for his 64th Test.

I have nothing against Mike, Embers or indeed Richard Illingworth as people but I felt I had a far better case for inclusion than any of them. Richard Illingworth had had his chance and not taken it, but, as I said, there is no way I could have foreseen Watkinson as a possible candidate, in sight of his 34th birthday and 13 years since his Lancashire debut. A decade later I learned that age did not matter, but at the time I was devastated, utterly demoralised by the crushing news of his selection on the basis of an admittedly profitable county season but I suspect more because he was playing on his home ground. No wonder those of us in the county system who did not have Test grounds as their home felt aggrieved when players such as Watkinson were hoisted into the national limelight on the back of so frail an excuse. What made it worse was that Watkinson was so new to spinning after years of tight but not overly successful medium pace and had not done much of an apprenticeship. It was a real hammer blow and for a month I did nothing for Hampshire, my mind preoccupied by what I thought were the injustices of the selection process.

To make it even worse for me, Watkinson fully justified his 'inspired' and almost unprecedented choice, taking five wickets in the match as England levelled the series in a six-wicket win. Not surprisingly he retained his place for Trent Bridge, where he took another three wickets and got a plucky half century, and for the Oval where he went wicketless in another draw. The series ended 2-2 with some exciting cricket being played and by the time stumps were drawn at the Oval in late August I was in danger of becoming international history. Watkinson even finished top of the England batting averages thanks to an 82 not out, while Richard Illingworth, recalled for the fifth Test, took a further four wickets and patriotic shouts from Hampshire for me to be given my opportunity, not least from the recalled Robin Smith, had long been drowned out. I finished the season feeling distinctly sorry for myself and consoled only by the prospect of two winter tours, the main party going to South Africa and an A team heading for Pakistan. I had to be on one of them. This inclination to optimism was based on a conversation I had with one of the selectors, who understanding my frustration and disappointment at getting so close, had told me: "There are tours. Be prepared." But after so many setbacks, I was not counting any chickens.

As another season drifted into late summer, the waiting began, so too did the conjecture about the composition of the respective squads and since I was largely ignored by the papers, I could not have been overly taken aback when the touring party to South Africa contained Watkinson and Illingworth but not me. True enough, I had not expected to be chosen, although I felt my county record deserved recognition, but it still did not stop me from being disappointed. Deep down I could not figure out what it was the selectors had against me or did not like about me. It was being said, I think, that I only took wickets with my quicker ball, that I lacked variety. But in championship matches alone, ignoring one-day competitions, I had taken 256 wickets in the four years from and including 1992 so I must have bowled an awful lot of quicker ones. At least Robin Smith had retained the place he won back in the summer against the West Indies before being injured and I knew how much he was looking forward to returning to South Africa as a fully committed England player. Robin had been domiciled in England for at least ten years but I know he also felt was some trepidation about going back, fearing the sort of hostile reception Kevin Pietersen was to get later from South African crowds who saw him as a traitor. Pleased though I was for him, I reckoned I should have been on the plane with him, so it was something of a sop when I was given a place instead on the A tour.

It was as if the selectors were saying, "We have not forgotten you," and while representing England at any level is an achievement and a source of pride, I cannot say I was best pleased.

As it happened, neither Watkinson nor Illingworth got the chance to prosper in South Africa; Watkinson played in only one of the five Tests and Illingworth in three, although he did take nine quite cheap wickets. Four of the matches were drawn and the last in Cape Town resulted in a ten-wicket win for the South Africans. It was Robin's last match for England, not that we knew it at the time. He got 66 of England's 153 in the first innings and came home with a batting average from the series of 36.28, but it was not enough to save his international career. It was as if the England selectors had something against the pair of us. Did our Happy Hampshire reputation get in the way?

I first came across Nasser Hussain when I played that one summer for Surrey's youth side and it was clear that here was a talented and focused young batsman, determined to force his way right to the top. He was also a man in a hurry. Picked by England at 21, he was regarded, with good reason, as something of a prodigy, but had drifted out of contention for a couple of years and was thirsting for another opportunity. After a tremendous championship season with Essex in which he scored six centuries and averaged 52, Nasser has some justification in believing he was due for a recall, but, like me, was only partially appeased by being chosen for the A team, albeit in his case as captain. I have to admit having had a bit of a 'run-in' with Nasser. I got him lbw when he was playing for Essex and, as usual, he did not think he was out. I pointed to the dressing room and advised him to go there and that made him extremely angry. "Enjoy your moment Udal," he responded, adding a few expletives for good measure. Our 12th man and backroom staff heard him shouting, "Doesn't he know who I am?" when he got back to the dressing room as he carried on cursing and swearing about me.

I am not sure in any case Nasser wanted to be with us in Pakistan - and not just because of me. He wanted to be in South Africa and his displeasure was evident when we reported for a pre-tour get-together in Tewkesbury. Nasser appeared to be in a constant huff, watching television on his own, always the last in the bar and difficult company. The feeling was that the wickets in Pakistan would take turn so the squad of 15 contained myself, Ian Salisbury and Richard Stemp as regular spinners plus Craig White, who could bowl off spin if required. This was reflected in the choice of John Emburey as team manager, although the Rev Mike Vockins from Worcestershire was the figure-head tour leader.

Vockins was a good man and we all liked and respected him, for this was not going to be a winter 'jolly' for him. It was the first time a professional England cricket side had toured Pakistan since the infamous Mike Gatting finger-wagging incident with local umpire Shakoor Rana and there were bridges to mend. The full tour party was Nasser Hussain, Gallian, Giddins, Headley, Irani, Knight, McGrath, Ostler, Piper, Pooley, Salisbury, Mike Smith of Gloucestershire, Stemp, White and myself. Of that group, all by now tested and proven in county cricket, only three - Ostler, Piper and Pooley - did not go on and play in Test cricket to a greater or lesser extent, mostly lesser. Only Hussain, it has to be said, went on to enjoy a substantial Test career and the rest of us, bar Nick Knight, could barely muster a handful of games between us. Even so, it was going to be a great experience and if Hussain nursed a grievance about being overlooked for South Africa, it was still a good tour to have on the CV.

When I went back to Pakistan in 2005, it had developed rapidly from the country I first encountered a decade earlier when the poverty hit me like a smack in the face. The Pakistanis could not have been more welcoming or eager to please on either occasion. The ever-present fear of stomach upsets prompted all kinds of drastic culinary action. Jason Pooley of Middlesex took enough canned meat to have fed an army and then there was Nick Knight and his baked beans. One day, Nick handed a hotel waiter a can of Heinz finest and told him to put them on some toast for him. Five minutes later the waiter came back, his task apparently fulfilled. On Nick's plate were two bits of toast and, yes, the can of beans unopened on top of them. For all the precautions and best-laid plans, we all got stomach problems and I was hit hard in Multan. I never liked the spicy food anyway, but you can feel a long way from home when you spend days in a toilet. Considering we were playing in a 'dry' country, it was a bit odd that our main sponsors should be Tetley Bitter, not that we ever saw their products. To get any kind of alcoholic drink at the time, we had to sign a form saying we were dependent on it as registered alcoholics. There was a bar on the roof of one of our hotels and in Islamabad we were able to slake our thirsts at the British Embassy, but generally we had to get used to the fact that alcohol was off the menu.

The tour was a disappointment for me. In fact it was a nightmare for more than one reason, not least because I had to come home early again for the second successive winter. I got on well with Emburey, who had been England's number one off spinner of his generation, but it was noticeable that in the major games, Stemp and Salisbury were preferred and my opportunities were as limited as they had been in Australia a year earlier. I could see myself slipping down the pecking order behind my rivals. We were not just trying to beat our opponents, we were all trying to outshine each other and that inevitably caused a certain minor tension among us. Nasser was eyeing a call up to South Africa as a replacement and I think Knight was another who coveted a late opportunity, but when it came, it was Jason Gallian who was sent for, playing the fourth Test in Port Elizabeth. The summons for me, only half expected, to follow Gallian never came. Instead there was further irritation when Neil Smith was called to South Africa for the internationals. My appearances in Pakistan were intermittent, scoring a half century against a Combined XI in Karachi and playing in the third unofficial Test in Peshawar, but I had a lot of time to reflect on the way my career was going and I had to be honest, it was not going forward.

My mind strayed home, as I suppose it was bound to do, because Emma was having our second child and on November 11, Rebecca was born with me about 4,000 miles from her hospital bed. There was a mixture of emotions, euphoria at having a second daughter and disappointment, perhaps a little guilt, at not being there, as I had been when Katherine was born. But duty called and as the tour began to peter out, Emburey and Hussain told me I would be playing in the last three one-day internationals, the final fixtures condensed into five days, so that at last I had something to prepare for. I had played so little of consequence for two weeks that I was almost rusty, but the internationals were big games and now there was the incentive to produce a good set of figures and issue a belated challenge to Stemp and Salisbury. On the day before the second of those matches, Emburey and Hussain took me aside and said there had been a change of plan. I would not now be playing. It was a blow, but not half as bad as another I received at 6pm the same day. I had a call from home. Emma was upset and in tears because our new baby had been taken into hospital with breathing difficulties. Rebecca was six weeks old and struggling in an incubator. I was in turmoil, desperate to go home and not knowing how or when I could. I was indebted then to Mike Vockins who made it all so much easier, sensing that I badly needed help. Vockins smoothed a potentially tricky path and in 24 hours I was home, staring at our stricken Rebecca for the first time, fighting for her very existence in the incubator. As Rebecca gradually won her battle with what proved to be a bad attack of bronchialitis, a breathing condition which affects children under the age of one. I had all but forgotten about Pakistan. I may have missed the last five days of the tour, but in the circumstances it did not matter. It was only a game of cricket after all and the fact that I was also left out of the World Cup squad made not a blind bit of difference.

While I had been away there had been changes at Hampshire. Mark Nicholas had retired at the end of the 1995 season and John Stephenson, who had been drafted in from Essex for Nicholas's last season as captain-in-waiting, duly took over. Why we had to look outside the county I do not know. Paul Terry had led us on occasions and while Gower had retired also, we still had Robin Smith, although at the time, we had no reason to believe he did not have an England future. I thought Terry should have been captain because of his great knowledge of the game and because he had the respect of the dressing room. Stephenson was a committed cricketer, a fierce competitor and determined to be a winner. Unfortunately for him, the Hampshire side he inherited was breaking up rapidly. Gower and Marshall had gone, Nicholas had now followed them, Terry was approaching the veteran stage and many of our younger players had not come through. Jason Laney, Paul Whitaker, Sean Morris, Richard Dibden, Matthew Keech, Darren Flint, Martin Thursfield and James Bovill did not fill the gaps as we had hoped they would and were destined to fall by the wayside. We were no longer competing for the major prizes and in retrospect the side was going nowhere but down.

From my perspective, I had not realised just how much I relied on Nicholas for support, real and moral, until he had gone, because I was never able to build up the same rapport with Stephenson. At Essex he had been passed over in favour of Paul Prichard and he came to Hampshire on the specific understanding that he would replace Nicholas after his year's 'apprenticeship'. The Essex players told us he could be a selfish cricketer, although that might just as easily be interpreted as a longing to be constantly involved, and 'Stan', as he was known universally, certainly led from the front, bowling more than he had ever done in his career bearing in mind that his solitary England cap came as an opening batsman in 1989. While Nicholas understood and got the best out of me, I never came to terms with Stan's captaincy or what he required of me so that for the first time I started to doubt myself.

I look back now on 1996 as the start not just of Hampshire's period of decline but my own. It was not until Shane Warne arrived that I began to believe in myself in the way I had done in my own apprenticeship under Nicholas. Spinners need nurturing, as I cannot emphasise enough, and I never felt I enjoyed Stephenson's confidence. It did not help that he kept holding up Peter Such as an example of what I should be doing, and while I have never been a massive turner of the ball, I like to think I was every bit as good as he was. Stephenson was a hard man to read and being an introverted sort of guy, he was not always good at getting across his message or what he wanted me to do. But a look at my figures will show how far I fell away. In the next three years I took only 84 wickets, of which a mere 16 were gleaned in 1998. England? Forget it. Looking for excuses, the change in captaincy and the loss of my mentor were undeniably big reasons for the drastic reduction in my success rate. I still got runs, 447 in 1996, but I was not getting anyone out. Only once did I get five wickets in an innings that year and my 34 wickets cost 46.52 each, not the sort of figures which were going to detain the thoughts of those in power for long, and rightly so. In fact, by September of that year, I was no longer even commanding the attention of the Hampshire selectors. Stephenson and Jimmy Gray took me aside after a particularly poor sequence and told me they were leaving me out and that I needed to work to get my place back. My pride badly hurt again, I did not like it one little bit.

Another significant reason for the way I fell from England candidate to Hampshire outcast in the space of a few months was that I started to enjoy myself too much. I hit the booze, not in a big way, but because I was feeling sorry for myself. Once or twice Robin Smith joined me but he could at least busy himself with his benefit year. Robin had been jettisoned after the South Africa tour, even after he had stood up so courageously against Allan Donald at his fastest and most furious, and it mystified him why. While this was admittedly not the sort of thing well-paid athletes should have been doing, least of all those with international aspirations, but we both felt badly let down. Becky was getting better so I could not blame any malign home influence, but I think, at the back of my mind or deep in my sub-conscious I realised that I had not done enough in Pakistan or Australia to demand retention and that the England selectors must therefore be looking elsewhere for their spin bowlers.

It was a salutary experience. If they studied the county scorecards, as they surely must have done, they would have seen that I was hardly stating a case for another chance. Robin was still banging on the England door by averaging 48 in county matches, but I drifted from one county venue to another, failing on the field where I had once succeeded and heading for the bar as soon as was feasible. Adie Aymes was a regular companion, but Adie never let his level of performance drop or his concentration waver. David Lloyd, now in a position of power with England, clearly did not rate Robin or I and, as the summer wore on, we became resigned to our fate. I probably could only call myself to account since I had flirted with the England set-up and not succeeded, but Robin was wounded by his omission more badly than he let on, even to me when we were alone. Judge had cause to feel snubbed because he had done all that had been asked of him and more, and had been just about England's best batsman for eight years. I, for one, cannot believe he did not have at least another four in him as an England player, but it was not to be. I also carried on drinking and winding down among my friends in Basingstoke and if it had not been for the sobering influence of Emma and my children, I am not sure how I would have fought back. Every player has a crisis, a blip when nothing goes right and I was not prepared for mine.

At the time of my downfall I was still only 27 and in spinning terms a few years from my prime. I had had nothing but success from the moment I broke into the Hampshire side as a novice, with a couple of cup finals, a couple of England tours, one-day internationals, big crowds and enough accolades to make me think it was forever. The measure of a player and his personality is how he copes when things start to go wrong and in 1996, when I could not take wickets in sufficient quantities, I did not know how to respond. Where once I had been almost cockily positive about myself, and my ability, I now wondered where I had blundered and why. I suppose it might have helped had there been strength around me, but Hampshire were going through a rough period and there was no one, other than Robin, to whom I could turn for support and advice. I was left to find my own way out of the hole I suddenly found myself stuck in.

After being dropped by Hampshire for two matches in September, I even feared I might not get another contract, but, luckily, Hampshire were not so well off for players that they could consider such an action and my record until 1996 had been impressive enough. It was a relief, nonetheless, when Stephenson told me at the end of the season, "We know you have had your troubles," and said my agreement was being extended until the end of the 1998 season. That winter I returned to my printing business and I was not even sure where England were touring since it would have been astonishing had I been involved. All I had positively to look back on was my 300th first class wicket, a landmark of sorts, but there was precious little else to warm the heart.

In many ways the season got worse because I got into an altercation - I hesitate to call it a fight - while playing for Camberley in a Surrey league match with Epsom and I was banned. It was the first of two such bans, and in fact I am still suspended from playing in any match in the league. I liked to play for Camberley when I could because I had family and friends there and because I got top order batting and early bowling chances I did not always get in county cricket. I was in the pavilion bar after the match when I reacted to a comment about my dad being banned. Someone from Epsom had rung the papers and 'the grass' was probably playing against us. I pushed one of their players and, to my dismay, the umpires felt obliged to put it in their match report to the league's management. Camberley were subsequently told to do something about my conduct and they were almost apologetic when they instituted a temporary ban.

Of course, I regret it now, as I did another incident playing for Camberley a few years later, but it was a case of frustration boiling over. In a way it summed up my whole year, which had been little short of a disaster. There had been my failure to make an impression in Pakistan, Rebecca's serious illness, a poor county season, the many changes at Hampshire and finally being dropped by them. I had seen Camberley as a bolt hole, ironically, from the world outside and while the incident and ban did not affect my career as such, it was not something to brag about, although I have to say I think the umpires made more of it than they should have done. No excuses, I put Camberley in a wretched position having to suspend me, and it was another miserable episode in a bad year. I hoped 1997 would be a better year (it could not have been worse) but I am sorry to say any improvement was only marginal. Not until 2006 did I have a year to rival 1996 and in hindsight it all contrived to set me back a long, long way.

Chapter 12

Australian Lessons

MATTHEW HAYDEN was a real example of the difference between the Australian and the English attitude. Hayden, a tall and powerful opening batsman, had broken into the Australian international side and then lost his place. When he joined Hampshire as an overseas player in 1997 he had been snubbed and rejected by Australia in much the same way Robin Smith and myself, to a lesser extent, had been by England. But did he sulk? Did he brood on his bad luck? Did he blame others? Not in the slightest. Hayden came to England to gain experience, to improve his all round cricket but also, and perhaps above all, he came to prove a point to the Aussies. Ten years later, Hayden was firmly entrenched again in the Australian side, one of the most formidable batsmen of his generation and assured of his place among the great Australian cricketers of all time. When Shane Warne came to us for the first time in 2000, he brought with him the same urgency, the same desire to compete and the same instinctive pride in performance. Unless there is the occasional injection of overseas players, county cricket can become stale and complacent, but there is such a regular supply from abroad these days that we are constantly invigorated and learning.

Hayden had lost his place at the top of the Australian order to Matt Elliott but harboured no grudges and swept into Hampshire like a man determined to show the selectors they were wrong. To that end, I never saw a player work as hard as Hayden did, preparing himself for each match, inflicting on himself a gruelling regime of preparation. If he was not in the nets, hour after hour, he was in the gymnasium, putting his large body through a series of demanding exercises and stretches. And then there was the running, lap after lap of the County Ground until his feet must have been sore and his tree-trunk legs aching. Hayden was a man on a mission and it was hard for us not to be impressed by his sheer

146

professionalism and determination. I liked the way he went about the business of cricket and there were those among us who attempted to copy his example. If this was the way to succeed, then we must adopt it. The Aussies were, after all, the best team in the world in the 90s having taken over from the West Indies and have stretched their dominance well into the next century. All the while Hayden and Justin Langer were just about the most durable opening partnership in world cricket.

In fact, Hayden did not immediately make the most of all his hard training when he first started with us during a sequence of low scores, but by an immense will to make up for his disappointment in being passed over, he came back strongly and finished with the high number of runs expected of him, averaging 57.52 in championship matches, including an unbeaten 235 against Warwickshire. I know Hayden was impressed by the county championship and found it to be a challenging competition, but I know also that he had one eye on the Australian tour of England, which was happening simultaneously, and there was no one more disappointed than he when he failed badly in the tourist match, scoring only six and two in a heavy defeat by an innings and 133 runs. When he went home later to Queensland from a profitable English summer, Hayden was a stronger and better player for his Hampshire experience and I am happy to say the relationship had been mutually beneficial.

I, for one, owed him a big debt because it was in the same innings that he got his big double hundred that I got my first, and to the start of the 2007 season, only century. It was a high scoring match on a typically flat Northlands Road wicket and Hayden guided me over the finishing line. My dad thinks I should have batted more for myself over the years, been a little selfish at times, but my own belief is that impatience has cost me dearly. Twice I have been out in the 90s and many more times in sight of a century and pushed on only the once. Silly shots at bad times have been my undoing and there was never any point in trying to convince influential people I was an all-rounder all the while my best score was 94. Here against Warwickshire's tiring attack, Hayden took the trouble to come down the wicket and talk me through it. "Don't give it away now," he kept saying. "Concentrate." And I did, eventually sweeping Ashley Giles, of all people, to take me to the magical three-figure mark. I was 117 not out when we declared after putting on 205 with Hayden and I only wish it had been the first of many.

I have to say, though, the real reason I played a good authentic innings that day was as much to do with fearing the wrath of my father. He knew, as I knew, that there would never be a better chance to score a century and I dread to think what he would have said if I had given away my wicket. A a measure of Hayden's supreme mental and physical toughness, though, came in our second innings, chasing an artificial, declaration-fed 335 when he scored 119 in a draw. Could I have done that?

John Stephenson, to his credit, pushed me further up the order that year and I responded with 600 runs and four half centuries but my bowling went further backwards as 34 wickets at 53.23 gave some indication of just how far. While Stephenson cannot be blamed for my continual demise alone, my professional relationship with him deteriorated to the point of no return when he criticised me at Scarborough in front of a full dressing room for bowling the wrong line. All the wickets had been taken by seamers yet for some reason he singled me out, the sole spinner, for criticism. The place was hushed as he told me to improve and, if he was angry with me, I was even angrier with him. It did not make sense at the time and it still does not. All captains become frustrated at some time or another with their bowlers, but the best ones keep any fury to themselves and deliver a reprimand at the appropriate time, usually in private. To be attacked so publicly was humiliating enough, but he was obviously a man under pressure because our results had been, at best, moderate. He tried everything to make it work, dropping himself down the order and bowling at every available opportunity as if he trusted no one else, but his detractors would say he often bowled at the tail. Relaxing with a drink in his hands, Stan could be great company but the Hampshire leadership proved to be a heavy burden, although it must be said that he could count himself unlucky in that the successful team of the Nicholas era had been reduced to an ageing rump.

One incident in particular summed up the short-lived Stephenson captaincy. We were playing Glamorgan at Southampton in the NatWest Trophy and struggling to defend what should have been a match-winning 302-6 from 60 overs. The match had reached a crucial stage with Glamorgan six wickets down and getting uncomfortably close to their target. I was bowling and a throw to me at the stumps from Hayden had Adrian Shaw reaching desperately for his crease. I broke the wicket with my hand accidentally, not with the ball as I should have done, but the umpire, Ray Julian, gave him out. From his position, square to the wicket, Shaw had failed to make his ground and he cannot have seen my failure to collect Hayden's thrown cleanly. As the batsman made his way slowly back to the pavilion, convinced he had been unfairly dismissed, Steve James, the Glamorgan batsman at the other end, angrily remonstrated with me and accused me of cheating. Hayden and Robin both said Shaw was not out, I knew he was not out, but Stephenson told me in no uncertain terms to go along with Julian's decision. I was in a very difficult position. James was threatening all kinds of retribution but, in the end, my conscience got the better of me and I recalled the batsman as he was about to leave the field. Stephenson was furious, all the more so when Glamorgan won with two balls to spare and Shaw was a not out batsman. When we got back to the dressing room, Stephenson vented his anger, accusing me of letting the side down, making the umpire look silly and costing Hampshire the match. I felt I had done the right thing in the spirit of the game, but Stephenson was so apoplectic with rage he threatened to resign. The next morning, his temper restored by a good night's sleep, Stan was big enough to phone me to apologise and promptly rescinded his resignation.

I had my moments that year in one-day matches, recording my best batting figures of 78 in the Axa and Equity Sunday League against Surrey, 34 in the Benson and Hedges against Gloucestershire and 39 not out in that ill-fated NatWest Trophy match with Glamorgan. I also took a competition-best three for 13 against Cambridgeshire at Wisbech, but in the bread and butter business of the championship, I failed to take five wickets in an innings for the first time since 1991, in effect since I had become established.

At the end of a nothing year for us, Stephenson proffered his resignation again and this time there was no going back. Not even the prolific Hayden could change the course of our season or keep Stan in a job. There remained the task of replacing him as captain and both Robin Smith and I fancied our chances. Robin had the greater experience, of course, and he was available to us far more than any of us had expected because his England career had collapsed, but I was not sure how much he wanted to be the boss. Robin is such a nice guy and I know he found it hard telling players they had been dropped or left out and, as for a Stan Stephenson-style dressing room rant, there was no chance. I should say right away there was absolutely no disagreement from me when Hampshire decided his vast international experience could be put to good use and I thought it was an excellent decision. My 'consolation', if such it can be called, was to be made his deputy, which was the best news I had received for some time. After two poor years when my commitment was not as good as it could have been and my bowling productivity slumped, this was a massive pat on the back and a great incentive to start afresh, shedding the prolonged sense of injustice once and for all.

David Graveney's name had long since drifted from my consciousness so I was surprised to receive a call from him to say I had been selected for an England team for an international Cricket Max tournament in New Zealand during the winter of 1997/8. The game was the brainchild of the great Kiwi batsman Martin Crowe, but I am sorry to say it never took off in the same way that Twenty/20, for instance among recent innovations, did. The England team contained Graeme Welch, Dominic Ostler, Matthew Maynard and Mark Nicholas was captain. Each side had two innings of ten overs each and for every straight hit the number of runs scored was doubled. We got quite involved and enjoyed the experience but the competition was not destined to thrive and I think a good opportunity was lost. Since this was a full ECB tour and selected by Graveney, long forgotten England ambitions suddenly stirred within. On our return I made a conscious effort to get myself fitter and mentally ready for the new domestic season, something I had not done since the Pakistan tour. I realised I had let myself drift in more ways than one, so I joined a gym, got back into the nets and pounded the streets. Self-pity is a dangerous beast and I had fallen foul to its destructive charms, blaming others without proper justification and ultimately letting down my teammates at Hampshire. In many ways this winter was a turning point but Robert Croft was well entrenched with England now and I could not see beyond him. The responsibility of being vice captain gave my own game an extra dimension because I had to start thinking about the performances of others for the first time and not just myself.

This was probably just as well since I mustered only 16 wickets in 14 first class matches in the summer of 1998 at 34.31, in respect of a bowling average, better than the previous year but still nowhere near the standards I had expected from myself. We had recruited the West Indian quickie Nixon McLean, while the veteran Yorkshire pace bowler Peter Hartley came down for a south coast swansong - and very useful he proved. Their arrival meant that I bowled far less than in previous years (191 completed overs in first class matches compared with 627 the year before) and my main achievements that year lay in the one-day competitions, where my four for 20 against Dorset was a NatWest Trophy best and the five for 43 against my favourite opponents, Surrey, was a personal milestone in the Axa Equity and Law League. The season will be remembered for my first taste of captaincy when Robin Smith was injured. I relished this opportunity, absolutely prayed for it, and then almost missed it because I had a stomach upset and was far from well when I led the Hampshire side at Edgbaston in the middle of July. We were shot out for 80 in our second innings, losing by a substantial margin of 225 runs, and on that basis it was a result best forgotten, but Robin was still missing for our next game at Portsmouth and I think I felt it was time I made my mark.

Portsmouth's United Services Ground, now no longer on the county itinerary, could provide hard and quick wickets and I know I took a big chance when after calling correctly at the toss I decided I should make Nottinghamshire bat first. There is always an element of gambling when choosing to bowl first, and even after consulting as many senior players as possible, I was not certain I had done the right thing. But after winning by seven wickets I was happy to take all the praise for my tactical acumen. That apart, the season was not especially memorable, but off the field I was becoming more established, having quit Omega Printers and my directorship, just about getting my money out of the ailing business, and moving to the Karran Group. Tony Britten, the man behind the company and later a close friend, lived near me without knowing who I was or what I did for a living and offered me the chance to spend the winters as a salesman at his Guildford office. But it was another winter activity which got me into a lot of bother.

Officially I broke an ankle in January 1999 while out running. The story I told Hampshire was that I had fallen off a kerb, and to this day this is what they believe happened. The real story, which can now be revealed, is that I broke it playing football. Hampshire did not mind us indulging in contact sports like football up to Christmas but expected us to take a responsible attitude in the New Year by refraining from anything likely to cause a serious injury. Having given up the goalkeeping of my schooldays, I was now a striker and in terms of goals a successful one in the Basingstoke Sunday League for a team called Highdowns. I knew, of course, of Hampshire's unwritten rule but I was implored to play and I relented, thinking one extra game would not hurt. Hurt? I had never known pain like it when I collided with the opposition's goalkeeper as we competed for a loose ball. I knew straight away it was broken, but refused to believe it and even drove Tony Britten's Jaguar XK8 from Brighton Hill, where we were playing, back to my home using only my left foot, hopping from one pedal to another in excruciating misery. Emma put a bag of frozen peas on it in a bid to reduce the swelling but I was crying out and we both knew I had to go to hospital. There I was asked on a scale of one to ten how bad was the pain. Twelve was the answer through gritted teeth as doctors placed the fracture in plaster for six weeks only after inserting a metal plate and two screws. I will never forget Tony's kindness, driving me to work once I had recovered enough and paying me all the while even when I was laid up.

As vice captain, it was hardly the example to set among the younger players so I stuck with my story about the kerb and milked the sympathy when I was at last able to report for pre-season training at the County Ground. The metal plate was a companion for the entire season, which did not help, and at the end of March I was told I needed six weeks further rehabilitation before I could even consider playing again. Guilt probably played a part in this, but I pushed myself back quicker than I should have done. In mid-April I played against Oxford University when I was not physically able, and against Surrey I was run out when my injured leg let me down.

I have to say that playing football has got me into trouble more than the once. I would be less than honest if I did not record my disciplinary problems over the years with Highdowns, for whom I reckon I was scoring at the ratio of more than one a game. We were playing at Tadley in the north of Hampshire and I was through once more in a one-on-one with the goalkeeper. To his credit, the keeper made a good save and even he must have been surprised when the referee gave a goal kick. "Open your eyes," I said to the ref in exasperation and he promptly sent me off for swearing. I went to see the referee afterwards to apologise and to ask for an explanation but he would not change his mind and the red card stood against my name. The following week we were playing the league leaders and I scored to put us one up. The centre half marking me was doing a good job in trying to cripple me and he must have booted me 20 times without a foul once being given against him. The same defender scythed me down again and this time I lost my rag, kicking him in furious retaliation. The referee had not much option but to send me off. Full of indignation about my first sending-off, I appealed to the Hampshire Football Association on what I thought were good grounds. I had not sworn. But to my horror, a £20 fine and a 14-day ban were doubled. The Hampshire FA sent me packing with a stern lecture about my behaviour, but only after demanding £40 and telling me I was suspended for 28 days. The ban and doubled fine made big news in the Basingstoke Gazette where I paid the price for my minor local celebrity in column inches.

Our coach at Hampshire in those days was Malcolm Marshall and 1999 was the year of his slow decline and death from cancer in November aged 41. Even now I cannot talk easily about him without a lump appearing in my throat. Everybody liked him, even his opponents, because he was a man without malice and admired as much for his many personal qualities as for his supreme cricketing skills. Only Chris Broad irked him, for some reason, while I was a colleague at least, and he never wasted an opportunity to fire a barrage of bouncers at him when they met. Rehan Alikhan, then of Surrey, once tested the great man's legendary patience beyond endurance when he played and missed four times in an over, the last delivery striking him on the shoulder. Maco could take it no more. "Send him a bigger bat," he shouted, but it was a rare outburst from a humorous, even-tempered man, slow to anger and quick to praise.

I cannot comprehend, almost eight years on, how quickly he went downhill. He had been complaining of stomach pains for some time before he was diagnosed with the dreadful disease in May, not long after the season had got under way. For two months after an operation, he recuperated at home and when he was finally fit enough to call in at the County Ground, it was a terrible shock. We could scarcely recognise him, so thin, wasted and gaunt had he become so quickly. Through it all he was sustained by Connie, the woman who was to become his wife as the end neared, and by their son Mali. Robin Smith could sense, as I suppose we all did, that this was one battle Malcolm was not going to win. I remember Robin saying, "He's slipping away," and we all knew what he meant. A year or two later, after he had been laid to rest in his beloved Barbados in a little church near the airport, I went to see his grave. On the black marble plinth is a poem written lovingly by Mali in his father's final days. I had been to the wedding of Mali's parents, and now I was staring at his father's tombstone and I broke down and sobbed unashamedly.

He was a good man and sadly missed to this day. It was his bad luck to be coach of the West Indies as they fell from grace and of a Hampshire side similarly breaking up from a period of strength. There was not much he could do about either, but as a result he was not acknowledged for his coaching ability as readily as he was as a player. Some advice he gave me was typical: Be patient. Maco said that as a spinner my job was to be different, to be content with maidens and not necessarily to try to get batsmen out as a priority. This went against my competitive instinct, but I could see the sense. "Set them up for others," he said. What annoyed him more than anything else while he was coach were no-balls. Maco started a fines system so that even if we bowled no-balls in the nets, we would be one pound worse off. He hated bowlers over-stepping the line in practice, a frequent habit that many counties allow to develop, and came down hard on those that did at Hampshire. Pete Sampras was the big tennis player of the time and Maco used to say, "You don't see Sampras serving from in front of the baseline when he is practising. Why should cricketers be any different?" I am so pleased we won him the Benson and Hedges Cup in 1992 for him and it brings a tear to the eye again when I recall how much it meant to him.

As poor Malcolm fought for his life, the season was clouded by his battle for survival, but there were, thankfully, lighter moments such as our trip to Swansea to play Glamorgan in a championship match. We had a massive party which went on for two nights and even included some of our opponents. Robin Smith, as our captain, decided we should have a fancy dress-themed evening after the second day's play so we went into town and hired costumes. Robin and I were Tweedledum and Tweedledee while others were even more exotic. John Stephenson stole the show as Elvis and there was even an appearance by King Henry VIII. The captain's orders were that we should not return to our hotel at least until the pubs had closed. From pubs we went on to a restaurant and then to a club so that by the time we all fell into bed after a fantastic time, it was 4am and we were due back at the ground five hours later.

Matthew Maynard, still just about Glamorgan's best known batsman and captain, was among those who joined us and we figured that if we filled him with enough drink, he would be sure to struggle - and he did. We may have discarded our costumes, but we were a bedraggled outfit when we reported for duty next morning with thumping heads and bleary eyes. The smell of strong drink was unmistakable.

Robin decided to abandon the warm-up routine but Maynard was not so lucky. Duncan Fletcher, then Glamorgan coach, did not need to be a sleuth to discover that Maynard was considerably the worse for wear and ordered him to run around the pitch and when he had done that, to go through a rigorous set of exercises. We felt bad just watching him, but Maynard could not contain himself and threw up all over the advertising boards in front of bemused and horrified spectators. I joined Adie Aymes at the crease and I have never felt so unwell while batting, not that I did so for long before we were blessedly all out. But if we thought we were in for a long hot day in the field, we were wrong. We held some fantastic catches, Maynard came and went quickly to our and,I suspect, his relief, and suddenly Robin was enforcing the follow-on. Glamorgan were six down in their second innings at the close and we headed straight to the bar at the start of another long night's drinking. To the accompaniment of more throbbing heads and dry throats, we polished them off in no time to win by an innings and six runs on the morning of the last day. My part in all this, apart from consuming a huge amount of alcohol, was a total of nine wickets including a season's-best six for 47. That season, it was not the only devastating social event while on the road. All part of being Happy Hampshire, I suppose.

Glamorgan have always been one of the more hospitable counties and there are still a few, mostly in the north, who appear to enjoy their cricket in the way that we all did when I first started. The Durham boys are good fun, and Yorkshire and Lancashire like a drink or two at the end of a day's play. But overall the social side has been sacrificed on the altar of competition and expediency. If teams stay for a drink, it is often among themselves and not mixing as much with the opposition. But I can recall learning so much by listening to the older professionals as they supped their pints. Experienced players, not least Malcolm Marshall, were always willing to discuss the game until the cry of last orders. The emphasis now is on fitness, healthy eating, warming up and warming down, on water to re-hydrate and on energy drinks like Powerade. By the time umpires remove the bails at 6.30pm or thereabouts, I am ready for a proper drink after six and a half hours in the field. Shane Warne likes a Budweiser or two, John Crawley and I chat into the evening with whoever wants to join us, but younger players tend to go home as soon as they can. There is a fear factor among too many of them, not wanting to be seen drinking alcohol or unwinding after a hard day. I feel sorry for them because there is much to learn, arts to perfect and still plenty of older players ready to pass on their knowledge. It is a shame not more of them take advantage of this great wealth of information available in a bar at the end of every day's play.

But then, and this is where I begin to sound my age, youngsters move in different circles. There are 20 year olds of my acquaintance with agents as advisers at a time in their careers when they have done nothing and might never achieve anything. I am continually baffled by this, as are my contemporaries, because I never had an agent even at the height of my earning powers. When I wanted that Duncan Fearnley bat as a youngster I got in touch with them directly, albeit cheekily, and I did not need to pay an agent to do it for me. Whether or not they need the security of an agent, I cannot be certain, but I do not think their increasing involvement is a healthy development.

Anyway, 1999 was a good year with 50 wickets in the first class season, because I was turning my arm over a little more slowly, with five-fors also against the New Zealanders and Gloucestershire at Bristol from 15 matches once I had fully recovered from 'falling off the pavement'. There was a great sense of optimism in the air after a period of stagnation at Hampshire, with grandiose plans for a £20m new stadium on farmland at West End on the outskirts of Southampton and talk of signing Shane Warne, the best player in the world, as our overseas player. The new millennium promised a wonderful fresh start. I only wish Malcolm Marshall had been there to see it happen, but in September, newly married to Connie, he headed back to Barbados and we knew we would not see him again. Two months later came the announcement that he had faded away and died, and while it was not unexpected, it was still a shock. Robin, Mark Nicholas, who gave by all accounts a marvellous valedictory, Tim Tremlett, Cardigan Connor, Paul-Jan Bakker, David Newman, our physiotherapist, and John Stephenson were among the mourners and part of the club died with him when Marshall's body was gently lowered into his grave. Those of us fortunate enough to know him will never forget him or the incredible contribution he made to cricket and in particular to Hampshire.

Chapter 13

Warne Arrives

SHANE WARNE might have joined Lancashire, he might have gone to Sussex, but in the end he chose to join Hampshire and now it is his final mission in a spectacular career to bring a trophy or two to the Rose Bowl, not least the county championship for the first time since 1973. His signing by us was the result of a lot of hard work behind the scenes, starting in 1997 when Robin Smith and I, the two Hampshire players he knew, met him during the tour match and sounded him out. We had heard that he fancied a year or two in county cricket and in the County Ground bar we discussed the possibilities of him signing for us as an overseas player. Before we met him we feared we might lose out to one of those clubs with a Test match ground, but we were greatly heartened when he told us how he fancied playing for one of the smaller clubs with ambition. Being aware of our plans to leave the antiquated County Ground for the Rose Bowl, we fitted his requirements perfectly. Robin sold the club to his old adversary with a glowing list of our plans and the wooing was completed when Ian Botham recommended Hampshire to him in the strongest possible terms.

Even so, it was another three years before he finally committed himself to Hampshire and in the interim, other clubs tried to do what we had done. Sussex made big efforts, I understand, in 1998 and Lancashire actually outbid us, but the money aspect was never the key to his decision. Of course, he wanted a financial package that was commensurate with his undisputed status as the best cricketer in the world, but he wanted to play for a club where he felt he might be happy and where his family could settle. Brian Ford, our chairman at the time, met Warne at Buckingham Palace in June 1999 at a World Cup reception and again floated the idea of him playing for us. We chipped away at him and got together a healthy package on incentives and by the end of the

1999 season, a gap appeared in his crowded calendar for the following English summer, which allowed him to play most of it for Hampshire. We knew even then that we were about to pull off one of the major signing coups of all time and drew attention from all over the world when it was announced at Derby where we were playing our last match of the season that he would be coming to us.

It was only later that I began to have second, selfish thoughts about his arrival. On the one hand, he would provide a great boost to the club, to the county game and to those of us who were about to become his colleagues. But on the other hand, I thought, "Hang on a minute, this affects me more than any other player." I had, in effect, played a prominent early role in signing a spin bowler to replace me and, let us face it, there was no better spinner than Shane Warne. I had just returned to known form and suddenly there was Warne, ready, willing and able to take my place, so while I was excited by the fantastic news, I was also slightly fearful of its implications. Even if Hampshire decided to go into matches with Warne and myself, there were not going to be many opposition groundsmen preparing pitches to suit spin, and with this in mind, I confronted Robin about my prospects. "You will play in the one-dayers," he told me, but his words were not exactly placatory. Time would tell.

For those who see Shane Warne on television or in the flesh, he comes across as the ultimate self-confident Aussie, but on the day he arrived early in 2000 there was a nervousness about him I had never seen before. Robin and I picked him up at Heathrow with Simone and his young family in tow, trailing a huge array of luggage and met by a phalanx of Press. Only then did I truly believe we had got him and realise just how well we had done. Warne may have been the biggest signing in Hampshire's history, but even on that first day, he was proving to be worth every penny in terms of interest and coverage generated. We took them the 65 miles to the De Vere Grand Harbour hotel on Southampton's dockside near to where that great nautical icon, the Titanic, set sail 88 years before. We had to hope there was not going to be the same sort of result. There were yet more television cameras, radio microphones and newspaper reporters from all parts of the globe awaiting him at the County Ground, which he handled with his usual competence and forthright charm, but he was still apprehensive when he joined the rest of the team for lunch in the old Phil Mead stand. The sea of faces were nearly all new to him and his initial, understandable, discomfort was plain to all, but then, we were just as anxious to impress him. This was the last year of the County Ground at Northlands Road, our home for more than 100 years, and the rickety old dressing room was certainly something he would not have been used to, but it was not long before he was occupying a spot near the window so he could indulge in his constant smoking, and it was not long before he fitted in, as if he had been one of us for years.

That first evening we travelled to Chelmsford for his debut next day and he was visibly more relaxed in our company after dinner, going to bed at 10pm in a bid to beat jet lag and, it is fair to say, he has been a committed Hampshire man ever since. At Chelmsford, I even managed to out-perform the great man, taking two for 27 to his nought for 44 in a five wicket win in the Benson and Hedges Cup, a fact which I remember Sky TV were not slow to exploit.

Hampshire had also invested heavily in Alan Mullally, the Anglo-Australian who was still at the height of his bowling powers after leaving Leicestershire. With Warne and Mullally we should have been more of a force in 2000 than we were but we were let down time and again by some poor batting. Only our vice captain Will Kendall reached a modest target of 1,000 runs, and for Robin Smith no centuries in 29 first class innings and a final average of 20.51. Warne himself was often surprised to be padded up by lunch, even when batting at eight or nine, so that to be relegated, as we were, in seventh position was a severe setback when we had expected instead to be challenging for honours. To win only three of our 16 matches when you have big stars in their prime was a terrible waste and hardly justified the huge hype before the season or the financial commitment at a time when we needed every penny in readiness for our increasingly expensive move to the Rose Bowl.

My own fears about being overlooked were only partially endorsed, playing in 12 first class matches for 30 wickets, and nearly all the one-day matches, and sometimes I think I was a little lucky to play as many times as I did. The team made a poor start, hardly winning a match for about six weeks and when our recovery came, it was too late. We began to fear that Shane might not want to come back for another dose of county cricket after a dismal introduction, and there were in addition enough problems off the field in his personal life to occupy his attentions, moving house from Rownhams to Chandlers Ford nearer

Southampton and then hitting the tabloid front pages with allegations concerning a nurse in Leicester and explicit text messages. Shane kept his own counsel on this matter but, with Simone in Spain, I know how annoyed and angry he was. We only ever heard the nurse's side of the story but we rallied round Shane as a team, offered our support and shielded him from the prying and probing eyes of the red-top press - many sent from Australia - which followed him for the rest of the summer. Anyone else would have buckled, but such is Warne's incredible strength of mind that he could put it behind him and get on with his sporting life as if nothing had happened.

Once he was on the pitch, no thought beyond the winning of a cricket match appeared to intrude and nothing affected his good nature for long. I even had the privilege of captaining him once or twice and blush even now when he asked me, "Shaggy, can I have another slip?" Him, asking me. More often, it was a case of learning from him, snapping up crumbs of wisdom when ever possible. "Spin it up spinner," was a favourite phrase. "Always spin the ball upwards." No one had ever said that to me before, and at 31 I was still learning about my craft from the master. Above all I was astonished by his confidence and his aggression on the pitch and I felt in 2000, even when I was the captain, that should he ever return to Hampshire he should be our leader, and so it proved. On his own admission he is not liked or as admired as much in Australia as he is in England, curious when you think what he has done to our cricketers over the years, but take my word for it, much of the gossip written about him - and plenty is - can be described as utter bollocks. I like Shane immensely and the Hampshire players are devoted to him and a compliment from him can make you feel 20 feet tall.

The sad thing was that the Leicester nurse incident, little more than tittle-tattle, cost Shane the Australian vice captaincy and probably, in time, the captaincy itself, which I believe deprived cricket of seeing what he would have been like as an international captain. The game is the poorer for that. The Ashes tour to England in 2005 could and perhaps should have been led by him, as indeed the return in 2006/7 when the Australians gained such handsome revenge. I spoke to Shane after every day's play in the fantastically exciting series of 2005 and never once, even in an unguarded moment, did he criticise Ricky Ponting. Those in the media, including ex players, who felt there was some animosity between them, based on his thwarted captaincy ambitions, were wrong in so far as I was aware. I just think it sad and unfair that he was never able to fulfil his destiny by leading his country in Test matches.

We became friends and much later I was privileged when with Rod Bransgrove, our chairman, I went to Cape Town as Shane's guest to see him play in his 100th Test. He had hired a hospitality box for the whole match and we wined and dined at his expense, which says something for Shane's great generosity of spirit and his appreciation of those who appreciate him. It was here that I got some valuable insight into what made Shane Warne the man. I met his mother Brigitte and his father Keith and could see traits in them both that have emerged in their son. Keith was a lovely guy, good humoured, well mannered, polite and easy-going but there was a hint of fieriness in his mother, which we have all seen on occasions in her little boy.

As we lurched towards the ignominy of relegation in 2000, the County Ground was in the throes of being vacated and the bulldozers waited metaphorically at the gates to flatten the prime building site in readiness for development of expensive executive homes. There was sadness in the air matched by anticipation in our move to the Rose Bowl. Shire ponies were grazing on the site when we bought the land from Queens College, Oxford in 1995 and now Nigel Gray and his groundstaff were preparing it to host first class cricket. There was great excitement tinged by leaving behind so many great memories of the County Ground. Our move out to West End meant that we also had to say goodbye to our out grounds at Basingstoke and Portsmouth, each of which had provided its own highlights over many years. My best snapshot of the County Ground was in beating Somerset in 1992 to help get Malcolm Marshall to a Lord's final for the first time. It was also the scene of my only century, so there was much to cherish and savour and the ghosts of the past were properly remembered in a special dinner held on the playing surface itself after the last ball had been bowled. But while we all looked forward, as well as back, we had not realised just how close the whole Rose Bowl project was to collapsing. For the fact that it did not, and is now looked on as one of the world cricket's great new sporting venues, there is only one person to thank and that is Rod Bransgrove, the other key man in Hampshire's rapid progress over the last six or seven years. Without Rod Bransgrove's financial expertise and his determination to make the Rose Bowl a Test match venue, I think we might well have gone out of business. I suspect no one had realised just how the Rose Bowl would devour money in the same greedy manner as those shire horses had eaten grass from the same field. The huge lottery grant of around £7m seemed to answer all our problems, but in fact they were only just beginning.

At the County Ground, Tony Baker and Mike Taylor seemed to do most of the administrative work with the minimum of full time support and Nigel Gray even admitted to mowing his beloved pitch on a particularly balmy Boxing Day. But at the Rose Bowl a much bigger staff was required and the building work was far more costly than anyone among a well-meaning committee had ever anticipated. It did not help that having sold the County Ground more cheaply than we should have done to a major construction company, we did not get anything of the vast profit they made when they sold it on. I felt sorry for Tony Baker, our chief executive, who laboured hard and long for the county over many years and who could see the colossal bills mounting and threatening to drag us into oblivion. Rod Bransgrove was the white knight who saved the Rose Bowl from becoming a white elephant. Rod is the best businessman I have ever known, making fortunes from pharmaceuticals and then the entertainment industry and now devoted to making Hampshire the county championship's top club and the Rose Bowl the greatest modern arena. As he has said often enough, if he had had any sense he would never have got involved in cricket, but it is a labour of love for him now and I believe his incredible inner drive will carry him and us through. I am not alone in being convinced that Hampshire will be a top club while the Rose Bowl is already coming out of a concrete chrysalis on the way to becoming a beautiful stadium.

Along the way, Rod has fought many a battle, to assume command from an amateur county committee and then against the English (and Wales) Cricket Board's establishment, who seem to fear his ambition and his passion. He will win, I feel sure, but I know he endured sleepless nights when his plans to bring international cricket to the south coast were held up and baulked for no obvious reason except, it seemed to him, envy and the trepidation of him turning the cosy cricket world upside down. I first met Rod at a party of Paul Terry's in 1992 and even then it was clear he had a deep love for the game that would not stop at being Hampshire's number one fan. Rod and his wife Mandy became social friends and drinking companions. They can party until dawn with the best of them. Later, his team 'The Staggerers' used to play at Camberley where I assembled the opposition in the form of the 'Old Lags', a strong squad often made up of big names like Hayden, Marshall, Connor, the Smith brothers, Neil Johnson and Terry. Mullally even played on the day he rejoined us. Later he helped Robin Smith set up Judge's Bar in Romsey and got involved in benefit year activities until it became clear he was the only man who could save the club from extinction.

Rod can be great fun. He once bought an evening with Steve Davis, the snooker player, at a sporting auction. Davis showed up at Rod's house and was anything but boring, cracking jokes and proving to be witty, charming and intelligent company. After dinner he took on Robin, me, Mandy and Rod, giving us each 40 points start and beating us easily during a superb evening which went on until the early hours. Rod's country home reflects his huge interest in the sports and entertainment worlds with rooms devoted to his memorabilia. I know Rod has been hurt by public criticism, many supporters out of ignorance think he is somehow in it for the money or the glory, but there is precious little of either. As he has said, how much money does he have to lose before people are convinced? I have seen the caring, considerate side of him. Whenever he speaks to me, his first concern is for Jack's welfare and when my private healthcare credit ran out at a time we needed it for Jack's treatment, Rod organised it so that we got a couple of extra sessions without having to pay for it. Rod is my boss now, we don't socialise as much as we did, and one day he might have to tell me I have reached the end of the line. But that will not stop me from applauding what he has done for Hampshire and hoping the Rose Bowl, in time, becomes a proper monument to his commitment and his desire to turn the club into a real force.

Jimmy Cook became our coach in 2000 and it was his bad luck that we were still a team in development so that, even with Warne, we were relegated in his first season in charge. It was also hard for him taking over from the recently deceased Malcolm Marshall and the emotion his death generated, and all the more difficult because his appointment was by no means universally popular among those influential at Hampshire. Cook's playing misfortune was that South Africa's exile from Test cricket coincided with the major part of his own career as an opening batsman and his only three caps came in 1992 and 1993, long after his heyday.

Instead, he went into retirement with a batting average in excess of 50 and anyone who saw him playing for Somerset would testify to the belief that he might have become one of the all-time greats had he been able to play regular international cricket. Those who remember him take on and destroy Marshall at Taunton were witness to a high-class talent. But when it came to the Hampshire coaching position, I know Robin wanted his close friend Paul Terry to succeed Marshall. Paul had built up a big reputation as a coach in Perth, to where he had emigrated after leaving Hampshire in an acrimonious hurry. At the time, his return did not seem feasible in that it was too soon after he had fled the country, so Cook was something of a compromise.

As a coach, Cook was methodical, organised and as much in love with the game as any of us. He believed that hard work and preparation were the basis for success, but the tactical side of the game often eluded him and it did nothing for his desire to win over the doubters when he spent hours feeding a bowling machine for his son, Stephen. Cook also ruffled a few feathers when he was responsible for dropping the redoubtable Adie Aymes and replacing him with Derek Kenway for the one-day matches in the belief that Kenway was an inferior keeper but better batsman, enabling us therefore to bring in an extra bowler. Kenway should by now be being hailed as one of Hampshire's greatest players, because he could have been. But he went into premature retirement without fulfilling one of the most natural talents of my time. Kenway's early progress was such that he even got on the first rung of the England ladder when he was sent out to the academy in Adelaide, but came home early and never got another chance after Rod Marsh, the coach there, expressed his concern to the club in Derek's tour report about his lack of desire to succeed. His failure in Adelaide reflected badly on Hampshire in many respects and we will never know why he did not improve or buckle down and work harder. Nottinghamshire wanted to sign him when he was struggling to hold down a regular place with us, but at the time we said we could not afford to lose him.

The pre-season tour of South Africa, organised by Cook, was Kenway at his most frustrating. We were all given the task of getting fit through the winter in readiness for bleep tests prior to leaving. We could only take a certain number of players and when it came to those tests, Kenway failed abysmally, failing to reach the modest required level by some distance. Poor old Robin, who so hated imparting bad news, had the job of telling Kenway he was not fit enough to travel, but typical of him also, decided to give him another chance. All Kenway had to do was improve his bleep test and he was on the plane. His second effort was no better than his first and Robin even ran it with him to help push him to his target. With a couple of teammates, I turned up to encourage him as best we could, but once more he failed and missed the trip. With this kick up the backside, I don't think it was a coincidence that 2001 was one of his best years for Hampshire. Only Derek will know deep down what his failings were. Desire, passion, commitment are all words that have been mentioned, but only he knows the reason why someone so unbelievably good could end up given up to club cricket at the age of 27. It remains my biggest regret, in terms of other players, that Derek Kenway did not go on and become an England player as his ability demanded. I wish him well, he is nice guy with a lovely family, but the question will remain, how good could he have been?

By the time we set off for South Africa, I had already been abroad to New York on an all-expenses paid trip with Emma as reward for being named as the Karran Group's salesman of the year. Karran had taken over Seven Corners and I had brought in £700,000 from five big accounts, though they only paid me six months' salary. I still loved cricket, it goes without saying, but I had got to the stage where I felt I needed to develop my business career for the years ahead. Unlike pampered footballers, there was no way I could make six months money last a whole year; I needed to work.

None of us were in the best of condition, though better than Kenway, when we joined Cook in South Africa for that pre-season tour. Cook, who thought nothing of running huge distances to keep fit, made us do the same and we were heavy-legged and sore and lost all three of our matches. I cracked a finger and missed the last of them, but by then it was not the only injury I was nursing. The other hurt was to my pride because, for no reason that was obvious to me, I had been dropped as vice captain. Will Kendall was kind enough to describe me as man of the tour for my batting and bowling, but that might have been because he had just nicked my job. Will was the nicest bloke in the world, a good batsman at the County Ground and not to blame for replacing me as vice captain. But I was in no way prepared for the day when Tremlett and David Robinson, the cricket committee chairman, called me to a meeting in one of the Rose Bowl's many portakabins and told me

Kendall was taking over. At the time I said something diplomatic like how I was "extremely disappointed", but in truth I was in total shock and felt terribly let down. I had captained the side in 2000 and, on the word of others, I had done a good job. At 32 I thought I was in poll position to take over from Robin when he retired, so to have Kendall promoted from nowhere above me was a setback I could never have anticipated. Hampshire saw Will as the next captain, not me. After all, he had the right credentials, public school and Oxford and was liked by all the players. Tremlett and Robinson said they wanted to give Will a chance and once the 'extreme disappointment' had subsided, I rang Will and offered him my full support, and I meant it, but I could not help but feel that for the first time, Hampshire had done the dirty on me.

What stopped me from storming out and joining another county was the news that I had been granted a benefit in 2002, having delayed it a year to accommodate Stephenson's, so to depart on a furious whim would have been very costly. I rang my dad, as I often did with good and bad tidings, and he told me, "get on with it," and he was right. Sadly, and I take no pleasure in saying this, Will led the side only once at Cheltenham and was having problems with his own game, partly I suspect because he was being undone by the vagaries of the Rose Bowl's pitch, which caused us all great concern for the first few years until it settled. Will had the technique for a reliable and predictable wicket, hence his success at the run-filled County Ground, but at the Rose Bowl he struggled more than most. That season he averaged only 23.62 in championship matches and made only 638 runs, not the sort of record expected of a front-line batsman. But, much more, Will was just too pleasant to be a leader of a group of professional sportsman as disparate as a multi-national, multi everything cricket team. Once in a while, as I had discovered, you need to be able to shout at people and Will was just incapable of doing that. I remember telling Mullally, recently restored to the Test side, to shut up on Will's behalf and I think it was clear quite quickly that he was not the man for the job. Hampshire knew it, but there was no one there brave enough to admit they had made a mistake, and I take no satisfaction from that. I wonder if Tremlett and Robinson now admit that they made a mistake.

That year, 2001, we were promoted at the first time of asking, finishing second behind Sussex, winning seven of our 16 matches, as much through our bowling - three of us took 50 or more wickets - as for our batting in which only Neil Johnson reached 1000 runs. The Rose Bowl was difficult enough for us, but it proved to be even worse for our opponents once its reputation as an unreliable batting surface spread around the circuit. My own season, relieved of the vice captaincy duties, was a good one with 54 wickets at 29.81 with a best of seven for 74 at Derby, but the highlight of it was surely the visit of the Australians, Shane Warne included. The sheer strength in depth of Steve Waugh's team and the concern over the durability of the pitch led Robin Smith, with the commercial aspects of a short match in mind, to plead with Waugh to make sure it went the three-day distance. Smith might well have batted first when he won the toss had it been a county match, but reckoned the Aussies would bat for a day and a half, long enough to satisfy full houses. What none of us had reckoned on was them capitulating in front of our eyes, all out for a staggering 97 on the first morning. Alan Mullally took five wickets and James Schofield, on his debut, three more including Hayden with his first ball. By the close of the first day we were 238-3 with Smith on his way to the first century against the Australians that summer.

It was a wonderful reminder of his glorious heyday. Even with a first innings lead of 257, nothing against a team as strong as Waugh's was ever guaranteed and, their pride wounded, they took advantage of injuries to Mullally and Mascarenhas to make 389 before Waugh declared at the fall of the ninth wicket. He need not have done since the last pair could have ground it out during what little was left of play, but on the other hand they could have been all out next ball. Because of the injuries, I bowled 47 overs unchanged and took four for 149 (including ex Hampshire men Hayden and Simon Katich), and there might even have been a fifth had Jason Gillespie not been dropped. That would have added nicely to my five-wicket hauls against the touring sides of South Africa, New Zealand and India. We were left with 26 overs to get 133, but with an attack containing Brett Lee, Gillespie in his pomp and the incredible Warne that was never going to be straightforward. They whittled their way through us, but true to the spirit, we went after the runs and when it was my turn to go the crease, I was confronted by Warne. "I am trying," he said, and I soon found out he meant it. Robin was struggling with a rib broken in the first innings and made only ten and no one was staying in for long. It was all getting a bit tense.

Warne Arrives

From 111-6, Mascarenhas and I put on ten vital runs before Warne, coming round the wicket, bowled me with the best ball I have ever faced. Only he could have produced a delivery which pitched half a yard outside the leg stump and clipped the top of my off stump. I might say the quality of that ball was wasted on me since it would have beaten anyone. Waugh said later it was better than the famous ball which bamboozled poor old Mike Gatting. Even in 2001, there were critics suggesting Warne was a spent force but I said, with some irony, afterwards to Glenn McGrath and the coach John Buchanan, "They say he's finished."

The rest is Hampshire history. Iain Brunnschweiler, our reserve wicketkeeper, swept the blue-haired Colin 'Funky' Miller for four to seal the county's first win over the Australians since 1912. There were nine balls remaining and we celebrated in style a two-wicket win. The Aussies took it in their stride, staying behind to sign everything big enough to get a signature on and congratulated us on our achievement, but I think deep down Waugh had the lurking suspicion we had somehow stitched him up. Warne took four wickets of course, as we feared he might, and showed no signs of pleasure at our surprise win. As I was saying, he is a very competitive man.

Chapter 14

Benefit And Ban

MAJOR RON Ferguson and Colin Ingleby-Mackenzie were two incredible characters who played selfless roles in my benefit season of 2002 and it is sad to think that both are now dead without reaching old age. Ron was a wonderful man, much loved by all those of us fortunate enough to know him and not at all like the old buffer military man depicted sometimes in the press once he had had international celebrity thrust upon him in the wake of his daughter Sarah's marriage to Prince Andrew. Ron liked cricket and cricketers and when I set about the task of making my benefit year a financial success, he went out of his way to help. Not for him the casual donation, that was not Major Ron's way. Sensing that I needed an office from which to organise the many events of a cricketer's year, he gave me a converted milking shed at his farm at Dummer in the north of Hampshire, free. All I ever paid was the telephone. I am indebted to all kinds of people for the eventual raising of £241,000 in recognition of 13 years service but Major Ron's kindness was typical of the generosity shown by so many in the county and beyond.

The Major, as I called him affectionately, was my patron, and he called me 'Shaggy' in a posh and resonant voice and the saddest part of the whole year was seeing him deteriorate before our eyes with the wretched cancer which was to kill him. He spoke on my behalf at the launch of my benefit and vowed to do the same for Robin when he began his testimonial season in 2003. Before then he endured long spells in hospital while he fought the disease with the same courage as Malcolm Marshall in the knowledge there was only ever going to be one winner. Once in hospital, the major 'died' for 17 seconds before he was revived and he much enjoyed telling the tale of his brush with mortality. Very ill, tired and a shadow of his former ebullient self,

Major Ron was as good as his word about Robin and showed up at his launch in a wheelchair, keeping a promise he had made a year before. It was an obvious struggle, but he would not have missed it for the world. He gave a little speech after I had introduced him and reduced us all to great laughter when he made light of the creeping menace of cancer. "I have seen the pearly gates," he said. "And they are not all they are cracked up to be." Robin and I attended his private funeral at the request of his lovely wife Susan, daughter Sarah and Prince Andrew. Prince Charles was another mourner and later, at a memorial service at Odiham, I was an usher, a duty I was privileged to carry out. I am fortunate enough to say, Ron adored me and I felt much the same way about him and he will go down as one of the most wonderful men I ever met, completely without malice and who wanted only the best for other people. A real man's man.

Ingleby-Mackenzie was part of Hampshire folklore long before I was even born. As the man who led Hampshire to their first county championship title in 1961, he had inspired a whole generation with his deceptively easy-going approach to captaincy. His famous quote when asked how he prepared his team for a big match was "in bed by breakfast", summing up his life's philosophy. Whenever he introduced me at functions it was as "the best off spinner in the world?" and how I wish I could have believed him. There was this tremendous enthusiasm about Colin, this wonderful zest, a trait he shared coincidentally with Major Ron. The greatest compliment I can pay him is to say that I would have loved to have played for him. Colin was one of those rare people who lit up a room when he came into it and it was he who ceremonially handed me my cheque as cricket members' club president, a Hampshire record amount, and it was a real shock when we learned of his illness and then death from heart problems at the age of 72. When he died I was with England in Mohali for the second Test and I suggested the players wore black armbands as a mark of respect. There was not a word of disagreement. In many ways he personified Hampshire cricket, the man who first put the happy into Hampshire and set the tone for the style the club has since sought to emulate. At other counties he might never have made the same impact, or had the scope to play the game the way he wanted it played, but his legacy is always apparent.

The way had been cleared for me to work through the winter of 2001-2002 on those functions, dinners, matches, golf days and sundry other activities which make up a benefit by the news that Martyn Ball of Gloucestershire had been preferred for the tour of India when Robert Croft pulled out. I have explained elsewhere what a nonsensical decision that was, based I feel on rewarding an individual player for collective achievement. David Graveney said Ball was "the right man" and after that I lost all hope of playing for England. Besides, I had plenty of other things to do.

The cricket benefit concept was meant as a way of thanking players for long service and to ease them into civilian life and I don't mind admitting that it is seen as a little outdated, antiquated even, bearing in mind that salaries have improved and there is always the winter in which to augment funds. It can encourage players to hang on beyond their shelf life and I know that when Hampshire gave one to Alan Mullally after only six years, there was some public resentment. Spider's injuries dissipated his value to us and he was unable to sustain his brilliant Hampshire start during which he regained his England place. The Professional Cricketers' Association, the players' union, has a pension scheme, which is welcomed by the rank and file, but sport can be cruel and not everyone plays long enough to qualify for a benefit. Cricket is a great life, but often a short one. My benefit year was made easier by a fantastic committee and by the secretarial support that allowed me to concentrate on my game without being hindered by inevitable organisational problems. In consequence, my phone hardly ever rang. Lisa, Clare Britten, Anthea, they all occupied the old milking shed far more than I did and it was them I thanked when Ingleby-Mackenzie presented the cheque.

There were many others, not least an old friend Chris Evans, who oversaw the fund-raising as chairman of the committee, which was all the more praiseworthy considering he ran a bank in Moscow. Then there was Rod Cousens, who put on a dinner at the famous Four Seasons restaurant when the comedian Jim Davidson helped bring in some £70,000. Rod did so much for me in my benefit year and became a true friend to whom I still talk regularly. He gave of himself unfailingly to help me and my family and I shall always treasure his friendship. Every time I ask him to help, he always says yes. A great man. I had a boxing evening at the Café Royale, a golf week in Spain, cricket fan and impressionist Rory Bremner spoke for me (in the guise of many others) at a Christmas lunch, while Shane Warne and Merv

Benefit And Ban

Hughes did me a massive turn when they were the main speakers at a summer lunch. We sold 300 tickets on the back of their involvement and they performed for nothing, which was a fantastic boost.

Talking of guest speakers, this would be the right place to mention Ian Botham's superb effort on behalf of Camberley Cricket Club in 1994. Ian, as generous as ever, agreed to speak at their dinner and planned to fly down from his home in North Yorkshire. But a propeller broke before he set off and he got a farmer friend to drive him to another airfield at York so that he could fulfil his commitment. Lesser men would have pulled out, no questions asked. We put him and his pilot up at Lakeside and, in thanking him, made a donation to leukaemia research. 'Both' is a wonderful bloke and that incident is typical of him.

Nigel Butler, the hard working and experienced treasurer of my committee, was convinced I would have a good year in financial terms by the number of donations being made by members before the season itself had started, and so it proved. Nigel is one of life's gentlemen. He has been treasurer of Hampshire benefit committees for quarter of a century and deserves a benefit himself for his selfless efforts on behalf of others. Nigel never takes a penny from the numerous events and he was properly rewarded when he was elevated to a vice-presidency by Hampshire for services to beneficiaries. As a director of Chase Sport, I now work with him and enjoy his company enormously. What did it all do for me? We moved to a bigger house, had a holiday and looked forward to the future with less sense of uncertainty.

But while I had a good year in terms of money raised, Hampshire had another poor year, in the main, in the continuing absence of Warne. Relegation, promotion and now relegation again, we were showing no signs of developing into one of the major counties. In the championship we won only two matches, not one of us scored 1000 runs and I was the only bowler to take more than 50 wickets. From a selfish point of view, it was an excellent season because in addition to my 56 wickets at 33.17, I also scored 516 runs, including 88 against Kent on a then still-torrid Rose Bowl batting surface. My tally of wickets was the best since 1994 and the highlight was undoubtedly figures of five for 59 against a very powerful Indian batting line up. My victims were Sehwag, Laxman, Bangar, Ganguly and a certain Sachin

Tendulkar and, while my celebrations were good, they were not as extravagant as they were in Mumbai when Tendulkar prodded that catch to Ian Bell. The Indians were deeply suspicious of the wicket and declared their second innings rather than risk injury to important batsmen, but I am not sure their fears were justified. We failed to qualify for the knockout stages of the Benson and Hedges Cup, were third from bottom of the second division of the Norwich Union National League and Marcus Trescothick knocked us out of the C & G Trophy at Taunton with a big hundred. No, 2002 was not a good year for Hampshire and 2003 was a good deal worse. How much we were missing Shane Warne.

The plan was for Shane to return to Hampshire in 2003 but our planning, based around his considerable presence, was thrown into chaos when he was found guilty of taking a banned diuretic. I find the whole episode incredible even now. As if Shane Warne, of all people, needed a performance-enhancing pill. But the evidence suggested he had, and his punishment was a year's ban, thereby depriving us of his services for the whole summer. Emma spotted the news on television and after I had recovered from an initial incredulity, I rang him to find out more. "It's not as bad as it looks," he said, but the damage had been done and we needed to find another captain and another overseas player in double quick time. Robin Smith was coming to the end of a great career and had been looking forward to returning to the ranks and handing over the captaincy to Warne. Robin's game still revealed flashes of his old flamboyant self but it was clearly hard for him to maintain the high standards he had set for himself. With him a non-candidate, I felt the task of replacing Warne rested between Kendall, John Crawley, who had been captain of Lancashire, and myself.

All of which was a nice welcome present for Paul Terry, who had taken over as coach from Jimmy Cook following our relegation, with the new title of manager. Paul had been away from Hampshire sufficiently long to be rehabilitated. Robin and Rod Bransgrove believed Paul could herald a new era, but having to find someone to take over from Warne as captain and player was a massive undertaking. Kendall might have been favourite had he not have been struggling to find his form at the Rose Bowl and in the end it lay between Creepy and me. I really thought the captaincy, something I had always craved, was mine but Paul called me over and said the decision had gone in favour of Crawley for his previous experience in leading a county and because he said, "I was one of the lads." Creepy was more distant, it was true, and I knew what Paul meant, but it was a setback and there is no point in pretending it was not.

As it happened, it was a very good year not to be captain and I ended up feeling slightly sorry for Creepy as he attempted to make a team of us. The choice of overseas player, necessarily late and after most of the best players had found counties, was the great Pakistani all-rounder Wasim Akram. We needed a big name to replace Warne and we got one in Wasim, but sadly it was not the Wasim of old, one of the great players of the 90s. In his glorious heyday Wasim had been a devastating left arm bowler and a thunderous batsman, capable of destroying any international attack, but not any more. I must admit I thought he would prove to be a great signing but, in basic terms, his body was knackered. Years of travelling around the globe, spearheading the Pakistan attack, and valiant service for Lancashire had taken a toll and it was obvious from the start that here was a spent force. Twenty wickets in five first class matches sounds more than adequate but he was often not well and he was not enjoying his cricket, so that it was no great surprise when he retired, no longer able to cope with the four-day game. It was a real shame, but there was no point in him continuing and, nobly, he even paid back some of his moving allowance because he had felt he had let us down.

Creepy also had to contend with Ed Giddins, a surprise winter signing, who had played for several other counties and for England, but who was also coming to the end and who brought with him the baggage of drug and illegal betting allegations. I can say here that I have never come across anyone quite like him in cricket, in fact anywhere, but his heart was not in it and he too failed to last the course. We had numerous injuries, which did not help, not least to Chris Tremlett who was beginning to make a name for himself as an outstanding pace bowling prospect. In total we used 24 players in first class matches, calling up players from club cricket, and only Dimitri Mascarenhas enhanced his reputation. As an all-rounder he should certainly have played for England in one-day internationals and it remains an injustice that he has not, but Duncan Fletcher said he was not a quick enough bowler.

My own contribution of 42 wickets and 488 runs was not bad, I suppose, but I failed for the first time since 1998 to take five wickets in an innings in what proved to be, in first class cricket at least, as bad a year for the county as I could remember. We finished second bottom of Division Two and I am not sure even Shane Warne would have made much difference to the outcome. We were knocked out of the C&G Trophy at the first time of asking, came bottom of our zone in the newly-instituted Twenty20 competition and our season was saved only by coming third, and being promoted, in the National League, giving us some kind of compensation and relief for Crawley who always knew he was keeping the seat warm for Warne. The Rose Bowl pitches were still causing problems, knocking back Crawley's international aspirations, and I know he found the whole season a tense and largely unhappy experience. These days he has found his very best form again and is relaxed and happy and fulfilling his destiny as one of the best batsmen of his generation. His form later in 2006 was absolutely outstanding.

Sadly, Robin left us at the end of the 2003 season, despite averaging 37 in ten first class matches, and in many ways his departure brought to an end the most prolific era in Hampshire's history in terms of trophies won. He had become at the finish more of an accumulator of runs, grinding out scores in a way unrecognisable from his very best, but I know he felt he had another year in him before Paul Terry, his close friend, had the unenviable task of taking him aside for a chat in his role as team manager and advising him to retire.

My own season was marred by another incident at Camberley, which this time led to a lengthy ban. Much has been written about it, some of it wrong, so this is the time to set the record straight. I am not proud of what happened and it should never have occurred, but it did and in some ways I am still being punished down the line. I always enjoyed playing for Camberley, where I am president, and I stress that I was not paid. Indeed, I handed over my subs, as all the players did. We were playing Cranleigh at the end of July and their Australian leg spinner, Alex Wyatt, had already riled us as a late order batsman with his silly, deliberately aggravating comments to our fielders. I am used as a professional to all manner of 'sledging' in the county game, so that nothing much disturbs me for long. I have heard it all before. But this guy irritated me, and the rest of our team, and continued to do so when it was our turn to bat.

Benefit And Ban

Chasing about 180, we were eight for two when I came out to bat and Wyatt was bowling. He was calling me 'big gun', among other things, which I could handle, but what I could not handle was the way he was chipping away at Craig Muir, who is disabled by being deaf and wears a hearing aid. Craig was the batsman at the other end and I kept looking at the umpires, expecting them to tell Wyatt to tone down his comments, which in my view had gone beyond gamesmanship. Craig, whose parents Dave and Rina are Hampshire members and lifelong friends, was dropped at mid-on off Wyatt, who promptly took out his frustration by calling him a "fucking spastic". I followed him to square leg and said, "you are so out of order," but he took no notice and did not deign to apologise. I spoke to the umpires to ask them to do something about him, but they did not.

In Wyatt's next over I hit his first two deliveries for four but missed the third and looked up to see Wyatt celebrating what he thought was the wicket of Big Gun. The ball had clearly brushed my pad and the umpire agreed but that did not stop Wyatt from calling me a cheat. I don't mind admitting I was infuriated and I threw him to the ground in a blind rage. I told him he was a disgrace to Australia and poked his chest, but I knew from the moment I laid hands on him I was in big, big trouble. The umpires should have been stronger but on the other hand I should not have taken the law into my own hands and I feared the consequences even as I made a hundred in a victory. I remember one of the Cranleigh fielders saying in consolation that he was amazed it had taken so long for someone to sort out Wyatt, but afterwards I was in a real state because I knew I had blundered badly. I had been defending Craig and sticking up for principles but an altercation on a pitch was no way to resolve a dispute and I anticipated swingeing repercussions.

In a bid to prevent further damage, I got a jug of lager and eleven glasses and went into the Cranleigh dressing room but Wyatt refused to shake my hand, offered in reconciliation. If he had said those horrible words in a public bar, for instance, I dread to think what could have happened to him. Even so, their captain said the matter was at an end. I took the precaution of informing Tim Tremlett and Paul Terry and hoped it was all over, but the umpires had put it in their report and it became public when someone from Cranleigh rang the Sun's cricket correspondent John Etheridge, who had played in the Surrey League and who then wrote about it in his paper after accusing me of punching Wyatt, something I strongly denied. I was all the more annoyed because Cranleigh had given assurances about the affair being closed. Inevitably it came before the Surrey League disciplinary committee, as I knew it would, and I was suspended for three years. Wyatt was banned for two matches, suspended for six months, as the instigator and I got three years. Was that justice? I don't think so. Peter Boot, the Camberley chairman, wrote a letter of appeal but it was ignored, and it was clear they had made an example of me because I was a professional.

What made it worse was the committee, having punished me once, then got in touch with Hampshire saying they were disappointed I had not also been disciplined by them. As it happened, I had. Terry and Tremlett had dealt with me internally and I accepted the punishment they also imposed on me. Sadly, the whole affair rumbled on even to the day I was chosen for England for the tour of Pakistan in 2005. There was an article in Charles Sale's column in the Daily Mail in which a prominent Surrey League official was quoted as saying he was disappointed England had selected a player with a conviction for trouble-making on the field of play. From what he was quoted as saying, this guy wanted to deny me the belated chance to play for England, in my view an evil and nasty sentiment. I thought who the hell do these fuddy-duddies on that committee think they are trying to stop my dream of playing for England coming true. They are sad old boys without lives of their own who tried to ruin mine. I have no respect for any of them and only hope I never bump into any of them as I would not be responsible for my actions. Not on the pitch, though. David Graveney saw the Daily Mail article and told me to ignore it, but it wasn't easy to do so and showed, two years after the ban was implemented, that there must still be some lingering animosity towards me.

One day, perhaps sooner rather than later, when my county career is over, I will be free to return to club cricket. I had planned that to be at Camberley, the club of my father and my brother. I fear now this may never happen. Shane Warne even got to find out about it via the internet and rang me to discuss the issue. I told him the culprit was from Melbourne and he said, "Don't worry, I'll get the lads to sort him out." It was the one bright moment in a tawdry affair.

Benefit And Ban

Warne breezed back into Hampshire's life in 2004 as if he had never been away. But while he had been a foot soldier in 2000, feeling his way into English domestic cricket, this time he was captain and in complete charge from day one. He flew in, his own ban completed and an international tour behind him, determined to make up for lost time by leaving an imprint on us, and the championship. Hampshire were at a low ebb and in need of a boost and Warne was just the man to provide it. There was a massive sense of expectancy about his arrival, a feeling that if anyone could lift us out of a certain gloom which had descended, it was him. He did not let us down. After being snubbed by the Aussies over the captaincy, this was his big chance to mould a team in his image and to weld together a group of players who were not without talent, but without a sense of unified purpose. Paul Terry, as manager, had been worried about a certain 'culture' which had grown up within the club and felt it might inhibit any progress if it was allowed to continue. Paul wanted to rid us of the Happy Hampshire tag.

This was all the more ironic because the prime mover, until he left in 2003, was a Yorkshireman, big Alex Morris. Alex was a good cricketer, an all-rounder of considerable commitment and ability, but who was just as committed to a vibrant nightlife. 'Almo', as we knew him, was beaten in the end by a long list of injuries, but while he gave of himself fiercely on the pitch, he was ever-ready for the bar at close of play. Almo liked a pint or two or three, and while he was fantastic fun, he embroiled others in his boozing schools and drinking games, perpetuating the belief around the circuit that Hampshire's attitude was somehow faulty. To single him out as the only culprit would be unfair because he was great company and did not often drink alone, but it was probably felt he was not the best of influences. To make sure the late night drinking and frolics did not become habitual, a curfew had been imposed on away trips and we expected it to be rigidly enforced by our new captain. On the contrary. We had a meeting with Warne soon after he arrived and his first action was to abandon the curfew. His belief, and it was obviously inherited from the Australian camp, was that a player should be accountable to himself and to his team mates. In other words, if a player performed poorly as the result of drinking heavily the previous evening he was letting down his friends and those who relied on him. "Why can't I stay out if I want?" he said - and who were we to disagree. The burden on each of us was to look after ourselves and look out for our team mates. "I am giving you personal responsibility. I trust you."

Our other overseas player was Michael 'Pup' Clarke, the brilliant young Australian batsman who brought with him the tag, and the burden, of being the next Ponting and, while it was clear he had breathtaking quality, he struggled to cope with the Rose Bowl wickets and did not do his considerable natural talent proper justice. Shane took him under his wing, nurturing his left arm spin and helping him gain the experience he is now using to such good effect on the international scene. Together they made a formidable pair in the second part of the captain's strategy, which was aimed at getting in the face of the opposition. Shane wanted to us to be positive, to be aggressive, to be confrontational where necessary and win without fear of losing. This philosophy rubbed off immediately, and while I don't think we went from being happy Hampshire to hateful Hampshire, we were a lot more competitive and intimidated by no one.

We won 'stupid' games, matches we had no right to get anywhere near, on the basis that we were simply not interested in drawing. We won at Headingley, where Kendall was captain, for the first time and at Taunton in an extraordinary sequence of events in a total of nine victories in 16 championship matches, enabling us to finish behind Nottinghamshire in second place and fulfil our pre-season target of promotion. Tremlett was fit more often than not, Mascarenhas could be devastating at the Rose Bowl, and then of course Shane gave us a whole new dimension. More often than not we played two spinners, and my figures were again good, 488 runs and 39 wickets at 22, and much to my surprise and pleasure the captaincy came my way when I least expected it. Will Kendall, in his last season before early retirement, was failing to hold down a regular place. Shane had recommended me to be captain in his own absence and I got a call on the golf course, making me proud indeed because I had thought the honour had eluded me after I had been stood down originally in Kendall's favour.

I was leading the side when we played in the first of two controversial matches with Somerset that season. At the Rose Bowl, Somerset lost Richard Johnson and Keith Parsons through injury and we were deprived for the same reason of Shane Watson, who scored an awesome century on his debut, and Dimitri Mascarenhas, so that it was nine versus nine. Shane and I put on 150 and it was also the first time ever that I got two half centuries in a match. Somerset were 146-8 in their second innings, but neither Johnson nor Parsons could bat, giving us victory by default by 275 runs. The return at Taunton will be remembered not so much for the incredible finish as for a bizarre outburst by Peter Bowler, the experienced and respected Somerset opener, raised incidentally in Canberra. As Bowler came out to bat he turned to Shane and said in his Australian accent, "How are you today, you big fat ginger Aussie?" I have no idea why he embarked on this tactic but he made a total fool of himself, believing he could somehow browbeat the biggest name in world cricket. Shane has seen off bigger people than Bowler and then proved it by bowling 30.4 overs, almost half, after setting Somerset 351 to win in 85 overs. On surfaces other than Taunton's amiable County Ground, it might have been a tall order, but with our ex batsman John Francis hitting 110, Somerset reached 300-3 without our captain ever once believing we would not emerge as winners. Shane kept his nerve, Somerset lost theirs and we won by ten runs with eight balls to spare. Shane finished with six for 127, but it was not just his bowling which was masterful, it was his leadership and his demeanour.

Shane wanted the opposition to hate us, as Bowler evidently had, but that incident at Taunton was nothing compared with the blasting Essex got at the Rose Bowl in a National League match. It was fun to watch as Warney, with Clarke joining in, gave the Essex boys a lesson in on-field aggressive talk to a level I had never previously encountered. It was quite an eye-opener, even to someone like me with the best part of 20 years in the game. Shane did not like Essex much, since I know he did not get on with Nasser Hussain or Ronnie Irani, who happened to be the Essex captain that day. "Mister Essex," Shane called him, and it got right up the nose of the volatile Irani. "I'm going to ruin you, Warne," was Ronnie's reply and here was a man not going to back down. Some of Shane's victims are intimidated and frightened by him when he talks to them, but against Essex our ploy worked. Attempting to overhaul our 184, they were 104-4 and then 153 all out. Call it sledging if you must, Shane is a master at it, doing just enough to wind-up the opposition and never allowing them to settle. It is a legitimate weapon in his bowling armoury. Certainly English umpires, wearily used to long but largely trouble-free days, were shocked by his level of appealing for lbw decisions, and by their duration. But then Shane sets himself high standards and reckons that over the years the appeal has been counter-productive at times in that umpires have been reluctant to raise their fingers in assent, even when they know the batsman is out, to show him who was boss.

My own season had another highlight when Jack was born. We had been playing Northants in the National League at Milton Keynes, where I took four wickets, and then moving on to Chester-le-Street where we were playing Durham in a championship match. Emma had been in labour and I flew down from Newcastle to be with her and then back again, so that I saw the son I had always wanted for three hours only. Ironically, it rained for the first two days of the Durham match and I got back for the third without having missed a ball. As for England, at 35 it never entered my head that my day in the sun might lie ahead. I followed England avidly as a supporter, an ardent fan, but nothing more. It was not for me.

Chapter 15

Captain At Lord's

FOR THE BEST part of two decades I have played with and against the best players in world cricket. As such, it has been a massive privilege and never for one day have I taken my good fortune for granted. To have shared a dressing room with people like Shane Warne and Malcolm Marshall, Freddie Flintoff and David Gower is incredible for a lad with my background. Cove is not a cricket hotbed. Choosing my best side is no easy task, but in batting order, this is the Shaun Udal XI: 1 Chris Smith, 2 Matthew Hayden, 3 David Gower, 4 Robin Smith, 5 Kevin Pietersen, 6 Andrew Flintoff, 7 Nic Pothas, 8 Malcolm Marshall, 9 Shane Warne, 10 Wasim Akram, 11 Steve Harmison. I have taken the immodest option of naming myself as 12th man because I would just want to be around these people, taking out their drinks. I would not mind being 12th man either to the best XI I have played against, again in batting order: 1 Matthew Hayden, 2 Rahul Dravid, 3 Viv Richards, 4 Sachin Tendulkar, 5 Brian Lara, 6 Ricky Ponting, 7 Adam Gilchrist, 8 Shane Warne, 9 Wasim Akram, 10 Curtly Ambrose, 11 Glenn McGrath. As a proper 12th man I would have to name Courtney Walsh who narrowly missed out to Ambrose.

You will notice Warne, Hayden and Wasim Akram are in both teams, but that is because their contributions have been so immense. Every time I would have Warne as captain even when there are plenty of good captains. Shane is simply the best ever, in my cricketing lifetime anyway. Why do I rate Wasim Akram so highly? On his day with Lancashire he was unbelievable, a genius in all conditions with his left arm variety. I recall him at Portsmouth when he took seven cheap wickets on day one of a championship match, consistently bowling at 85-90 mph in one of the best, sustained spells of bowling I have ever seen. Someone once said bowling to Hayden was like bowling to a sightscreen and I chose him ahead of Desmond Haynes and Gooch. Some people will be surprised at Nic Pothas being right up there with the best keepers of my career, ahead even of Jack Russell, and it might seem like a parochial consideration to the outsider, but I have thought carefully about all these names. Pothas averages in excess of 40 with the bat for Hampshire, which is better than any other I have played with. Jack Russell was a likeable bloke when I roomed with him in Melbourne and as long as he had his steak and chips and his Heinz baked beans (they had to be Heinz), he was happy. He washed his underpants in the sink and spent time sewing up holes in his cap and enjoyed his own company, which, being gregarious by nature, I found hard to understand. But then Jack was different. I played against him far more than I played with him and he could be a cunning opponent. Just as the bowler was coming in at you (and that could be Walsh), he used to clap twice and at the change of an over, scrape his foot in the playing surface in front of you. Quite recently, Jack, in his other guise as a noted painter, produced a wonderful print of my 'Mumbai moment', which I bought. As for the other keepers of my generation, chirpy Steve Rhodes was tough to play against and Adie Aymes made the most of himself and could not have been far from a tour. In my opinion Chris Read still has much to do.

One player who does not get the public credit he deserves but is much admired within the game is Rahul Dravid, hence his appearance in one of my teams. Aside from the fact that he is a real gentleman, polite and well-mannered, he is also a formidable batsman, not known as 'the wall' for nothing. Dravid averages more than 50 in 100 plus Tests and the reason for that is he places a heavy price on his wicket. For a time, perhaps two or three years, there was no one to touch Tendulakar and when I got him out at the Rose Bowl I thought that was going to be a career highlight. Lara was the quickest player on his feet that I ever bowled to, bar none, and a destroyer of spin. It would be great to watch if I had not occasionally been on the receiving end. Being on the receiving end of the great West Indian fast bowlers was no fun either. Walsh was fantastic, day in and day out for Gloucestershire, and broke my toe in a Sunday league match, but there was always a hint of menace about Ambrose. Once he let go a beamer at me, which hit me painfully on the elbow.. "Slipped," he said, but his Northants teammate Nick Cook apologised on his behalf because

Ambrose was never going to. Shoaib Akhtar and Brett Lee are the fastest I have ever faced. That day at the Rose Bowl when Hampshire beat the Australians, Lee was fired up and determined to beat us and I could not help thinking that had he been English, I doubt if he would have been as fast because our wickets and the weight of cricket might have toned him down. The others in my teams speak for themselves, but while Gilchrist may have been a better batsman and kept brilliantly, Shane himself says Ian Healy was the best to have kept to him at international level, although best of all was Darren Berry of Victoria. I first came across Ponting at Lilac Hill in 1994 and noted then the fantastic eye for picking length and the merciless way he hooked McCague. He broke my thumb when I attempted a caught and bowled, but you did not need to be a genius to realise that he was going to be a great player.

All of which leads me to Pietersen and critics of my choice might say with some justification that he has not proved himself yet, but I am positive he will. He comes across as brash and sure of himself, but he is neither in reality. Maybe sometimes in the past he has said things without thinking, but he has matured and for that his girlfriend Jessica must take some of the credit. KP can be anything in cricket, even one of the all-time greats, because all the requirements are in place, not least a strong mentality, the desire to succeed and the cricketing basics of an astonishing eye, wrists and hands. He believes that playing hockey at school in South Africa helped him develop his wrist-strength and it is all there when he goes on one of those controlled hitting sprees.

We at Hampshire were fortunate to get him although his international success has rebounded on us because we hardly ever have the benefit of his services. I first came across KP playing for Nottinghamshire at Trent Bridge and it was easy to see that here was somebody a bit special, and a bit different. Where all his teammates wore shirts and ties, KP was decked out in shorts and flip-flops. When it was clear he would be leaving Nottinghamshire for us, I kept in contact with him by phone and text throughout what proved to be a tumultuous tour of his South African homeland and there was great excitement when he came south. I know he wanted a progressive county but I think the real reason he signed for Hampshire was the chance to play with Shane Warne. It was a big selling point. From the night before he joined us when I had a beer with him at the Hotel Du Vin in Winchester, we have been good friends and I much appreciated his support and his company in Pakistan and India where life was never easy. I accept that he can be seen as over-confident by those who do not know him, but I think the flamboyance is a front for a much more sensitive person than his detractors realise.

Duncan Fletcher said he had adapted to international cricket quicker than anybody he had ever known and I am convinced that he will one day convert his potential into consistently big international scores. Did I say something about flamboyance? Well, he did show up at our C&G Trophy semi final in 2005 in a fluorescent yellow jacket and white, yes white, sunglasses, but then he does like to stand out in a crowd, even in very big ones. The by-product of his high-profile public persona is the tabloid press coverage which inevitably follows. Having turned himself into a personality, as much in evidence on the news pages as the sports, he had to live, like Warne, with some unsavoury stories, often emanating from women alleging to be his ex girlfriends, and I know he was upset by what appeared, as anybody would be. I know also how some of the Nottinghamshire boys were supposed not to be too upset when he departed, but he is hugely popular at Hampshire, when we see him, and is well regarded in the England camp. KP keeps in contact, often texting me to find out about Jack's progress, and there will always be a welcome for him at the Rose Bowl.

At the risk of going on about Robin Smith, there are two facts I would like to add. The first is that Curtly Ambrose said of him he was the player he most admired and that it was nonsense about him having a perceived weakness against spin. Warne got him four times in five Tests in 1993 but against India he averaged 63 and against Sri Lanka 67. He may not have had the softest hands, but the criticism of him being bamboozled by anyone of less than medium pace hurt him hard. I know, having had experience of it myself, that Robin would have thrived under Duncan Fletcher's regime and would have finished with 6000 Test runs and been better appreciated for his diligence and his courage in the face of hostile enemy fire. No one worked harder. By the time I used to arrive for matches at the appointed time, Robin had often been in the nets for up to an hour with his father firing the bowling machine at him. Cricket always came first.

Captain At Lord's

As for coaches, the best I have ever worked with were Troy Cooley and Bruce Reid and it is no coincidence that both were Australian. Cooley's defection to Australia from the England staff was a big loss, bigger than most people realised. When I was with England in Pakistan, Cooley said there were three aspects it was vital for me to get right as a bowler; namely, arm, feet and line. For two weeks in Pakistan he said nothing to me until one day he came up and quietly confided: "Number two is not right." That was all, and I simply went away and worked at what I had to do. Cooley assumed that if a player was good enough to be selected for England in the first place, he should be capable of sorting out his own problems, but was always available. Reid, a former Australian pace bowler who worked with us at Hampshire, was another in the same mould who kept his advice to a minimum but always had a sharp eye for developing faults. Reid and Cooley did not waste their time or ours by stating the obvious, unlike far too many coaches in the English county game who appear to speak for the sake of it. Good coaching is an art, but the best of them respect professional cricketers and do not try to blind with science. Paul Terry at Hampshire is a different sort of coach - his title is manager - and enjoys a good relationship with Warne. Paul is shrewd enough to let Warne run the Hampshire show because that is what he wanted when he came over. Paul's job is to prepare the way and clear obstacles so that Warne's only concern is what happens on the pitch.

There is a place for good coaching in cricket, of course. In my early years, I realise now, I was, as my critics suggested, getting too many wickets with my quicker ball and it still works for me to some extent. But then batsmen became wary of it and it was not as productive. For a couple of years around the time of my Ashes tour it became my stock ball, overused and unsuccessful, so that I had to adapt to survive. I decided to slow down from what had become almost slow medium, to introduce some variation, to get batsmen guessing again. While re-thinking my bowling technique I was also re-thinking my lifestyle, including looking more closely at my diet and my alcohol consumption. Once all that was in place I started to take wickets again and become a far better bowler, I like to think, than I had ever been. Experience plays a part too. In one-day matches more than the longer version of the game, you can develop a sense of when batsmen are about to come down the wicket at you. To counter this I take a slower run-up and Nic Pothas notices the extra taps a batsman makes with his bat as his impatience grows.

Psychology is so important in the little battles of the mind. For instance, I have never been at ease at Northampton and I don't know why because there is nothing wrong with the pitch, or Leicester where again I have never been especially successful. On the other hand I do expect to succeed at Trent Bridge, while Worcester is a classic English ground where I always look forward to playing. My favourite is Lord's, while Sydney and Melbourne are not far behind and Mumbai will always hold a special place in my heart. The best food is at Derby and that may account for me taking 26 wickets there over the years at 24. County cricket has been my bread and butter, if you will excuse the link, for so long now there is hardly a player I have not played against at some time or another and rivalries are bound to develop, sometimes for geographical reasons and sometimes because of the players involved. Lancashire versus Yorkshire has always had an historical edge to it, Somerset and Gloucestershire and Surrey and Middlesex spring to mind, but in 2006 our clashes with Sussex had more than local prestige at stake. Sussex deservedly won the league and cup double and for a time we pushed them close in the championship but every time we played them, no matter what the competition, there were incidents. Chris Adams, the Sussex captain, leads from the front and is a combative sort of guy who is never going to shrink from any confrontation. There is a saying in cricket that what is said on the pitch in the heat of the moment stays on the pitch, but when Adams went public with his criticism of us, and Shane Warne in particular, a lot of ill-feeling developed and was smoothed out only at the end of the season.

Trouble had been brewing since the previous year at Hove when Adams went to the press to brand Hampshire's behaviour a disgrace and said Warne had gone too far with his pressure tactics after we had twice got out the dangerous Matt Prior cheaply. Nothing had ever been said face to face, and we did not like it when he made his complaints without speaking to us. There had been words exchanged between Adams and Simon Katich and something of this resentment lingered into a C & G Trophy match at Hove in 2006. James Kirtley of Sussex is a highly capable bowler who earned England recognition, but his career was blighted when he was called for throwing and I know he worked extremely hard in the winter of 2005-6 working on rehabilitating his action. We knew it must have been tough for him but when he took three quick Hampshire wickets that day it was obvious to us that the quicker he bowled, the more bent became his bowling arm. In short, we thought he was throwing. When I was one of his victims he raised his arms in triumph and I said to him, "At least your arm is straight now," a remark for which I was reported, and with Michael Yardy getting involved, it all turned a bit nasty. In many respects it is hard to blame James because the 15 degrees rule, the angle which a bowling arm must not exceed, was designed with Muralitharan in mind. I came across the great Sri Lankan in the PCA Masters and I have to say in answer to his detractors that his wrist and arm joints are incredible in that he can bend them as no other can. However, to return to Hove, Kirtley's action that day was 'not right' and Warney went public to condemn it, refuelling the antagonism.

All too soon, we were playing Sussex again at Arundel in the Twenty/20 and there was another incident when Prior was run out by a throw from Chris Benham when he strayed from his crease wrongly thinking the umpire, Allan Jones, had called 'over'. I was captain that day and it never occurred to me to recall Prior because the umpire had already given him out. We drank with Sussex in the bar afterwards and were more than surprised when Adams again aired his views in condemning us for our unsporting behaviour. So with Warne again away, I was captain when Sussex came to the Rose Bowl for the return match in the same competition ten days later and it was hard to disguise the tension now existing. To resolve this issue and to prevent it developing further I spoke to Adams to clear the air. There appeared to be no hard feelings until Kirtley was caught in the deep in a Sussex collapse and I followed him off because his dismissal signalled the end of the match. Kirtley refused to shake hands. Later, over a beer, I had a drink with him because he was patently nursing a deep grievance. "I did not want to shake hands with you because I have been to hell and back trying to get my action sorted out. It's been an awful winter." It was clear he had been worried about his career, so to have us question it again had set him back. I was in no position to apologise for Shane, but I did apologise for my reaction at Hove. I regretted it, we shook hands and hoped that would be the end of a summer of hostilities between the neighbouring counties.

Towards the end of the season, with Warne now back, there was an excellent drawn match at Hove in the championship. Warne and Adams chatted, got over their differences and the game was played in a proper spirit. In many ways it was our most enjoyable match. Both sides spent an hour or two in the bar later and the whole tawdry catalogue of disputes was brought to a proper end.

Now that the end of my career is not far away I have the horrible feeling that I might be the last of a dying breed of finger spinners. People today ask me why we cannot produce another Jim Laker or Fred Titmus. Far be it from me to criticise someone who took 19 wickets in an Ashes Test, but I think if I had played on the uncovered wickets of Laker's day my career tally would be 400 better. Sadly it is more than just the state of the wickets which have changed so fundamentally. Players these days are far more proficient at dealing with spin with the reverse sweep, pioneered by the late Bob Woolmer, now an integral part of most batsmen's repertoire. In Laker's day also, there were much longer tails, often starting at number six, while we expect even number eleven to make some kind of batting contribution. I had a coaching session with Fred Titmus once and he made great sense and I wish it had been possible to exploit his great well of knowledge because I have lacked a mentor, someone to turn to in the way Warne turns to Terry Jenner. I worked also with John Emburey in the nets at Lord's and it would have been nice to have found my own Jenner.

Overall I am a little gloomy about the off spinning future. Batty and Swann are the best of the younger generation, in my opinion, and Alex Loudon is developing fast, but I fear the day is not far off when England and other international sides go into Tests without a recognised finger spinner. The vogue is for leggies or left armers coming over the wicket and bowling into the rough, as Ashley Giles has done so effectively for England, with the emphasis on economy. Heavier bats, better wickets and shorter boundaries all conspire against the off spinner whose stock ball is into the right-handed batsman and a look at the casualties, or the lack of progress, of the off spinners among my contemporaries shows that the decline has already started. What happened to Richard Dawson, the bright young Yorkshire hope? And where are Harvey Trump, Neil Smith and James Boiling? James Middlebrook is a decent cricketer and I hope Swann fulfils his potential and carries the torch for our calling. Robert Croft got an extended run in the England team but his career average was worse than mine and he was always more worried about conceding runs than getting batsmen out, a legacy I suspect from playing in a side which did not consistently win four-day matches. Croft was a talented batsman and may go down as the last off spin bowler to have played regularly at Test level for England. I hope not. Look around the world and the story appears to be the same, or around the counties where there is a dearth of spin prospects of any sort. Mediocre spinners can, and do, skip from county to county, naming their price because there is so little competition. Lawson and Rashid at Yorkshire have ability and I will watch their development with more than passing interest

What they must avoid is the sort of blip which halted my progress in the mid 90s. I did not realise that I had to keep working at my game, to keep improving, but I was too successful too soon and I failed to capitalise on a promising start because I just assumed it would continue. In retrospect, and it is easy to say this now, my mental approach was wrong and I did not train or practice when I should have done. The price for neglect was a heavy one. I did not begin my Test career until I was 36 and by then it was too late to make it last beyond one incredible winter. The tragedy is I thought I was the finished article at 26 and I hope Lawson, Rashid and any others with ambition do not fall into the same trap. But then, for young cricketers there is more than one trap. The difference between when I started in 1987 and now is colossal in terms of respect and expectancy. As an 18 year old I had to help the ground staff with menial jobs and would never have dared enter the first team dressing room without first knocking on the door. It made me all the more determined to be in that dressing room. I can recall watching the county squad go off to Barbados to prepare for the coming season and thinking to myself, "one day I will be with them." I know I am a generation older and there is no turning back the clock, but 21 year olds have sports cars and agents, are capped far too early and travel to away games in ripped jeans and t-shirts. They wear caps at lunch and show none of the manners assumed of us when we were juniors. Peter Sainsbury, who banned jeans, would have had apoplexy if he was coach now. He told us not to speak to senior players unless we were spoken to, and made it clear that our principle role in our worthless lives was to bowl to the first team in the nets.

My Turn To Spin

Am I attracted to coaching? Not really. I think I would struggle to work with kids as a spin coach, but if I did get involved in some way it would be to teach them about the mental side of cricket, about how tough it is to prolong a career. More appealing is cricket administration because I have been a company director and retain strong links with the business community from my benefit year. Duncan Fletcher once told me that the five years he had in Cape Town in business was one of the best things that happened to him and agrees with the assertion that all the best coaches tend to have been mediocre players. Umpiring appeals, if you will excuse the pun, and I have not ruled out applying to join the county list. Ex players tend to get more respect and the younger ones are more flexible and easier to approach than those nearing the end of their time. I get on well with Peter Willey, George Sharp, Neil Mallender and Ian Gould, while Ray Julian and David Shepherd were popular and competent. Peter Hartley, an ex Hampshire teammate, has made the transition to umpiring, but there is no getting away from the fact that when I retire there will be a big hole in my life. Adjustment is not going to be easy and I want to stay in the game in some capacity when it is clear the legs are no longer able to cope. I will miss the dressing room banter, the friends and the sheer joy of playing a sport I love. Replacing those things is going to be hard, very hard, and, yes, I fear it a little.

The Professional Cricketers' Association is aware of people like me, coming to the end, and are emphasising the need among younger players to make sure there is more to their lives than cricket. I don't doubt how useful it was for me to play club cricket in Australia for a winter but there are too many players who play the whole year, hopping on a plane for club cricket in Australia and South Africa the moment the English season ends. Their bodies never rest, their minds never switch off and injuries never get the chance to heal. The PCA has improved enormously over the years and encourages players to use the close season to explore other avenues so that when the time comes for them to quit, they will be able to cope with the outside world. I look forward from January onwards to the time when in early spring I rejoin the squad for pre-season training, but far too many players come back from stints abroad nursing injuries that have had no chance to mend.

I cannot end this examination of my cricketing career without mention of my greatest Hampshire day, leading the county to the C &

G Trophy final victory in front of a full house at Lord's. But I have to say it might never have happened. There was a time in that 2005 season when I was so surplus to requirements I was banished to the 2nd XI. Shane Warne was warming-up for the Ashes and the Rose Bowl wicket was still not the sort where it was possible to play two spinners. I was always in the squad but got used to carrying the drinks and was waiting for Shane to go so that I could reclaim my place in the county side. But for a match against Surrey I got a real shock to the system when I was omitted completely. I was told to go to Hove to play for the 2nd XI and I don't mind admitting I thought it signalled the beginning of the end. From this, the low point of my season, things picked up. The 2nd XI won, the first team were trounced and it proved to be a good match to miss. I was restored to the side and when Warne left us mid-term, I was named as captain. Warne actually told me I was to lead the side and although I knew I would never be as good as him, I could feel myself relax.

Straight away, having been promoted to the first division, we could see a huge difference in standard. I am a firm believer in two divisions and we found better bowlers, better overseas players and good competitive cricket. At Hampshire we recruited Craig McMillan, Andy Bichel, Shane Watson and Simon Katich from abroad in addition to or as cover for Warne, and while I would like to see nine players qualified for England in every county team, there was no denying what they brought to our drive for the championship and for the C & G Trophy. I thought then, and still do, that Shane Watson has the potential to be a top class all-rounder. Tactically I felt I was a capable captain and I knew from day one that the players were behind me so I could afford not to worry that an occasional mistake might cost me the job I had always wanted. On a hunch I gave Mascarenhas an extra over against Sussex just as he showed signs of flagging and he won us the game in an inspired spell. When Warne came back from the Ashes series, there was nothing he could do to prevent us coming a worthy second to Nottinghamshire but my own form had rarely been better. I finished sixth in the national averages with 44 wickets at 18.90 and felt happy, confident and in control. Along the way I became only the tenth Hampshire bowler to take more than 1000 wickets in all competitions.

And so to Lord's. Well, not quite. First we had to win four matches and that was never going to be easy, even with Pietersen and Warne available for the first two. Heath Road, Whitchurch has no claims to be one of the great cricket venues but it was here that we met Shropshire and dispensed with them in no time, by seven wickets, with Pietersen hitting six sixes and seven fours in a rapid 76. Pietersen was in form in the second round against Glamorgan at Sophia Gardens, although Nic Pothas's century enabled us to win by six wickets and with almost eleven overs to spare. At this juncture in the competition Warne metaphorically waved us goodbye in the knowledge that if we did reach the final, his Australian commitments would prevent him taking part.

The draw for the quarter final was not exactly kind to us. Surrey at the Oval is not the one we would have chosen and it looked as if we were heading for oblivion when Jon Batty hit a century in an imposing total of 358-6 from 50 overs after I had 'foolishly' lost the toss. The match was televised and I wonder how many people switched off when we lost Greg Lamb without a run on the board and Pothas at 41, but then John Crawley and Watson got us going and McMillan, Sean Ervine and young Kevin Latouf maintained the momentum in support of Watson. At 279-7 we were right back in it, but while the run rate was not a problem, we were also losing wickets and when I joined Watson we needed 80 off eleven in front of an increasingly noisy crowd. I knew I had to take a risk and the turning point came when I decided to walk down the wicket to Mohammad Akram. I tried to drive him straight but the ball flew to mid-on where it just cleared Graham Thorpe on its way to the boundary. From then on, everything went our way until Watson's fantastically-paced innings of 132 was ended when he was bowled by Tim Murtagh. He left as we required 17, but Chris Tremlett can bat and leant me valuable support as we whittled away at our target. There were 13 balls left when I struck the winning boundary and promptly collapsed on the pitch in part elation, part exhaustion. Chris Tremlett, all 6ft 7 inches of him, jumped on me in relief and happiness and the wonderful Hampshire supporters celebrated in style. I cannot pretend that in seeing so many of them in the ground before the start did not get the butterflies going, because I was aware of my responsibilities to them as captain. Now they could raise the roof because history had been made, it being the highest successful chase by any county in one-day competitions. Our astonishing final score of 359-8 is etched on my mind forever.

Captain At Lord's

If we had had to choose the perfect semi final draw it would have been Yorkshire at home and that is what we got. It was important to me as captain that if we were to reach our first knockout final in 13 years it came via a home win and events conspired against our opponents in an incredible sequence of mishaps. While we had four or five days rest, Yorkshire had to travel late the previous evening from Lancashire and then, next morning after not many hours sleep, the coach driver refused to take the team from the hotel because he had exceeded his permitted hours. The coach (and new driver) stuck in traffic, Craig White even ran the last mile to the Rose Bowl and it was clear when they warmed up that the Yorkshire camp was not a happy one. Once again it all went for us when I won the toss and made them bat and as I looked at their line-up I felt that if we could remove Phil Jaques early and get past White at five, resistance may only be sporadic. Watson brilliantly ran out Anthony McGrath and White ran out of partners. Jaques made 31 and from 103-2, Yorkshire were reduced to 197-9 from their 50 overs. At the interval my instructions were to make them wait for our wickets, but I need not have worried. In almost anti-climactic circumstances, Pothas and Ervine, who hit 100, polished off the runs in no time. Victory was by eight wickets and our fielding was from heaven.

Lord's here we come. By happy coincidence we met our cup final opponents Warwickshire in a championship match days before and trounced them by an innings and 86 runs at the Rose Bowl inside three days. I never thought that might happen when I declared at lunch on the second day, but Warwickshire did not appear to have much interest and the only decision I had to make was enforcing the follow-on, for which I apologised to the team. But I made up for it by taking a season's-best six for 44 and we headed to London with a day to spare. Warwickshire even trained at Lord's on the Friday, the day before the final, which I thought was odd. Pietersen was available to us and on Friday evening we had a relaxed meal in Hampstead High Street,a few social drinks with husbands and wives Smith, Budge, Burgess, Britten and Mandy Bransgrove. Rod was at another function. I headed back to the Regency Park Marriott for an early night. There I met Botham in the bar. "Have a drink, be natural," he said. I did and I am glad I did. My concern at the time was for my father who had been in hospital. I really wanted him to be there to see me lead a side out at Lord's. It would have been a high point for him as much as it would have been for me and when I spotted him in my binoculars with mum, mother-in-law Caroline, my friends from the night before, the entire Rose Bowl staff and what seemed like the whole of Hampshire, at once I felt at ease.

We had won the toss for the right to occupy the home dressing room and I remember it as a beautiful clear day when I felt nothing could go wrong. Rod Bransgrove came in a couple of hours before the start to wish us well but KP's presence was reassuring, Watson was calm, Bichel jovial and good for morale and John Crawley looked like a man who had played in numerous finals, as of course he had. Only Latouf, who had still to make his first class debut for us, showed signs of nerves and he had every right to do so. Latouf represented the only choice we had to make. There was a squad of 13 and it was between him as an extra batsman and outstanding fielder, Jono McLean and James Bruce for the last spot. Two of them had to be disappointed. Warwickshire looked stronger than when we had played them in the championship match with Ashley Giles, Ian Bell, Neil Carter and Trevor Penney coming into their side, but my only concern as we warmed up was what to do if I won the toss. At 9.10 I felt we should bowl and I told Terry and Crawley this was what we would do, but an hour later the outfield had dried and I changed my mind. It looked good for batting. Even as Nick Knight, the Warwickshire captain, and I walked out to toss-up, I was completely undecided and not bothered about the outcome. I called 'heads' and the coin came down 'tails'. Knight said he would bowl and I think I would have done the same, but to this day I am unconvinced. Mark Nicholas, in his television commentator role, interviewed me on the pitch and said I had deserved this day, while co-commentator Geoff Boycott said he would have batted first. There was the difficult job of telling Bruce and McLean they would not be playing and I remember this enormous sense of pride of being captain of a cup final team. Lord's was full, Emma, the children and my dad were out there and I thought suddenly of my grandfather. He would have enjoyed every minute. There was also, and I struggle to explain this, a rush of quite trivial things entering my head at this moment of high drama. I am not even sure what they were or why I thought of them, but I recall thinking how silly it was that they should be occupying my mind.

Captain At Lord's

I would like to say the match itself went according to plan and I suppose I would have settled for the 290 we made, but we lost our last seven wickets for 41 and I suggest 310 would have been a more realistic target after the marvellous start given us by Sean 'Slug' Ervine, who made 104 coming in at number three. Nic Pothas batted well for his 68 but I imagine Warwickshire felt 290 was catchable. Neil Carter, who had taken five of our wickets, was also going to be a key batsman. Warwickshire used him as a pinch-hitter at the top of the innings where he could be destructive. Creepy said getting rid of Carter was vital and when he hit Tremlett for six on his way to a rapid 32, I became worried. But then Ervine ran him out and Mascarenhas and I dragged us back into the match with some tight and accurate bowling. Knight and Bell were their best two batsmen and took the score to 166 for one with ominous authority. Our total at that stage did not look to be enough but our compensation was that they were not scoring quickly. The turning point came when Bell was struck down by cramp and Warwickshire were never quite the same force when, clearly incapacitated, he lifted a tired shot to Tremlett who had earlier dropped him at mid-off from my bowling.

As Bell made a weary, painful way back to the pavilion, I got our players into a huddle and told them, "We need another ten per cent. This is our moment". Trying to catch up with the run rate, Warwickshire lost wickets in the chase and there was a bizarre moment when the crowd stood to applaud Richie Benaud's last stint as a commentator in England just as Andy Bichel bowled Jim Troughton. Our fielding was immaculate, Watson's return to the attack lifted us and Bichel got a large and vociferous crowd on its feet as we sensed victory. But then came a big blow. In the 49th over, when we were coasting, we were 'fined' six runs for a slow over rate and there was a momentary panic until we all realised Warwickshire did not have the resources to take advantage.

Victory by 18 runs was comparatively narrow in a high-scoring match and credit to Warwickshire who played well, none better than Knight who made a match top score of 118. At the conclusion, I cannot remember being so ecstatic. To collect the trophy as the first Hampshire-born captain to win a major competition was reward in itself, but to see the unfettered happiness and joy of our supporters, our beleaguered chairman and our back-up team of Terry, Reid, physiotherapist Paddy Farhart and so many others was a fantastic feeling. Rod Bransgrove joined us on the pitch to sample the champagne and the lap of honour. I lifted my children on to the pitch and the tide of emotion was incredible.

About 20 or 30 miles away in Chelmsford, Shane Warne was 12th man for the Australians in a tour match. Within two hours of our win, he was on the phone to offer his congratulations, but by then we were deep into our celebrations. Gordon 'Giddy' Powell, whose company sponsor Hampshire, spent £100 on two bottles of champagne and told me to fill up the trophy, only to discover it was full of holes like a colander and leaked the precious liquid all over the floor. Mum and dad joined us in the pavilion, but by the time we had made a slow journey around the boundary, it took us an hour to reach the sanctity of our dressing room. Before that we put the trophy, holes and all, on the pitch and, surrounded by 50 friends and family, struck up a rendition of 'Glory, Glory, We are Hampshire'.

Back at our hotel, good friend and hotel manager Stuart Chappell and his staff came out to welcome us. There were still fans ready to greet us all around London and after Farhart led us in singing 'We are the champions', it was 4am before we got to bed. Four or five hours later, heavily hung over, I found at least ten people still in the bar where I had left them. Two days later, we played Middlesex at the Rose Bowl. I dropped Owais Shah and we lost. Cricket is a great leveller. Not long afterwards Shane Warne rejoined the club and I had some extra medals to dish out. McLean and Bruce got one each as squad members in the final but the last one was for Shane. He had played in the first two rounds and when I presented it to him he was deeply touched. Like Marshall and his Benson and Hedges medal, Warne had something tangible to show for his commitment to Hampshire and it was a surprise how much it meant to him. As for me, I thought this was the zenith of my career. Only an England cap would have made me happier and surely that was never going to happen now.

There is always a price to pay for a lifetime in professional sport, namely the toll injuries take on the body. As my career winds down and I look back on 20 years with Hampshire, there are scars, mental and physical. Every morning when I wake, I need time to come to terms with the aches and pains before I can go about the business of the day. How much longer I can do this, I don't know. There is pain in one ankle as a legacy of the football break and pain in the other from a freak accident while I was fielding at Northlands Road in 1998. I went over on it while running and a scan next day showed a small fracture. I was in plaster for ten days. Scar tissue remains also in my side as a daily reminder of the number of overs and balls delivered, day in and day out, through two decades of cricket. The result of all this is that I have trouble walking up stairs, carrying my young son and stepping over the stair-gate we use to protect Jack. I have been warned that arthritis, that bane of the ex-pro, awaits me in middle age. People don't understand how playing so much sport for so long can punish the unprepared body. I work hard at my fitness, as all players do now, but it is as much as I can do to get myself ready for a hard day in the field. One day I will have to surrender to the inevitable and stand down. The spirit is as willing as it ever was, but the body is struggling to cope with the demands of a hectic summer schedule of cricket matches and the travelling, even as Hampshire do, in a luxury coach. When that day comes it will be a sad day, indeed.

One day I hope Jack can understand what cricket has meant to me and appreciate it, but further confirmation of his autism came in March 2007 from eight leading experts in the field. I cannot write or talk about it without feeling emotional because I know there are hard times ahead for him. There are good signs. He shows affection and loves watching other children play, but there is no sign of him speaking yet and ten per cent of autistics never speak. We have to guess his needs. He is getting the best of treatment at a special play group two mornings a week but, as I write, the next months are going to be crucial in discovering the extent of his disability. Trained teachers are working with him but the poor boy cannot eat any food with lumps in it and everything has to be pureed. Through it all Emma has been as stoical as ever, a wonderful mother to all our children and a wife in a million to me. Never once has she reined me in. If I stay an extra hour in the bar at the end of a day's play, she never worries. Other players look at their watches and flee. Emma is the complete opposite of the footballing WAGs and their vacuous shop-till-you-drop philosophy. She is frugal and caring, laughs at the WAGs so-called glamour and, if she does come to the cricket, prefers to sit well away from the pavilion with our children. In so many respects, truly I have been lucky.

SHAUN UDAL - Statistical Summary

Compiled by Jim Baldwin

FIRST-CLASS CRICKET:

Tests (4)
England v Pakistan (First Test) at Multan 2005/06.
England v Pakistan (Second Test) at Faisalabad 2005/06.
England v Pakistan (Third Test) at Lahore 2005/06.
England v India (Third Test) at Mumbai 2005/06.

Debut for England
v Pakistan (First Test) at Multan 2005/06.

Highest Score for England
33* v Pakistan (Second Test) at Faisalabad 2005/06.

Best Bowling Performance for England
4-14 v India (Third Test) at Mumbai 2005/06.

Debut for Hampshire
v Oxford University at Oxford 1989.

Awarded County Cap 1992.

Awarded Benefit 2002.

Highest Score for Hampshire
117* v Warwickshire at Southampton 1997.

Two Half-Centuries in the Same Match for Hampshire
50 & 74 v Somerset at The Rose Bowl 2004

Best Bowling Performance for Hampshire
8-50 v Sussex at Southampton 1992.

Best Bowling Performance in a Match for Hampshire
11-170 (5-85 & 6-85) Hampshire v Nottinghamshire
at Nottingham 1995

Centuries (1)
117* Hampshire v Warwickshire at Southampton 1997.

Half-Centuries (28)

66 Hampshire v Worcestershire at Portsmouth 1993
79* Hampshire v Sussex at Portsmouth 1993
59 Hampshire v Essex at Southampton 1994
83 Hampshire v Derbyshire at Southampton 1994
64 Hampshire v Warwickshire at Birmingham 1994
94 Hampshire v Glamorgan at Southampton 1994
56 Hampshire v Worcestershire at Southampton 1995
85 Hampshire v Yorkshire at Southampton 1995
62* Hampshire v Northamptonshire at Northampton 1995
50 England 'A' v Combined XI at Karachi 1995/96
50* Hampshire v Worcestershire at Worcester 1996
58 Hampshire v Cambridge University at Cambridge 1996
58 Hampshire v Gloucestershire at Bristol 1997
91 Hampshire v Kent at Portsmouth 1997
54* Hampshire v Nottinghamshire at Nottingham 1997
66 Hampshire v Worcestershire at Southampton 1997
62 Hampshire v Leicestershire at Leicester 1998
85 Hampshire v New Zealand 'A' at Portsmouth 2000
59 Hampshire v Middlesex at Southgate 2001
81 Hampshire v Derbyshire at The Rose Bowl 2001
62 Hampshire v Middlesex at The Rose Bowl 2001
88 Hampshire v Kent at The Rose Bowl 2002
60* Hampshire v Durham at The Rose Bowl 2003
50 Hampshire v Worcestershire at The Rose Bowl 2003
57 Hampshire v Derbyshire at Derby 2003
52 Hampshire v Yorkshire at Leeds 2004
50 Hampshire v Somerset at The Rose Bowl 2004
74 Hampshire v Somerset at The Rose Bowl 2004

Five Wickets in an Innings (33)

8-50 Hampshire v Sussex at Southampton 1992
5-47 Hampshire V Oxford University at Oxford 1992
5-97 Hampshire v Nottinghamshire at Nottingham 1993
5-74 Hampshire v Nottinghamshire at Nottingham 1993
6-141 Hampshire v Warwickshire at Southampton 1993
5-131 Hampshire v Lancashire at Southampton 1993
5-75 Hampshire v Glamorgan at Swansea 1993
6-79 Hampshire v Lancashire at Manchester 1994
5-63 Hampshire v South Africans at Southampton 1994
5-46 Hampshire v Gloucestershire at Portsmouth 1994
6-85 Hampshire v Worcestershire at Worcester 1994
5-119 Hampshire v Northamptonshire at Southampton 1994
5-26 Hampshire v Surrey at Southampton 1994
5-137 Hampshire v Surrey at Southampton 1994
5-81 Hampshire v Kent at Southampton 1995
6-65 Hampshire v Gloucestershire at Bristol 1995
5-144 Hampshire v Worcestershire at Southampton 1995
5-85 Hampshire v Nottinghamshire at Nottingham 1995
6-85 Hampshire v Nottinghamshire at Nottingham 1995

5-82 Hampshire v Gloucestershire at Southampton 1996
6-47 Hampshire v Glamorgan at Swansea 1999
5-102 Hampshire v New Zealanders at Southampton 1999
5-96 Hampshire v Gloucestershire at Bristol 1999
5-58 Hampshire v Derbyshire at Southampton 2000
7-74 Hampshire v Derbyshire at Derby 2001
5-56 Hampshire v Sussex at The Rose Bowl 2002
5-59 Hampshire v Indians at The Rose Bowl 2002
5-59 Hampshire v Lancashire at The Rose Bowl 2002
5-69 Hampshire v Yorkshire at The Rose Bowl 2002
6-79 Hampshire v Derbyshire at Derby 2004
6-61 Hampshire v Gloucestershire at Cheltenham 2005
5-65 Hampshire v Surrey at The Oval 2005
6-44 Hampshire v Warwickshire at The Rose Bowl 2005

Ten Wickets or more in a Match (4)
10-171 (5-97 & 5-74) Hampshire v Nottinghamshire at Nottingham 1993
10-192 (4-51 & 6-141)Hampshire v Warwickshire at Southampton 1993
10-163 (5-26 & 5-137)Hampshire v Surrey at Southampton 1994
11-170 (5-85 & 6-85) Hampshire v Nottinghamshire at Nottingham 1995

CAREER RECORD FOR HAMPSHIRE

County Championship

BATTING:

M	Inn	NO	Runs	HS	Ave	100	50	Ct
222	311	58	6021	117*	23.79	1	25	106

BOWLING:

Balls	Runs	Wkts	Ave	BB	5WI	10WM
40918	20168	617	32.68	8-50	29	4

Other First-class matches

BATTING:

M	Inn	NO	Runs	HS	Ave	100	50	Ct
23	30	7	441	85	19.17	0	2	6

BOWLING:

Balls	Runs	Wkts	Ave	BB	5WI	10WM
4435	2110	77	27.40	5-47	4	0

TOTAL FOR HAMPSHIRE

BATTING:

M	Inn	NO	Runs	HS	Ave	100	50	Ct
245	341	65	6462	117*	23.41	1	27	112

BOWLING:

Balls	Runs	Wkts	Ave	BB	5WI	10WM
45353	22278	694	32.10	8-50	33	4

CAREER RECORD FOR ENGLAND

Tests

BATTING:

M	Inn	NO	Runs	HS	Ave	100	50	Ct
4	7	1	109	33*	18.16	0	0	1

BOWLING:

Balls	Runs	Wkts	Ave	BB	5WI	10WM
596	344	8	43.00	4-14	0	0

Other First-class matches

BATTING:

M	Inn	NO	Runs	HS	Ave	100	50	Ct
6	11	1	156	50	15.60	0	1	3

BOWLING:

Balls	Runs	Wkts	Ave	BB	5WI	10WM
941	558	8	69.75	2-95	0	0

(England tours: Australia 1994/95,Pakistan 1995/96 (England 'A') and Pakistan/India 2005/06)

TOTAL FOR ENGLAND

BATTING:

M	Inn	NO	Runs	HS	Ave	100	50	Ct
10	18	2	265	50	16.56	0	1	4

BOWLING:

Balls	Runs	Wkts	Ave	BB	5WI	10WM
1537	902	16	56.37	4-14	0	0

TOTAL FIRST-CLASS MATCHES

BATTING:

M	Inn	NO	Runs	HS	Ave	100	50	Ct
255	359	67	6727	117*	23.03	1	28	116

BOWLING:

Balls	Runs	Wkts	Ave	BB	5WI	10WM
46890	23180	710	32.64	8-50	33	4

LIMITED-OVERS CRICKET:

One-Day Internationals (11)
England v New Zealand (Texaco Trophy) at Birmingham 1994
England v South Africa (Texaco Trophy) at Birmingham 1994
England v South Africa (Texaco Trophy) at Manchester 1994
England v Australia (Benson & Hedges World Series Cup)
at Sydney 1994/95
England v Zimbabwe (Benson & Hedges World Series Cup)
at Sydney 1994/95
England v Zimbabwe (Benson & Hedges World Series Cup)
at Brisbane 1994/95
England v Australia (Benson & Hedges World Series Cup)
at Melbourne 1994/95
England v West Indies (Texaco Trophy) at Nottingham 1995
England v West Indies (Texaco Trophy) at The Oval 1995
England v West Indies (Texaco Trophy) at Lord's 1995
England v Pakistan at Rawalpindi 2005/06
(Note: Shaun Udal played two further Benson & Hedges World Series Cup
matches for England against an Australia 'A' team in 1994/95 but these
are excluded from official One-Day International records)

Debut for England
v New Zealand (Texaco Trophy) at Birmingham 1994

Highest Score for England
11* v Zimbabwe (Benson & Hedges World Series Cup)
at Brisbane 1994/95

Best Bowling Performance for England
2-37 v Australia (Benson & Hedges World Series Cup)
at Sydney 1994/95

Debut for Hampshire
v Nottinghamshire (Refuge Assurance League) at Nottingham 1989

Highest Score for Hampshire
78 v Surrey (AXA Life League) at Guildford 1997

Best Bowling Performance for Hampshire
5-43 v Surrey (AXA Life League) at Southampton 1998

Half-Centuries (8)
54 Hampshire v Middlesex (AXA Equity & Law League)
at Portsmouth 1996
50* Hampshire v Warwickshire (AXA Life League) at Southampton 1997
52* Hampshire v Worcestershire (AXA Life League) at Southampton 1997
78 Hampshire v Surrey (AXA Life League) at Guildford 1997
70 Hampshire v Sussex (AXA Life League) at Southampton 1997

51* Hampshire v Glamorgan (Norwich Union National League)
at Cardiff 2000
58 Hampshire v Gloucestershire (Norwich Union National League)
at Cheltenham 2002
58 Hampshire v Middlesex (Norwich Union National League)
at The Rose Bowl 2002

Four Wickets in an Innings (9)
4-40 Hampshire v Middlesex (Benson & Hedges Cup)
at Southampton 1992
4-64 Hampshire v Durham (Sunday League) at Southampton 1992
4-51 Hampshire v Northamptonshire (Sunday League)
at Bournemouth 1992
5-43 Hampshire v Surrey (AXA Life League) at Southampton 1998
4-20 Hampshire v Dorset (NatWest Trophy) at Bournemouth 1998
4-36 Hampshire v Surrey (Benson & Hedges Cup) at The Oval 2002
4-31 Hampshire v Sussex (Norwich Union National League)
at The Rose Bowl 2002
4-40 Hampshire v Northamptonshire (ECB National Cricket League)
at The Rose Bowl 2003
4-46 Hampshire v Northamptonshire (totesport Cricket League)
at Milton Keynes 2004

For Hampshire in Limited Overs Matches

*NatWest Pro40 League

BATTING:

M	Inn	NO	Runs	HS	Ave	100	50	Ct
242	165	49	1700	78	14.65	0	8	85

BOWLING:

Balls	Runs	Wkts	Ave	BB	4WI	Econ
10283	8062	279	28.89	5-43	6	4.70

+Cheltenham & Gloucs Trophy

BATTING:

M	Inn	NO	Runs	HS	Ave	100	50	Ct
47	23	9	312	44	22.28	0	0	16

BOWLING:

Balls	Runs	Wkts	Ave	BB	4WI	Econ
2468	1546	56	27.60	4-20	1	3.75

Benson & Hedges Cup

BATTING:

M	Inn	NO	Runs	HS	Ave	100	50	Ct
48	30	7	343	34	14.91	0	0	13

BOWLING:

Balls	Runs	Wkts	Ave	BB	4WI	Econ
2694	1738	54	32.18	4-36	2	3.87

Other Limited Overs Matches

BATTING:

M	Inn	NO	Runs	HS	Ave	100	50	Ct
5	4	2	96	35	48.00	0	0	1

BOWLING:

Balls	Runs	Wkts	Ave	BB	4WI	Econ
276	178	5	35.60	3-34	0	3.86

TOTAL FOR HAMPSHIRE

BATTING:

M	Inn	NO	Runs	HS	Ave	100	50	Ct
342	222	67	2451	78	15.81	0	8	115

BOWLING:

Balls	Runs	Wkts	Ave	BB	4WI	Econ
15721	11524	394	29.24	5-43	9	4.39

Notes:

* = Records include Refuge Assurance Lge 1989-91, Sunday Lge 1992, AXA Lge 1993-98, CGU National Lge 1999, Norwich Union National Lge 2000-03, totesport Cricket League 2004-05, NatWest Pro40 League 2006.

+ = Records include NatWest Trophy 1991-2000, Cheltenham & Gloucester Trophy 2001-06.

For England in One-Day Internationals

BATTING:

M	Inn	NO	Runs	HS	Ave	100	50	Ct
11	7	4	35	11*	11.66	0	0	1

BOWLING:

Balls	Runs	Wkts	Ave	BB	4WI	Econ
612	400	9	44.44	2-37	0	3.92

Statistical summary

For England in Other Limited Overs Matches

v Australia 'A'

BATTING:

M	Inn	NO	Runs	HS	Ave	100	50	Ct
2	2	0	18	9	9.00	0	0	1

BOWLING:

Balls	Runs	Wkts	Ave	BB	4WI	Econ
108	89	2	44.50	2-56	0	4.94

For England 'A' in Pakistan 1995/96

BATTING:

M	Inn	NO	Runs	HS	Ave	100	50	Ct
2	-	-	-	-	-	0	0	0

BOWLING:

Balls	Runs	Wkts	Ave	BB	4WI	Econ
90	70	0	-	-	0	4.66

TOTAL LIMITED OVERS

BATTING:

M	Inn	NO	Runs	HS	Ave	100	50	Ct
357	231	71	2504	78	15.65	0	8	117

BOWLING:

Balls	Runs	Wkts	Ave	BB	4WI	Econ
16531	12083	405	29.83	5-43	9	4.38

Career Record for Twenty20 Cup Matches

For Hampshire

BATTING:

M	Inn	NO	Runs	HS	Ave	100	50	Ct
25	18	7	188	37	17.09	0	0	7

BOWLING:

Balls	Runs	Wkts	Ave	BB	5WI	Econ
465	557	25	22.28	3-21	0	7.18